WE SHARED THE PEELED ORANGE

WE SHARED THE PEELED ORANGE

The Letters of "Papa Louis"
from the Thai–Cambodian Border Refugee Camps
1981–1993

LOUIS E. BRAILE, M.D.

Introduction by Hugh Q. Parmer, President
American Refugee Committee

SYREN BOOK COMPANY
Saint Paul

Most Syren Books are available at special quantity discounts for bulk purchases for sales promotions, premiums, fund-raising, and educational needs. For details, write:

Syren Book Company
Special Sales Department
5120 Cedar Lake Road
Minneapolis, Minnesota 55416 USA

Published by
Syren Book Company LLC
5120 Cedar Lake Road
Minneapolis, Minnesota 55416 USA

Printed in the United States of America on acid-free paper

ISBN 0-929636-34-1

LCCN 2004113990

Cover photo, Doug Hulcher
Inset photo, ARC staff archives
Title page photo, Jim Hubbard
Cover design, Kyle G. Hunter
Book design, Wendy Holdman
Project editor, Patricia Benson

To order additional copies of this book see the form
at the back of this book or go to www.itascabooks.com

Contents

Foreword

In 1981 I was working as a volunteer at Khao I-Dang, a camp for displaced Cambodians on the Thai–Cambodian border. My father, Dr. Louis Braile, arranged to come for a visit and to work as a short-term medical volunteer. Before he arrived, many of my Cambodian friends were surprised I would allow such an elderly person to come to this setting. Then my 59-year-old father arrived. He was much older than most volunteers, but had an energy we all admired and envied. He quickly was called "Papa Louis," a demonstration of love and respect, not just to a generation of Cambodian refugees, but also to relief workers from the United States and around the world.

This was the beginning of a love affair between my father and people in need that would take him 11 times to refugee camps on the Thai–Cambodian border, twice to communities in Cambodia, and finally once to Goma, Zaire, over the years 1981 to 1996.

Initially his tours were short, often two to three months, allowing him to continue his family medical practice in the Seattle area. Eventually, he retired from conventional practice and was able to spend longer periods overseas until a severe stroke, suffered in 1996, prevented further travel and work. My father died in 2002, leaving a legacy of hope and healing.

Before his seventh tour on the Thai–Cambodian border, which began September 1, 1986, with the American Refugee Committee, my father was asked to write a statement on why he volunteered to do this work. He shared his reasons in the following words:

> Why do medical professionals go to the Thai–Cambodian border camps? This is a question asked of me many times. It implies that surely the beauty of Thailand, the opportunity to travel and to live and work with a select group of Western medical workers is not sufficient reason to warrant exposure to the

Dr. Louis Braile (center), his daughter Peggy (left), and his wife Gwen (right).
Source: Braile family photo

risks and demands of working in heat and mud, of exposure to exotic diseases and the violence of men.

We deal with illnesses, some common and some peculiar to the tropics; we deal with the ugly wounds of war, the effects of ignorance and deprivation. The Cambodians are by nature a happy and friendly people. But in this scene there is an all-pervading sense of melancholy and hopelessness, brought on by the fact that these people are pawns, victims of the military and diplomatic goals of larger nations.

The medical work brings a slight vision to these people of a better world, a glimpse of love and compassion. In truth, it is this vision that is more important and effective than our medical striving.

And so I prepare for my seventh trip to the border camps, grateful for the opportunity to help in some way, grateful to family and friends who support me in this effort, and grateful to

those Americans who see the vision and through their donations make this effort possible.

While my father was doing his part around the world, my mother
gave of herself in her own unique way. My parents corresponded almost every day, very important in terms of mutual support during long
separations. Realizing that family and friends wanted to hear about the
daily life of Papa Louis, my mother began to copy his letters from each
tour and send them to friends and colleagues. These letters kept us informed about life on the border and in Cambodia, and also reminded us
of our responsibility to give back to others, having been blessed with
so much.

In my family we often describe an event or activity that provides pleasure as a gift. From both my parents, these letters have been a gift. We
now share this gift with you.

Peggy Braile
Gig Harbor, Washington
August 2004

Introduction

I never met Dr. Louis Braile, but I know him nonetheless. I saw him in the young Colombian doctor who left her wealthy family to run a feeding center for starving children in Angola. I met him greeting Kosovars as they walked the last 10 miles across the border into Albania and safety. I traveled with him up the Nile to teach emergency medical skills to Sudanese nurses. I rode with him in a truck filled with blankets and water containers as it crept carefully into southern Iraq. *We Shared the Peeled Orange* is uniquely the story of Dr. Braile and his amazing life of service to people forced to flee their homes because of war and oppression—the world's refugees. But this collection of letters is also a window through which we can glimpse the lives of thousands of unknown heroes, men and women, young and old, who work every day to help the 36 million people across the globe driven from their homes by conflict.

As it was for many humanitarian workers, Dr. Braile's introduction to refugees was almost serendipitous. In 1966 he read an article in the Journal of the American Medical Association called "Volunteer Physicians for Vietnam." At 44 years of age, with a wonderful wife, Gwen, his young family, and a growing medical practice in Washington State, Dr. Braile would seem an unlikely volunteer for the refugee camps of war-ravaged Southeast Asia. But a sense of compassion and duty, an adventurous spirit and an understanding wife and family led to his first step on a long road of service.

Off to Vietnam he went, as a volunteer doctor. He would return three more times over the next five years.

Meanwhile, in 1978 a Chicago businessman named Neal Ball agreed to "adopt" a refugee from Cambodia. Neal thought he had only agreed to send a regular check—until he received a call informing him that "your refugee is arriving at O'Hare Airport on Saturday!" He was up to the task, however, and that refugee led Neal to understand the terrible health conditions that plagued displaced people on the Thai–Cambodian border. With a few business and social friends he raised funds to send a team of health volunteers from the Midwest to those camps. That volunteer effort marked the beginning of the American Refugee Committee.

In 1981, Dr. Braile's daughter Peggy, by then a nurse, was working with the International Rescue Committee (IRC) at Khao-I-Dang (KID) Holding Center, the refugee camp for Cambodians in Thailand. Dr. Braile had already decided to join his daughter in service at KID. When he arrived, the IRC staff generously lent Dr. Braile to ARC to help this new humanitarian organization hit the ground running. There were so many in need, and Dr. Braile quickly became known and loved as "Papa Louis." From that day forward, all of his tours of duty were in partnership with ARC.

Besides being a skilled doctor and committed family man, Dr. Braile was many other things: a patient teacher, a creative chef, a passionate music lover, an adventurous traveler, a sensitive listener, a talented observer, and an indefatigable writer. He wrote letters home to his wife, Gwen, almost daily. The letters are an extraordinary record of what, for relief workers, is an ordinary day in the life of a refugee camp.

As a writer, he used all his senses to bring his story alive, to make us see, hear and feel the pain caused by the death of a baby girl from malnutrition, or the horror of trying in vain to save a young man who has stepped on a land mine. We go along for the jarring, desperate rides in an old, overheated ambulance. Through Papa Louis's words, we also feel the tropical heat, torrential rain, the sting and bite of insects. We see the emerald green fields. We hear the music of celebrations, smell the aromas of the market, taste the hard-to-find coffee and bread, the plentiful oranges, water buffalo roast and other exotic fare.

We could not print all of Papa Louis's letters in one, short book. The letters and excerpts we have chosen do flow chronologically, but regrettably, some individuals, events, and details from this man's remarkable story of a dozen tours of duty over more than a decade are not included. But, taken together, these fragments of experience create a colorful, memorable mosaic of life in a refugee camp from different perspectives—refugees, medical professionals, humanitarian volunteers, field staff, spiritual counselors, and the public and private organizations that work so hard to manage the unmanageable.

Most important, we are introduced to some of the unforgettable Cambodian patients who were helped by Dr. Braile. We meet the dedicated Cambodian medics who learned from him. We come to know colleagues and friends from around the world who walked awhile with him on this journey. We meet others who simply crossed his path, a few more threads in the amazing, global web of relief workers who, with little glory but plenty of guts, move around places most of us can't find on a map, helping people most of us easily forget.

The American Refugee Committee is proud to publish *We Shared the Peeled Orange* on the occasion of our 25th anniversary. This anniversary, however, is a milestone we might wish we'd never reached. We might wish that as Papa Louis once said, "We are, indeed, making progress in the treatment of the body. Would that we could make similar progress in healing the mind and heart."

Like Papa Louis, we must make peace with the human condition. Like Papa Louis, we must keep going with lots of hope and a little daring. He knew that, while powerful social, political and emotional forces may perpetrate terrible violence and loss, the resulting pain, death and disease happen one person at a time, one family at a time, until whole countries may be lost. This book reminds us, once again, that that's how the healing happens, too. A single human being reaching out to another human being, and thereby motivating others to step forward, is what makes the difference between life and death, between hope and despair in a world where the relentless demand for refugee services continues. Now it is our time, and our turn, to take the next steps.

When you have finished this book you too will know Dr. Braile. I hope that through him you will also better understand those volunteers in the field who risk their lives and health, who undergo great hardships, their work rarely recognized, and whose sole reward is often the gratitude in the eyes of those whose lives they have touched.

Hugh Q. Parmer, President
American Refugee Committee
September 2004

WE SHARED THE PEELED ORANGE

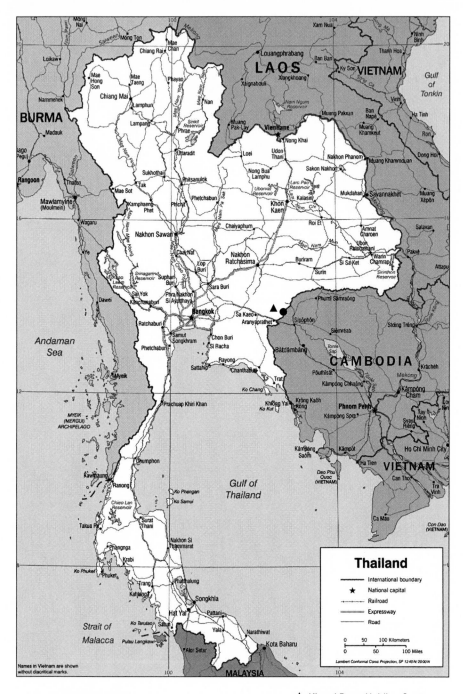

Source: CIA publications

▲ Khao-I-Dang Holding Center
● Nong Samet

Preface

Cambodia is bounded on the north by Thailand and Laos, and on the east by Vietnam. The long border between Vietnam and Cambodia has much to do with the modern history of these two countries. For many years Vietnamese merchants and traders crossed the border and set up mercantile centers. Vietnamese military followed the merchants; minor wars were frequent, and the border became blurred. Deep hatred developed between the people of the two countries.

During the colonial period of the 18th and 19th centuries, France was an occupying power in Cambodia and Vietnam. The Cambodians were considered to be a friendly people who lived in an idyllic country with an abundant supply of fruit and fish. Their inherited knowledge of rice culture resulted in more than enough grain for their own use and allowed for export to other countries.

Cambodia's government was a monarchy. The royal family, whose name was Sihanouk, lived at the height of luxury. They received the adulation of the peasants but did not respond to their needs. Opportunistic hangers-on surrounded the royal family, and bribery and corruption became the hallmark of their reign. In 1970, the monarchy was overturned, and, with the support of the United States, General Lon Nol staged a coup and took over the government. During the U.S.–Vietnam War, the North Vietnamese violated Cambodian sovereignty by routing the Ho Chi Minh Trail through Cambodian jungles for transporting troops and armaments. In an attempt to eliminate the Ho Chi Minh Trail, the U.S. mounted heavy bombing raids that caused great death and destruction. The Lon Nol government was very unstable at the time, and the bombings only increased the instability, making the situation ripe for the onslaught of the Khmer Rouge.

During the middle years of the 20th century, Cambodian families who could afford it sent their sons and daughters to Western countries, particularly France, for university education. Pol Pot went to Paris as a student and came under the influence of radical communism while there. He formed a cell of comrades determined to install communism in Cambodia. This was the birth of the Khmer Rouge (Red Cambodians). The Pol Pot organization was successful in overthrowing the Lon Nol government.

The communism of Pol Pot was of the most radical form, based on the convictions that the state—which they termed *Angkar*—was all-powerful and all-wise and that every facet of Western experience was evil and needed to be eradicated. The result was an era of terror in which several million Khmers died. The major targets of the Khmer Rouge were the educated and those who were connected with the Lon Nol government, its military or police. It was a chaotic time during which hundreds of thousands of city dwellers were forced to move to rural areas and work. There was complete disruption of food production; families were fragmented, and large numbers sought escape to other countries. Death from disease, execution, malnutrition and starvation was rampant in what became known as the "killing fields."

When the horrors of Pol Pot and his regime were followed by the Vietnamese invasion, thousands of surviving Khmers, rather than live under the rule of their traditional enemy, fled to the Thai–Cambodian border and crossed into Thailand. Thus, according to the Thai government, they were illegal immigrants and became a great problem. The government's response was to set up barbed wire–enclosed camps along the border under the management of a paramilitary organization called Task Force 80 (TF 80). As there already were many poor people struggling for existence in Thailand, the Thai government's concern was to make every effort to keep the poor Khmers from becoming de facto settlers there. The presence of these thousands of destitute "illegal immigrants" on the border, with no more to sustain them than what they could carry, presented tremendous problems. Provisions for security, shelter, sanitation, food and health services were urgently required.

Soon the rest of the world became aware of the tragedy being enacted on the Thai–Cambodian border. The UN and the ICRC [International Committee of the Red Cross] quickly became involved. Volunteer organizations were asked to send medical and life support teams on an emergency basis. These organizations were either secular philanthropic in nature, such as CARE [Cooperative for Assistance and Relief

Everywhere, Inc.], the IRC [International Rescue Committee] and ARC [American Refugee Committee), or religious in origin, such as the CRS [Catholic Relief Services]. This is where my story of service and adventure begins.

Louis E. Braile, M.D.

Editor's Notes

1. Dr. Braile's letters were written to his wife Gwen, unless otherwise noted in the text.

2. Following the communist victories in 1975 and continuing until 1995, over three million people fled the former French colonies of Indochina – Vietnam, Cambodia, and Laos. Thailand was country of 'first asylum' for over 237,000 Cambodians who arrived first at Khao-I-Dang (KID), a camp administered by UNHCR (United Nations High Commissioner for Refugees), with access security provided by a Thai paramilitary group known as Task Force 80. Resettlement of refugees from KID to third countries was eventually halted, yet KID remained a large holding center for many years. For Cambodians who chose not to enter Thailand/KID, or for those who chose to enter KID after it had been closed to new arrivals and resettlement, UNBRO (United Nations Border Relief Operation) constructed camps along the border to shelter the growing refugee population.

In 1989, Cambodian refugees on the Thai-Cambodian border numbered 306,000. By 1991, the Cambodian refugee population had reached 353,000 with another 180,000 Cambodians displaced inside their own country. Finally, in October 1991, a UN-sponsored settlement signed in Paris placed Cambodia under the control of UNTAC (United Nations Transitional Authority in Cambodia), pending national elections.

From March 1992 to May 1993, UNHCR coordinated a repatriation effort that succeeded in closing the border camps and KID and safely moving 360,000 people back to Cambodia in time for elections. On 3 March 1993, the last convoy of 199 refugees left KID and this camp, first opened on 21 November 1979, was officially closed. At the closing ceremony, then UNHCR Special Envoy, Sergio Vieira de Mello, called KID 'a powerful and tragic symbol' of the Cambodian exodus and the international humanitarian response. (In 2003, Sergio Vieira de Mello took a leave of absence from his position as United Nations High Commissioner for Human Rights to serve as Special Representative of the UN's Secretary-General in Iraq. He was killed there on 19 August 2003.)

After his first service at KID, Dr. Braile spent much of his time working for ARC at border camps (e.g. Nong Samet, which later became part of Site 2 after the Vietnamese attacks of 1984/85). This is reflected in the letters collected in this book.

The names Cambodia and Kampuchea came to have certain political and ideological overtones, but both names derive from the same Khmer word, *kambuja*, and are used interchangeably. For reader clarity, we have chosen to use the more familiar name, Cambodia, in this book.

Source: UNHCR, State of the World's Refugees, 2000

Of Love and War, Bread and Coffee

4 November 1981

Our transpacific plane landed at Bangkok International Airport. Befogged by long hours of travel and with some trepidation, I got off the plane; like a package on a conveyer belt, I was conducted through customs. The inspector opened one of my bags and found it full of the cookies you made. He had the most quizzical look on his face, but signaled that I could pass along.

The Bangkok airport's main hall was large and there was a constant hum of conversation. It reminded me of a beehive. In the rendezvous area, people pressed against the barrier, anxious to identify the arriving passengers they were to meet. There in the middle of that crowd was our daughter Peggy, who looked wonderful.

On leaving that area, we were followed by taxi drivers who grabbed our sleeves and sought to convince us they were the best and least expensive. Peggy gave me my first lesson in how to get along in Thailand when she told me to pay no attention. The second lesson followed when she approached a taxi driver who was standing by his vehicle. There I witnessed our sweet and gentle daughter in fierce negotiation with the taxi driver.

By the time we reached the Miami Hotel, it was 4:00 A.M. and my biological clock was totally confused, for I was both very sleepy and intensely hungry. Peggy and I had a light snack, and after I walked her to the IRC guest house where she was staying, I returned to the Miami Hotel and crashed.

5 November 1981

The Miami Hotel was no five-star hotel. My little room had a linoleum floor, and I could clearly hear the sounds of my neighbors getting up and beginning their day. Nevertheless, I was grateful for a nice sleep and there was the advantage of being close to the IRC office.

IRC, having accepted me as a volunteer member of its team, had certain responsibilities imposed by the Thai government having to do with security, my whereabouts, identification papers and other such red tape. All of this was taken care of efficiently and with good humor by the IRC staff.

It was early afternoon when we left for Aranyaprathet, traveling in an ICRC courier vehicle. It was packed with the maximum number of people and their baggage. Nobody seemed inclined to talk—which was just as well, for I soon fell asleep, and the four-hour trip passed without my seeing more than a blurred vision of the landscape.

Aranyaprathet, commonly called Aran, is located just 5 km from the Cambodian border. It is the nearest town of any size to the refugee camps and is the base for IRC and a number of other Volags [voluntary agencies]. Peggy took me to the house she shares with several other IRC workers, and a temporary bed was found for me.

7 November 1981

Today I moved to transient quarters in the office house. I will be glad when I can move into more permanent quarters. In order to shave here, one must first find some bottled water, heat it in a teakettle, then find a basin or sink to use. All in all it's a big procedure, so I have decided not to shave for the duration.

Today was my first day at Khao-I-Dang Holding Center. KID is located about 20 km from Aranyaprathet and also from the actual border with Cambodia. It is categorized as a transit camp, and theoretically all of the refugee inhabitants are potentially eligible for expatriation. The camp is under the management of the UNHCR [United Nations High Commissioner for Refugees].

Behind the camp is the dark and foreboding mass of Khao-I-Dang Mountain, from which the camp gets its name. This mountain has been the site of great tragedies in the lives of these Khmers. The camp itself is situated on several hundred acres of ground, from which virtually all vegetation has been removed. There are a few trees and some small garden plots. The remainder is red soil, lying exposed and ready to become mud when it rains, and to raise dust when it is dry and the wind blows.

KID is surrounded by a barbed wire fence. Barracks, offices, hospital compound and hundreds of huts, all constructed of a mix of wood, bamboo, thatch and blue plastic tarps, dot the ground. The entrance is guarded by TF 80 troops, some of whom appear friendly, others grim and menacing. The guards prevent Khmer inhabitants from leaving the camp and make sure that only authorized people enter. They also prevent contraband materials from getting in. Sometimes the guards wave the Volags in without any inspection, sometimes they insist on seeing passes. On rare occasions they demand that all people get out of the car, and a thorough inspection of the vehicle and contents is carried out. Violators may forfeit their passes for a short period of time, or worse, may be banished from the border area.

My first day in camp was spent meeting people and being shown around. One of IRC's responsibilities is the Admissions ward, where Peggy is the charge nurse. Dr. John Ho, born in China, educated in the United States and now a specialist in infectious disease, is the medical director.

The origin of the Khmer medics and their role here is very interesting. The medical volunteers who came to the border in the early days of the Cambodian refugee problem were small in number, but were faced with giving care to thousands of Cambodians. The refugees were suffering from disease, war wounds, malnutrition and psychological and emotional trauma. It was very apparent that, despite their dedication, this small number of volunteers could not make a dent in the massive problem.

Among the refugees there was the occasional person who could speak some English or French. In general these were young people from the well-to-do families, who had had the opportunity to continue their education.

These young Cambodians were invited to come to work in the hospital, and most of them were very happy to do so, for they became eligible for extra rations. They also welcomed the opportunity to associate with the foreigners, as many of these Khmers were hopeful of expatriation to the U.S. Most of them were males, but there was the occasional young woman who qualified. It was on-the-job training for these young, untrained medical workers, first doing menial tasks and then learning technical nursing, medical and laboratory procedures. It was not long before they were skilled in inserting IVs and performing spinal taps and minor surgery, such as abscess incisions and superficial laceration repair. Once the initial emergency was under control, the Volags began more formal training. A curriculum was set up and new candidates were trained in progressive steps: health worker, nurse and finally medic. It was here that ARC became known as one of the best of the Volags on the border in the field of medical training.

Transportation to and from KID is provided by an IRC van driven by a Thai driver, and I am gradually learning about the daily meal schedule. Virtually all of my colleagues are a generation younger than I, and many of them are female. Whatever the explanation, for most of them breakfast is no big deal. Some eat no breakfast, some drink a cup of instant coffee or hot tea, and some eat leftovers. Lunchtime at KID finds most people going across the street to a little Thai hut called the "Fly Palace." Food is cooked over an open fire, from which smoke rises to stain the chicken carcasses hanging from the rafters. There is always rice and a variety of cooked vegetables and sauces, which I could not begin to define. At rest on any edible surface or buzzing in the air are hordes of flies. If my fellow workers didn't eat in this place, I would not eat here myself. Dinner is something else. Little cooking is done in this little town of Aranyaprathet. Most foreigners associated with relief agencies (better known as "farangs") make their way to the peculiar phenomenon known as the night market on one of the downtown streets. During the day it seems to be an ordinary street. Late in the afternoon a great change takes place. Like magic, tables, chairs, benches and pushcarts with charcoal braziers appear. They occupy the sidewalks and flow into the street, leaving only a narrow passage through which motorcycles roar and cars make their way very closely to seated diners. The air is filled with the odors of charcoal fires and cooking seafood and meat. A Western public health food inspector would be challenged, for there are few refrigerators or iceboxes, and much of the meat and fish is either hanging or lying out in the open. Nevertheless, the food is mostly delicious, and I don't hear much about digestive problems.

In the morning, I get up at 5:00, and for a while I have the house to myself. It is dark, the hour of transition, and morning sounds commence.

Roosters crow, hens cluck, a variety of birds call, and a multitude of insects hum and buzz. Were you here, you would no doubt share my pride in our daughter. The Khmers with whom she works obviously love her. You may be assured that the world *is* a little better place because of her efforts.

10 November 1981

When people at IRC realized that I would be here for more than a month, they decided I should move into more permanent quarters. This evening I moved. My new domicile is only 1 km from where I have been staying. We rented a *tuk tuk* for the move. This is a hybrid vehicle powered by a motorcycle attached to a two-wheeled arrangement in the back with two seats.

It was early evening when I arrived, but no one was up. Trying to be quiet, I explored the house. We have two bathrooms of the slit trench type. There is no shower of the type we are accustomed to. Instead there is a rather crude little room in which there is a huge waist-high jar that is filled with room-temperature water. Using a long-handled pan, one pours water over the body, soaps and rinses.

11 November 1981

Tonight, TF 80, the local Thai paramilitary group, put on a party for foreign volunteers. Each Volag was asked to put on a short entertainment. Our group sang and danced a song called "Loy Kratong." The affair celebrates the day of Loy Kratong, which occurs on the full moon of November, and is a celebration of harvest and the beginning of a new year. It all went off very well, and it was a great evening. The full moon, the palm trees, the reflection pool, the chimes and the murmur of foreign words made me really feel I was in the exotic East.

Dr. John Ho is physician in charge of Admissions at the Khao-I-Dang Hospital. He was not sure what to do with me—an older, family practice physician. The other day he hesitantly asked if I would be willing to work for a short time in the OPD [outpatient department] with the French team, MSF [Médecins Sans Frontières].

Late in the afternoon, after finishing my work with the French, I go back to Admissions and help them finish up. Tomorrow I will go to the border camp where they have a small hospital.

At the French ward, whenever there is a break in patients waiting, I sit on a bench. Soon one of the Khmer diagnosticians comes and we talk. In a few moments, others gather. In a mixture of French and English, we talk of America and Cambodia and of the world. Yesterday we were speaking of war, and I said I did not like war. One young lady said, "It is better to make love rather than war." We all agreed. Shortly after I asked a young man about his family. He reported he had 1½ babies and with great laughter said that he was making love not war.

12 November 1981

This morning an ARC member invited me to breakfast at their house. I had toast and coffee. Toast is virtually unobtainable in Thai restaurants.

It is now early evening. I just had a very good Thai dinner prepared by the maid of this house. The custom is to pay her 150 baht per week no matter how many meals you eat here. One baht equals approximately five cents.

Before sitting down to write this letter, I wiped the table of a myriad of insects. By the time I sat down to write, it was covered again. There are so many mosquitoes I'm not sure I can finish this.

14 November 1981

Late yesterday afternoon we had a torrential, tropical rainstorm. For a half hour the noise of the rain on the tin roof made it impossible to talk. In that short time the roads and fields, which had been fairly dry, became quagmires. A light rain has continued through the night. As a result, there are far fewer bugs about at this time.

My life has settled more into a schedule now. I leave here about 6:20 and get into the van at Peggy's house about two blocks away. They drop me off about two blocks from ARC, where they provide me with breakfast. I help load the truck and van and then it's off to Nong Samet. It is about 45 km to this camp—15 km highway, 15 km bumpy and 15 km bumpiest. Arriving at Nong Samet, a border camp not far from KID, I spend the morning on medicine and surgery rounds. Lunch is bought in the morning at a Thai restaurant—rice or noodles and a few strips of chicken, pork or fish. Afternoons I spend in the OPD. We leave Nong Samet about 3:30–4:00 in order to clear the road before it is blocked by the military. Again the bumpy ride. The nice part is the earlier quitting time than KID. However, there is no regular day off.

15 November 1981

Today is Sunday and I work half a day. The ARC team encouraged me to take today off, but I insisted on working. Today I will be a pediatrician. I hope I can remember the pediatric doses. The regular farangs here have gone out of their way to make my schedule easier. After the first few days of fatigue I have felt very well. I do go to bed early unless there is some special thing scheduled for the evening.

In back of our house there is a large open field, part of a Buddhist complex. Of an evening on return from work I go there and sit on a little hillock. It is as near to being alone as I have been able to manage here. Yesterday as I sat and contemplated the distant scene in the gathering dusk, a Buddhist monk-student approached. When he was near, I said hello and he replied in broken English. He squatted near me. It was apparent he knew only a few English words. We fell to naming various items of clothing I had on and parts of the body, he in Thai and I in English.

16 November 1981

I cannot find words to describe the torrential rain that awakened me about an hour ago. It is accompanied by lightning and thunder, but the roar of the raindrops drowns them out. It brings some practical problems, for I must walk the dirt alley for two blocks to Peggy's house to get the van that takes me to ARC. We try not to walk in mud puddles, for groundwater harbors hookworm and other beasties. I am also trying to figure how to keep my wallet and instruments dry. Plastic bags would be fine—however, I don't have any here. I'll figure out something. Yesterday was Sunday and we work only half a day. We were invited to an engagement party and were served a delightful meal. Cambodian crepes consist of a patty of noodles and sprouts covered with an egg batter and fried. They also served green salad from their garden. I have tried to avoid uncooked or unpeeled food, but in these circumstances I could not refuse. I took some pictures of the interior of the house and of the prospective bride and groom. The Khmers love to have their pictures taken.

18 November 1981

I am again a pediatrician for three days. Kathy, the young pediatrician on this team, had been working a long stretch. Finding that I was reasonably able to take care of her ward, she took off for three days of well-deserved rest.

My little bed has a wooden platform topped with a grass mattress. The maid is accustomed to putting a sheet over the mattress, next a blanket or blankets, and then covering the whole with a second sheet. The result is that one is not able to sleep between sheets. For the first few nights, I patiently remade the bed each night. The maid's reaction was apparent, when I found blankets and sheets neatly folded and piled on the bed. We needed no interpreter for me to understand that if I wasn't satisfied with how she made the bed I could do it myself. Actually, we get along well and she takes good care of us.

Yesterday afternoon it was necessary for me to drive one of the vehicles home. Driving on the left turned out to be reasonably easy, with the steering wheel on the right. I did find it hard to gauge the position of the left side of the car, and the poor nurse who rode with me arrived home quite shaken—but safe.

19 November 1981

Yesterday was a tough day. As so often happens, we had a sudden influx of very sick patients with a variety of problems. The difficulty in management stems not only from the obvious language, equipment and supply problems, but also from the philosophy that—insofar as possible—we try to lead the Khmer health workers to arrive at the decisions about treatment themselves. This, of course, requires much discussion with these workers, who have limited English. We are forced by military regulations to leave by 4:00 P.M. I left Nong Samet with a nurse and transported one of the patients to KID, but left four behind—any one of whom may not have made it through the night.

20 November 1981

Yesterday started out a beautiful morning. Having passed the last military checkpoint and about 1.5 km from camp, I asked my friend and driver to let me walk the remainder of the distance. I trudged this red clay road, with beautiful meadows on each side of me, quite happily. Although there was the feeling of being miles out in the wilderness, I nevertheless met a continuing parade of Khmers carrying bundles and going to or coming from mysterious errands. These people, who have been through so much and have so little, are by nature friendly, and so in the beauty of this scene many early-morning greetings were exchanged. It was of little import that I understood none of their language and they understood none of my English or French. I came upon a beautiful garden patch, with symmetrical rows of green leafy vegetables contrasting in color with the rich fertile soil. A gardener was working here, and when he saw me pause to admire his work, he came and stood in front of me, smiling. I tried with words and gestures to express my admiration. In the middle of this exchange, my eyes fell upon his hands, and with a shock I realized he was a leper with only stumps of fingers left. I left in a humble state, feeling I had indeed experienced the saying, "I complained because I had no shoes until I met a man who had no feet."

22 November 1981

Today is Sunday. I slept an extra hour, made myself a breakfast of soft-boiled eggs and toast and hot chocolate. I came out to KID to see the craft center and renew friendships with the Khmer staff here in admissions, and in the French MSF where I had worked for a few days. The Khmers are smarter than the farangs—they close the handcraft center on Sunday, but the farang medical workers are on the job.

My health continues excellent. Working straight through from Monday to Saturday, I did end up rather tired yesterday. I will soon return to Aranyaprathet to do a little shopping, and then a nice Sunday afternoon nap. I allow myself one BM per day, and on that basis can maintain that I have not had the diarrhea so common among the farangs here.

After the first day or two at Nong Samet, the staff there has learned how to use me. The pediatrician uses me as a consultant in adult medicine, the internist for surgery, and the surgeon for OB. It's all good for the ego, and I feel I make a difference and it's worthwhile. Tonight Peggy comes to our house for dinner and Scrabble.

23 November 1981

The mosquitoes are fierce this morning. The repellent is very effective. One evening, shortly after I arrived, I offered Arivan, the old Thai gentleman here, the use of some repellent. He was profuse in his thanks and proceeded to take the bottle to his room. I could not think of a diplomatic way to straighten that out. Fortunately I have another bottle.

24 November 1981

Yesterday I arranged to remain in Aranyaprathet later than usual, in order to cash some traveler's checks. I went to a nearby restaurant and had rice, two fried eggs and a bottle of Coke. Coffee and tea are not Thai-type drinks, and bread is not part of their culture. At 8:00 A.M. each day the Thai national anthem is broadcast by radio and loud speakers. At this moment, anyone outside stops whatever he is doing and stands. Even traffic stops in place. Perhaps an anachronism, it is nevertheless impressive. The work goes well and my health remains excellent.

26 November 1981
Thanksgiving

Yesterday afternoon, a young man who had fallen from a high ladder was brought in. He had sustained head and chest injuries and a wrist fracture. It was quite satisfying to reach back into past experience, do an auxiliary nerve block, and reduce and plaster his wrist. I rode the bumpy 20 km in the ambulance with him. Last evening Peggy and I met in downtown Aranyaprathet. I bought a large bouquet of flowers for Peggy's house and one for ARC—flowers are inexpensive here.

26 November—later

It is unusually late for me to be up, but I am in the mood for writing and not ready to sleep. We were to work only until 1:00 P.M. today, but an influx of seriously ill patients kept us at Nong Samet until 3:30 P.M. It was an unusually hot, humid day, and during my 2.5 km walk home, the expected thundershower struck and I was drenched. I had intended to spend some time helping with dinner, but instead ate a quick snack and took a nap. By the time I had awakened, showered and dressed, it was 6:30 and dark.

As I made my way down JVA [Joint Voluntary Agency] Lane, a truck approached and stopped. I stepped aside to let it pass. An English-sounding feminine voice said, "Dr. Braile, go ahead and pass, we will wait." It was quickly followed by an excited voice crying out, "Dr. Braile, Dr. Braile, it cannot be." Out of the back of the truck jumped Rita Lampart, a volunteer nurse I met in Vietnam some years ago. What a joyous reunion we had standing in a mud puddle in JVA Lane. I quickly insisted that the three ladies come to dinner.

The dinner was perfect and everyone was happy. I sat with Rita and we discussed old times and mutual friends. It was a glorious evening, and I go to bed thankful indeed.

28 November 1981

It has been a busy time both at work and socially. Yesterday, after arriving at ARC house, I decided I must go into Aranyaprathet to shop. Aranyaprathet is about 1 km from ARC, and my steps were hastened by my devious plan. Peggy had introduced me to the Chinese Palace, which not only serves the Thai version of Chinese food but also has Foremost ice cream. And so to end a long hot workday, I proceeded there and happily sat at a garden table, and ate two scoops of chocolate ice cream and had a nice cup of coffee.

Thus refreshed, I proceeded into Aranyaprathet. I have enjoyed Thai food, but I must confess I regret that their culinary culture does not include bread and coffee. One can fairly easily find a replica of Wonder Bread in a few stores, but good solid bread—brown or French—is hard to come by. I searched the market area, wandering through narrow aisles of exotic and odiferous fish and bins of vegetables unknown to me. I finally had to give up and buy a loaf of Wonder Bread.

Next I went in search of a *tuk tuk,* to drive me home in what I consider Asian splendor. This splendor was augmented by barbecued chicken-on-a-stick—which I ate on the way home.

29 November 1981

Today, being Sunday, we worked only a half day. I made two ambulance runs from Nong Samet to KID. The first was with a young man with a gunshot wound, and the second a man with possible appendicitis. The ride over that bumpy road is physically difficult when one is well, but for the poor patients it must really be tough.

I returned to ARC about 1:30 P.M. The stovetop ovens apparently work well, so I decided to try to buy one for Peggy's house and one for ARC. I asked our Thai driver to write stovetop oven on a card, but he didn't seem to understand, until I said it is used to bake cookies. Thai people do not like to say they don't know or don't have any. At any rate, I must have been in every hardware store in Aran. Each proprietor read the card I presented and said something about cookies. The consensus as I get it was that there are no stovetop ovens in Aran and I must go to Bangkok.

After my shopping tour, I had chicken-on-a-stick and then went to the Chinese Palace for an hour of coffee, ice cream and the *Bangkok Post* to read.

2 December 1981

Peggy will spend today with me at Nong Samet. This is part of a program she and I have stimulated to make for closer relations between the various groups who work here. The ARC group has been most warm and generous to me. They insist that I share breakfast with them each day and will not let me pay for it. Accordingly, I proposed to provide breakfast on this day.

Last night, I met Peggy downtown and we completed our shopping. The menu for breakfast is omelet (fried boiled potatoes, onions, bacon, mushrooms and tomatoes), fresh bread (from the Khmers) and orange juice. After seeing Peggy home, I returned to our house. We had bought a half gallon of strawberry ice cream to treat Donna's nausea and vomiting. I left half of it there and brought the remainder home. My Thai friends were huddled in their rooms. It has been relatively cold here—60 degrees—at night, with great winds. I could entice only one of them to have ice cream.

I explained to Som Wit that I had to do some cooking for breakfast the following day. I'm sure this further confirmed in his mind that this was one peculiar American. He informed me that we were out of propane gas. He offered to help me get a charcoal fire burning in the hibachi. And so, on the back porch with the wind blowing fiercely, we huddled over the hibachi. Som Wit soon sought refuge from the cold in his bed. Slowly the potatoes boiled, while I peeled and chopped up the rest of the ingredients. Finally by 12:30 A.M., I had all the cooking done.

2 December—later

The breakfast went off very well. Peggy and I had a great day at Nong Samet. She works Saturday night and we leave Sunday. If I can arrange it, I will work with her. I will have to work hard on packing. I am faced with buying presents for our housemaid and the Khmer workers. Slowly but surely life begins to get complicated.

5 December 1981

I am sitting in a little fly-infested Thai roadside stand. I am at a cross-roads where the road to KID and Nong Samet intersect. In a while, the IRC van bearing Peggy and the other KID night workers will come along, and I will go to KID to spend my last night in this area with Peggy and her coworkers. I am tired from the busy schedule and a hard day's work today.

If my writing is worse than usual, it is because I have an abscess at the base of my middle finger, right hand. I got a lesson in surgery from my Khmer surgeon friend, when he refused to lance it yesterday, saying it was too early. It is painful but not serious. I have hot wet-packed it.

Later at KID, as I finished the above, I suddenly noted that my watch had stopped, and I feared the van had passed without me. I hastened out to the road and they soon came along. I am sitting in the lab writing this. I don't believe I have remarked about the constant hubbub of noise that goes on. It is similar to voices in a crowded theater before the play begins.

I do not plan to work here tonight unless they really need me. I am tired and hungry. Fortunately, the hot-bread lady just came by and I am munching on a small loaf that is a reasonable replica of French bread. Now if I could find a cup of coffee.

The Road to Nong Samet

(To friends at the American Refugee Committee)

The road to Nong Samet is neither long nor famous.
It is smooth in parts and rough in others.
It passes through scenes that remind us of home,
and scenes that are pure Orient and Tropics.
We have passed the time in talk.
We have traveled in silence.
We have shared the peeled orange.
We have traveled that road,
rested in the morning and weary at evening.
At the end of that road, we have shared some triumphs,
and some failures.
I am grateful to the Thais and the Khmers
for the road to Nong Samet.
But mostly I am grateful to you,
for you have shared of yourselves.

Return to the Border

2 April–30 May 1982

To friends and family:

The lives and fate of the Cambodian refugees were very much on my mind during the months following my return from my first tour to the border. As soon as Stateside arrangements could be made, I would try to return. Only this time it would be different, for my wife, Gwen, would come with me. I called the IRC and they quickly accepted our proposal. We would go as unpaid volunteers. Gwen had no formal medical or nursing training, but it seemed probable that IRC would find some clerical work she could do in support of the medical team.

The first leg of our journey was to fly to San Francisco. Our plane was delayed for one hour by bad weather in California. When we finally landed in San Francisco, we were surprised to be told that our transpacific plane would take off from Oakland, and we needed to get there in a hurry. With some difficulty, we engaged a limousine and were treated to a fast trip through San Francisco, across the Bay Bridge, and on to the airport. We arrived just in time.

In those days, the ICM [Intergovernmental Committee for Migration] contracted with World Airways to provide air transportation for Khmers migrating to the United States. Khmers are small in stature, and the airline had modified the 747 jet accordingly. To avoid flying empty back to Thailand, seats were made available to personnel from NGOs [nongovernmental organizations], and any remaining seats were offered to tour groups. When we boarded the plane, it appeared to us that we took the last two remaining seats. We were so tightly packed in it hardly seemed necessary to fasten seat belts.

Instead of heading west over the Pacific, our plane turned north. We were frustrated when we learned that the plane would land in Seattle to pick up a few more passengers. In the transit lounge, Gwen bought a Washington State apple to take to our daughter, Peggy, who would meet us at the Bangkok airport. Peggy was serving a one-year tour with IRC and indicated in her letters that she missed apples. We then stopped at the Anchorage, Alaska, airport before heading to Taipei, Taiwan.

On landing in Taipei, we were kept in the plane, vaguely aware that there was some dispute going on. It turned out that somebody had goofed in the arrangements for one of the tour groups and that they would not be allowed to leave the plane. They were irate, but things settled down when several gun-bearing guards came aboard.

Hong Kong was our scheduled overnight stop, and after 24 hours in that plane we were ready for it. Contact was made with the local IRC office, and we traveled through the dark and narrow streets to the Holy Carpenter Hostel. Gwen and I were assigned to a humble but very adequate and clean room. We were hungry and went out in search of a restaurant. Good fortune was with us, for we found a little seafood restaurant that fed us very well.

Gwen and I both slept well, but about 3:00 A.M. we experienced that bright awakening that is part of long-distance jet travel. I decided to get up and search for a cup of coffee. It was to no avail. In the lobby, I found the two attendants sound asleep and the door securely locked and wired shut.

At 6:00 A.M., we headed for the airport and boarded a Thai Airways plane to complete the last segment of our journey. There was great contrast between World Airways and Thai Airways. On Thai Airways, all the ladies were given mini-orchid corsages; once aloft, a very good American-style breakfast was served. Seated by the window, I could look down and make out the tortured land of Vietnam, where in a sense all of this had started for me.

Customs and immigration procedures at the Bangkok airport were time-consuming but without problems. As we slowly made our way from one line to another, we could see Peggy waiting for us in the crowd behind the barrier. En route, we had become acquainted with several other IRC people, and we gathered together and piled into the IRC van that Peggy had arranged.

It seemed to me that the traffic in Bangkok had not changed much since my previous visit—perhaps a little more congested if that were possible. The van driver delivered us to the Federal Hotel. Gwen and Peggy went sightseeing, but for me it was naptime.

Susan Walker, country director for ARC, and Irma Fiordalisi, a pediatrician with IRC, joined us for the evening, which was to be devoted to dinner at a famous seafood restaurant. We were indeed privileged to have Susan Walker with us, as she had lived in Thailand for 14 years and speaks the language well. Sukhumvit is a major thoroughfare and at that time of evening was very crowded. As a result, our little group became separated. Suddenly I heard Gwen's voice, in great stress, calling, "Peggy, Peggy." I could only imagine that something terrible had occurred to our daughter. I ran as quickly as I could through the crowd and came up to Gwen, who was pointing to the street. There was Peggy, struggling with a Thai man. I started to dash out there, but by then the man had jumped on his motorcycle and taken off.

Peggy came back with a look of anger and despair. Unwisely, she had been carrying her wallet in her hand. The thief, riding with his cohort on a motorcycle, spotted this. The cycle driver stopped. The man in back dismounted, ran to the sidewalk and grabbed Peggy's wallet. Perhaps because it contained $200, or perhaps because she was made of sterner stuff than the thief expected, Peggy ran after him and tried to hold him or knock over their cycle. In the scuffle, she was thrown to the ground, but she did manage to knock her assailant's glasses off and tore off his wristwatch. One of the passersby had noted the license number of the motorcycle, but Susan told us it was unlikely the stolen items would be retrieved.

The fancy seafood restaurant featured many aquarium tanks, which held a great variety of sea life from which we could choose our menu. Gradually we got over the negative feelings engendered by the street incident and enjoyed our dinner.

The balance of our time in Bangkok was spent in errands, napping and completing necessary forms. We traveled to Aranyaprathet in a very crowded ARC van. Gwen was particularly thrilled to see some elephants and water buffaloes. We arrived late in the afternoon and made arrangements to stay in Peggy's house. We were tired, but I was eager to take Gwen to the night market, where we had a nice dinner.

We were assigned to live in House 21, a typical middle-class Thai house on stilts. Our housemates were Seig and Lois Muehl, schoolteachers from Iowa, and Andrea, a British lady with great international experience who was working in tracing. She worked very hard, and we did not see much of her. Tracing is a function that comes into play when there has been disruption of a society and there is need to try to reunite families. In the performance of this, people like Andrea interview persons who are seeking family members and a file is made. It was most interesting and surprising to learn of their successes.

At KID, I found I was assigned to OPD 23, which had been under the management of IRC for a number of months and was functioning very well. In OPD 23, most of the Khmers were of mixed ethnic heritage—Cambodian and Chinese. Dr. Lois Visscher was the attending physician, and I quickly realized she would be a hard act to follow. I guessed that she was somewhere in her early 70s. Despite her age this tall, majestic, gray-haired lady moved with great vigor, and obviously had the respect of the Khmer workers. She had spent most of her professional life in India as a missionary, and in the few overlap days we shared, I did my best to learn all I could from her.

While I was getting settled in OPD 23, Gwen was being introduced to the office staff of IRC. Administration there, like administration all over the world, developed paperwork that requires typing. A Thai lady by the name of Supawadee was the secretary and did most of the typing, and Gwen wasn't sure what she would find to do—but I was confident she would work herself into a job.

Many times an outpatient facility is the first construction in the development of a health service. In KID there were several OPDs. The theory is that with a medical facility in the neighborhood, people are more apt to come at the early signs of disease or illness. Another function of the OPD is to decide which patients have an illness more suitable for hospital treatment. Our building was constructed of bamboo. Inside it was divided into a number of small examining rooms, an office and a pharmacy. Benches for patients waiting their turn lined the central hall. A metal barrel-like structure with a spigot at the bottom was provided for hand washing.

The IRC work schedule was five full days per week, with Sunday and Monday off. I was, of course, desirous of going out to the ARC camp at Nong Samet and was able to get a pass to go there the first Monday I had off. It was wonderful to see my Khmer and farang friends once again. There really was a palpable difference between Nong Samet and KID. Perhaps it arose from the wilderness atmosphere. Perhaps it was the presence of the ancient ruins, or perhaps it was the fact that these people, unlike the KID residents, had little hope of expatriating. I talked with the ARC people, and they were delighted when I offered to come out on Mondays to work with them.

I was assigned to work in the OPD at Nong Samet, and on my first day of work I met Nora. Stately and taller than the average Khmer woman, she had the Khmer smile and she spoke very clear English. She quickly told me she was a graduate in French literature from the University of Phnom Penh. In a short time, we formed an excellent working relationship. A number of the patients we saw were new arrivals from Cambodia, many having gone through great tragedy and bearing the marks of malnutrition, starvation, wounds and tropical disease. When I was in medical school, our professor of pathology was Spanish and had spent a number of years in South America. He insisted that we study tropical medicine. In those days, I was skeptical that I would ever make use of what we were learning, but here in this dirt-floored bamboo hut I was seeing many of the conditions about which our professor had lectured us.

My work in OPD 23 was also challenging and interesting. The Khmer medics were all very intelligent and eager to learn both medicine and the English language. Barbara Behrens, the IRC nurse in charge, had been there long enough to have things well organized. In general, the patients were not as seriously ill as those I saw at Nong Samet; but living so closely together, there was lots of infectious disease, particularly in the children. Malnutrition was also common amongst the children.

Across the courtyard from OPD 23 there was an MCH [maternal-child health] unit operated by Christian Outreach. The personnel in this group were English ladies, and I soon found they brought to this work dedication, practicality and love for their clients. Essentially, their service was not only to the individual mothers and children but in a larger sense to families. I soon learned that the cause of malnutrition and many of the diseases we sought to treat really originated in the social and political situation thrust upon these poor people.

An IRC van was assigned to us, and often when I left for lunch or at the end of the day I would offer a ride to the Khmer health workers.

Having grown up in the Methodist Church, I often whistle the old hymns that I dearly love. One time when I was driving a load of my colleagues, I was whistling one of those familiar hymns when I suddenly realized that many of my friends were singing the tune, of course using words I could not understand. I was so surprised that I stepped on the brakes and turned to look at them, asking how they came to know these songs. One of them, with the great smile so typical of these people, said to me, "Papa, did you not know we are Christians?" He further explained that Baptist missionaries had converted his ancestors to Christianity many years ago.

Naiveté is a common quality among people thrust into a totally foreign community, and I was not without that quality. As a result, in those early days I often told my new Khmer friends to tell me "if there were any way I could help them." This wasn't very smart, since obviously there were many problems they wished to be helped with, but in most cases they were things I could do nothing about. It was my naiveté that led to my "Nora experience" during the second week of this tour.

Early one morning, as I parked near OPD 23, who should approach the car but Nora. I couldn't imagine how she had managed to come from Nong Samet, and in response to the surprised and questioning look on my face, she told me that they had made a perilous and illegal nighttime journey. It was all the more surprising because Nora's family included her mother, who was blind, and her teenage sister. How they made their way along that rough trail on the side of Khao-I-Dang Mountain I could not imagine.

Of course, before we parted I asked Nora if there was any way in which I could help her. Her response was that if she could get a job in KID, she and her family would become legal residents and receive rations and a place to live. Sometimes over here it seemed that the Almighty took charge of incidents like this. I had just recently become friends with a man high up in the UNHCR organization, and he told me that they had great need for interpreters. I told Nora I would go talk to this new friend and perhaps it would work out. Indeed it did, and in short order Nora and her family were legal residents, had a hut to live in, and the promise of daily rice distribution.

Having helped Nora and her family to get settled in KID, I thought that I had completed my services to them. To my surprise, a few mornings later when I arrived at OPD, there was Nora waiting for me. In my usual fashion I asked, "Nora, what can I help you with?" Her reply was, "It's the jewels." "The jewels?" I responded in questioning tone. Nora explained that in preparation for her dangerous trek from Nong Samet to KID she had given her jewels to Ray, a well-regarded member of ARC, for safekeeping. Nora was asking if I would get them from Ray and bring them to her in KID. With a mixture of apprehension and a sense of beckoning adventure, I agreed to see what I could do.

I did not know Ray well at that time, but when I went to his house that evening he did indeed have the jewels and seemed quite happy and relieved to turn them over to me, wrapped in a soiled handkerchief. Feeling like a participant in some intrigue, without looking at the jewels, I stashed them in my pocket and took them to my house. There in the privacy of my room, I undid the handkerchief and found a large, garish wristwatch, very popular with Khmer men, two necklaces, a bracelet, several women's rings, and some loose stones. Totally unfamiliar with the value, I nevertheless assumed that in the Khmer economy this was a significant hoard.

Several times that night I awakened pondering what I had got myself into and visioning passing through the gate to KID wondering if the Thai gate guards would choose that morning to do an unusually thorough inspection of persons seeking to enter KID.

On that fateful morning, I placed that rather bulky handkerchief package in my pants pocket, deciding that the punishment would be less severe if a search was carried out and the incriminating object was not found in some cleverly concealed place. As often happens in life, my worries were needless, for the guard waved us in without a search. I exhaled a great sigh of relief when I handed that burden over to Nora. I saw her only one time after that, only a glimpse as I passed her office. A few weeks later, when I had business in the office where she worked, I learned that she had been expatriated quite promptly.

My only other direct action that facilitated expatriation of one of my Khmer friends had to do with San. He was one of our medics, and with the exception of his younger brother, had lost his entire family to the fanaticism of Pol Pot. San had made several unsuccessful applications for expatriation, and in desperation approached me for help. At this time, the power to accept or reject resided in a Thai lady, high up in the diplomatic world. I went to her office, where a young lady, who was the secretary and who determined whose pleas would be heard, interviewed me. She listened with a compassionate look in her eyes and agreed to give us an appointment. I went with San to this office on that crucial day. The secretary had told me that it was her observation that the official seemed to attach considerable importance to the general appearance and deportment of the applicant. One of the remarkable things about these Khmer health workers was that despite their poverty and difficult living conditions they always appeared neat and clean for work, and that was San's appearance as we walked to the site of this important meeting. The waiting room was filled with applicants, many of whom crowded toward the door to the interview room. After registering San with the secretary, I took him to the back row of chairs and told him to sit patiently. We sat for about one hour and began to wonder if we would get in before closing time. Somewhat to our surprise, San's name was called and I watched him go through that important doorway. It was only a few minutes, but it seemed longer, when San came out with a beatific smile on his face. All was in order and he would leave on one of those early-morning buses within a few days, headed for Phanat Nikhom transit camp and from there by plane to California.

On the appointed morning, I went to the assembly area and found San and his young brother, each guarding a small satchel that contained all of their worldly goods. "Bittersweet" describes many of the situations of life in the refugee camps, and the word certainly applied here. San's face alternated between that lovely smile and an expression that said he realized he was leaving his friends to embark on a journey that would determine the quality of the rest of his life. There were many Khmers gathered to see their colleagues off on the buses. I left with the feeling that I had done well in helping San. But I also realized that in this crowd of Khmers there were many others who, like San, had gone through terrible tragedies and who also had great hopes to escape the life in the camps. What about them?

During this short tour, I followed the schedule of one day in Nong Samet and five days in OPD 23 in KID. The waiting room in the OPD would usually fill up by 8:00 a.m, the opening hour. Patients were registered and summoned to an examining room. The patient was seen by a medic, a history taken and appropriate examination done. If the medic felt unsure, Barbara, the IRC nurse, or I would be called to see the patient. Sometimes, when none of us were satisfied that we knew the diagnosis or appropriate treatment, we would take the patient down to Admissions for consultation. This long file of sick and ailing would continue pretty much uninterrupted through the day. Every day, along with the routine, there were a number of "interesting" cases. Mountain climbers use the word "interesting" to denote a mountain that presents a challenge or when the possibility of a successful climb seems dubious. Somewhat the same usage of "interesting" occurs in OPD medicine in tropical areas.

On the wards at the Nong Samet hospital, the routine was early-morning rounds. Patients were presented by the Khmer medic in a priority schedule, with critically ill presented first, followed by new admissions, and then patients who had been in the hospital for one or more days. My role was to check the history and physical findings, concur in the diagnosis if appropriate and comment on the treatment plan. One of the recurring satisfactions in having the opportunity to be here was to note the progress in development of skills in these medics. None of them had more than a high school education, yet they had absorbed and retained the medical training that ARC had provided them.

While I was spending my days in OPD 23 and the Nong Samet hospital, Gwen was doing secretary work in the public health office and the IRC office, where she was very much appreciated. I stopped in there one morning and was talking to Ailsa Holloway. Suddenly her eyes dilated and her mouth fell agape. I could tell she was startled by something on the wall—which I was standing very close to. I quickly moved away and saw a snake entwined in the bamboo. There was much excitement for a few minutes. A Khmer took a forked stick and dispatched the snake, which was identified as a Malaysian pit viper—very poisonous.

For Gwen and me our tour was very interesting and satisfying. Once again, as I went through the process of leaving, I had the sense that I would be back.

Two Worlds, One Heart

16 September 1982

Here I sit in first class on the 10:13 A.M. flight, perhaps an auspicious sign for the balance of this trip. A number of factors make me question the wisdom of this trip. I suppose the reason I am sitting here is mainly selfish; however, I can honestly state that I do feel a real commitment to the poor Khmers and to the Western workers there on long-term tours. At no time in my professional life have I felt more fulfilled than during the two previous trips to Thailand. I am ready to get to Aranyaprathet.

22 September 1982
Aranyaprathet

We are sitting around the table at ARC House 2. The young people are talking, and I must say that much of the conversation goes over my head. I am afraid our communication is not so good this trip. This may be true partly because life is complex. ARC has car problems, and as a result there is no transportation available in the evening. Tuesday night I slept in a temporary room; Wednesday I moved into a nice room of my own. Both evenings I spent delivering cookies, which involved walking many kilometers up and down the highway.

25 September 1982

Last evening ARC had a big party for Ray, a favorite, longtime medic. It started out in minor key with radio communication about shelling at Nong Chan—a border camp about 6 km from Nong Samet. There were 10 wounded. Food for the party was pizzas purchased from a Thai restaurant whose cook had been instructed in the art of pizzamaking by an Italian surgeon. There was much palaver, drinking, and dancing to raucous music. All in all it was not my sort of thing. I kept busy making coffee and driving to the store.

On Saturday and Sunday the team divides in two—each half working alternately Saturday or Sunday. I work today and it will be busy, for I shall be surgeon, internist and pediatrician, to say nothing of consulting for OPD seeing 250–400 patients per day. Further, the Khmers know that OPD is closed on Sunday, so they crowd in on Saturday and Monday.

A schedule for my life is developing. I am first up at 5:30 A.M. and make myself a cup of instant coffee and start the percolator for regular coffee. While washing up, I boil two eggs and fix some toast. We leave here about 7:30. At camp I make rounds wherever I am needed. Then lunch. In the afternoon it's OPD. We get back to ARC House 1 about 5:30 P.M. I usually have an errand in Aranyaprathet. These young people are very disorganized about eating. Consequently, I usually go by myself to night market. I try to be in bed by 9:30.

The landlord, who lives nearby, has a flock of dogs, which of course make themselves at home here. There is also a house cat named Wanda.

26 September 1982

It is Sunday morning and I am waiting for the KID noon bus. Yesterday was a very long, hard workday filled with satisfaction. I was pediatrician, surgeon, internist and consultant to OPD. In addition, a French physician named Philippe came by. He is medical coordinator for MSF border camps, and it fell to me to escort him around Nong Samet. As he left, he invited me to an MSF party last night in honor of his birthday. There were only a few special guests besides the MSF personnel, so it was quite a privilege. The MSF provided great food—open-face sandwiches, kabobs and the best chocolate cake I have eaten in a long time. The only entertainment was dancing, so while the others danced, I gorged. I was there four hours and thoroughly enjoyed it. French dancing appears to be an uninhibited combination of ballroom, jitterbug and acrobatics, and it was beautiful.

Today is a day off for our half of the ARC team. We went to breakfast at a new restaurant in the night market that features foreign, or "farang" as the locals would say, food. I had scrambled eggs and bacon. Subsequently I had my picture taken (very small for new ID cards), and bought a small kettle for boiling my eggs in the morning.

27 September 1982

It is 7:00 Monday morning. Breakfast is accompanied by the loud meowing of Wanda. Ray, who left for the U.S. yesterday, was her benefactor—to the degree he kept chicken-on-a-stick to feed her. I try to avoid feeding her, but this morning she was persistent and I yielded.

Laundry here is a hit-or-miss proposition. I'm sure that every day I am wearing at least one piece of clothing belonging to someone else.

I am sleeping quite well. As usual there is a bottom sheet but no top.

28 September 1982

Last night a group of us went to dinner in honor of [nurse] Jean Jachman's 41st birthday. We went to Ploen's, a new farang restaurant in the night market. I had spaghetti, which was quite good. They also have "pig entrails and pickle soup." If I am brave enough, perhaps I shall try it sometime.

Yesterday we had our first big rain. The road from Nong Samet was slippery. One of our cars slid into a ditch, but the car I was riding in was following, and we were able to haul them out.

Yesterday I awakened with a severe sore throat that developed into sinus pain. I was able to work through the day. Three tabs of aspirin and a nice nap and all is well. Today all I have is a runny nose. There has been much respiratory disease and dengue amongst the staff.

29 September 1982

I'm happy to report I have my watch operating perfectly, including the alarm, the date and Big Ben. I went to the farang market last night. I bought chicken-on-a-stick. I was in the process of bargaining with a *tuk tuk* driver for a ride home when Jill Butler called to me offering a ride. It is nice to know so many people here.

My cold has matured into a full-blown upper respiratory infection, with profuse nasal congestion, discharge and cough. Despite this, I feel quite able to work, eat and nap. I don't get quite as much walking exercise due to the rains and mud. Work and life continue quite satisfying here, and all goes well.

30 September 1982

One of the problems doing internal medicine is that one always has one or two patients whose disease defies diagnosis and whose course seems irrevocably downhill. Currently we have a 15-year-old girl who has rheumatic heart disease that is progressively sapping her of life. I search for some brilliant flash of insight, but none comes. No mail has reached me as yet.

1 October 1982

Can it really be October? It seems a long time ago that I left Seattle, but each individual day flies by and soon this tour will have ended.

Last night the maid cooked. We were served rice, fish, fried vegetables and a chicken stew. It was delicious. Slowly but surely I'm getting this house organized.

It rained all night, but today promises to be clear and hot. The pour-on shower is a little colder every day, but thus far I have resisted heating water as most of the others do.

3 October 1982

Friday night there was a Task Force 80 party at the army base in town. We arrived late, the food was all gone, and there was nothing doing except drinking and dancing. After a short time, Jean Jachman and [her sister] Katharine Donohue and I left. Katharine is a bit younger than Jean and is a Catholic nun. They are both nurses, and it is a joy to see them sharing this adventure together. Jean is married to a Northwest Orient pilot. After dinner, we returned to our house and played Scrabble.

Saturday morning I went into town, bought a newspaper and had a nice breakfast at the farang restaurant. I was planning on making a pot roast dinner for tonight, so I headed for the market. A young girl at the farang market told me it was a Buddhist holiday and not a good day to buy meat, so I decided to postpone the dinner.

4 October 1982

At the end of October, IRC is sponsoring a 3.2 km run to benefit underprivileged Thai children. I am going to try to get in shape for it.

Today was a hard day. It was muggy-hot all day until finally it rained late this afternoon. I worked in Surgery, OPD and the Vietnamese clinic.

NW 82 is an infamous concentration camp immediately adjacent to the hospital, housing about 2,000 Vietnamese. They live under tents, with 1.4 square meters of land per person. Jean is the Vietnamese clinic nurse, and I see their more difficult patients. The reasons for the existence of this inhuman situation are complex, but certainly it is nothing the UN can be proud of.

5 October 1982

I am distressed that, despite repeated attempts, I am unable to discipline myself to write to you at a regular time each day. As excuses, I can mention that work demands vary from day to day, the temperature and humidity are variable, and of course the social life of this house is unpredictable. About the only thing I can predict is that when I get home I am ready for a nap. This evening we have an ARC business meeting.

6 October 1982

The hot muggy weather continues, and at 8:20 P.M. I am perspiring freely. Today was a good day. At present I am the surgeon at Nong Samet, for Noun Yim LyRath, medic, is at KID on a training course. Surgery rounds took most of the morning. We are receiving one or two gunshot wounds or land mine injuries each day. After surgery rounds I worked OPD. Lunch at CRS is getting hard to take. It usually consists of noodles or rice and some thin soup with vegetables and a few scraps of some kind of meat. The saving items are a nice roll and plenty of cold water.

After lunch, I saw several patients and then headed for OPD. En route, they came running for me. A new mine injury had arrived. I was very impressed with the efficient manner in which the Khmer staff handled it. I rode in the ambulance with the unfortunate victim. The driver drove as carefully as possible, but it was all I could do to brace myself and hold the poor man's stump of a leg.

By the time we were through at KID it was time to go to Aranyaprathet. I ran/walked 3.2 km in 22 minutes, returning home thoroughly soaked with perspiration. A nice shower and a nap and I was ready for dinner. I drove into town and bought chicken-on-a-stick and tomatoes and some ice cream as a treat. This, plus a nice pineapple, made a delicious dinner augmented by *Fiddler on the Roof* played on Lori's [an ARC nurse] large stereo. Some of the girls couldn't resist dancing, so we had a floorshow as well.

My weight is down a little, but I am feeling quite well. I am off this Sunday and plan to do some shopping for T-shirts and sarongs. Thus far, I have resisted the Buy-Me Girls [charming but aggressive street vendors selling all manner of useful and useless local goods].

7 October 1982

This has been the hottest day yet. I'm sure I perspired gallons. I worked in Surgery and OPD, and it was very busy. I saw a number of very interesting cases, most useful for teaching the Khmers. Savong is one of our health workers, a few years older than most of his colleagues. He speaks reasonable English and French, but his work is hindered by a lack of self-confidence, resulting in reluctance to make decisions. Today I walked from OPD to the hospital with him, and he told me that he teaches English to Khmers at his house—earns 400 baht per month. Once again, I am impressed with the ambition and ingenuity of some of these people.

Tonight I went to a pediatricians' dinner at the farang restaurant. I had fried vegetables with cashews and rice. I am again impressed with how well I get along with so little meat.

9 October 1982

Saturday a marauding band of Khmers fired on a Thai military unit and the Thai town, Bong Samet. We set out for camp as usual but found that in retaliation the Thai had closed the road. We did not know how long it would be. Parked by the side of the road, we waited. As the hours passed, we gathered in small groups—some talking, some singing, and some reading or writing. Noontime came and we became hungry. A Catholic Relief Services truck was in our caravan, and amongst the food being transported were a number of chickens. The Thai drivers built a fire and trussed the chickens between split branches. I, of course, hovered around, eager to supervise, but was forced to keep quiet since they obviously had great experience. Soon we all gathered near the fire, and enjoyed a picnic of delicious chicken and a variety of other foods scrounged from individuals' emergency food, which we all carry. Of course, we had no utensils and became quite greasy as we ate with our fingers. Ironically, in the middle of this meal, a fancy car drew up bearing some Japanese visitors. When they saw this strange group of grubby Americans, they hastened back to their car and returned armed with Canons and Minoltas, and took pictures of this scene. Finally, at 2:30 in the afternoon, we were told we would not be able to go into camp that day.

After two days, we were allowed into the camp again. The Khmer staff had done very well in some respects but not in others. They had received three patients with gunshot wounds, two with chest wounds. Saeroeun was the most experienced health worker present. He diagnosed the cause of respiratory distress in one of the chest injuries as intrapleural bleeding, inserted a chest tube, and no doubt saved the man's life.

I haven't seen much in the way of birds here, but there are a number of animal stories. For instance, recently at Khao-I-Dang, in a rat control program, a small bounty was offered Khmer children for rats brought in dead or alive. This proved good business for the children, who promptly built pens and bred rats by the litter. The other morning sitting in the van, I felt my left shoe to be unusually full. On removing it, a frog jumped out. On another morning, on opening the pharmacy at camp, a baby cobra was found—very upsetting since it was probable that the mother was nearby.

11 October 1982

Yesterday was Sunday and my day off. The roads to Nong Samet remained closed by the military, so none of our team worked. I went into town for shopping. Sunday apparently is not a good day to buy meat. I finally found a market with reasonably good-looking water buffalo roasts. I then bought a variety of vegetables and flour. I put the roast on low flame at 11:00, aiming at a 7 o'clock dinner. In the afternoon, I went back to town and bought a volleyball and net, two of those basketry kickballs (the game is called Takoo) and two KID T-shirts. I had talked to the ARC coordinator about providing our Khmers with the volleyball—which may be my major contribution to this situation. Late in the afternoon, the ladies joined me in peeling potatoes, onions and carrots. The roast continued to cook but remained tough. One of the ladies suggested that, in the absence of cooking wine, we put in some gin. By 6:30 the roast was tender. The dinner turned out beautifully. We had saved two bottles of wine, enough for each of us to have a small taste. It was a very nice evening.

This morning it appears we will be allowed to return to Nong Samet. We wonder what we will find. Please do not worry about this episode. Thai authorities are very anxious to ensure our safety. At any rate, by the time you read this, this episode will be long past.

13 October 1982

This morning I got up to a gray, rainy day, and I did not feel my usual enthusiasm for getting to work. An epidemiologist, Barbara Behr, came by to ask if I could attend the BCMG [Border Control Medical Group] meeting at 10:00 A.M. The team agreed I should attend, so I have an easy day.

Yesterday was a good day. An internist from IRC came out to see Nong Samet—name of Bruce something or other. I took him in hand as part of my belief that there should be closer cooperation between ARC and IRC. We saw all of the camp, plus I managed to put him to work enough that it was a good day for all of us. We saw the Vietnamese clinic patients. Living under much stress and more sophisticated than our Khmers, they have much more in the way of functional complaints than the Khmers.

14 October 1982

How can I write to you without dwelling on food? I can't. Yesterday morning the team decided, as I told you, that I should go to the BCMG meeting. Jokingly, they suggested I would have time to fix dinner. I bought four cut-up chickens. I salted and peppered them, added garlic, and put them on very low heat to simmer all day. At the meeting, Becky (medical coordinator) decided to go out to Nong Samet in the afternoon. I could not let her go alone, because of the terrible muddy roads and the unsettled political situation. On returning to Aranyaprathet, I did some last-minute shopping. We made mashed potatoes and a very good gravy, and had tomato and cucumber salad. It turned out to be an excellent meal. The team has voted that I should rent a stall in the night market and open up "Louis's Cuisine."

19 October 1982

Today I shall tell you more about Wanda. Wanda is a male cat, black with white paws and chest. His original name was Walter, but apparently Wanda was felt to be more euphonic. Ray, medic and philosopher who left here two weeks ago, was Wanda's original sponsor. Ray fed Wanda on chicken-on-a-stick. When Ray left, Trish took over the responsibility, but now she is gone. None of the rest of us is a cat lover. Right now, Wanda is brushing against my toes and meowing in a demanding tone. At a house meeting yesterday, we discussed Wanda's fate. At first, the general consensus was that Wanda had to go. Then someone brought up the mice and rats Wanda catches. Wanda has won a reprieve, but who will buy him the chicken?

I am in charge of CME [continuing medical education] for the Khmers, and thus far it goes well, with my colleagues volunteering to take classes. Teaching is top priority here.

After considerable political turmoil in the camp, things are settling down. One of the Khmer leaders was assassinated while on a trip last week. He was in disfavor with most everyone, and perhaps when the tension settles down things will improve.

20 October 1982

My major contribution to ARC this tour is completed—the volleyball court is constructed and in action. For a while, it looked like this project would never come about, since installation was delayed repeatedly. By late afternoon yesterday, it was done and the Khmers were happily playing.

Minolt is a Thai ambulance driver. We are good friends, since we have shared the road to KID many times. Yesterday, with an air of urgency, he beckoned me from across the courtyard. Using some words, he handed me a plastic envelope, neatly stapled and labeled. Inside were some light gray and white chips. Cookies? Candy? Geological specimen? How nice of my friend. Then a farang nurse said, "Bones." A patient of ours had died at KID and Minolt had brought back the crematory remains for the family. Such is life in Nong Samet.

LyRath is back from his two-week surgical CME at KID. He is disappointed that they did not have him wield the scalpel while he was there. He did learn something, however, for yesterday, as he strode into the little surgery in Nong Samet, he looked about and began to issue orders about cleaning up the place. His disdainful expression as he stared at the cobwebs in the overheads revealed that those Swedish nurses at KID surgery had reached him.

21 October 1982

We have a 15-year-old Khmer girl on the medicine ward dying of intractable heart disease. Nutrition is a problem for her. One thing she will drink is strawberry syrup obtainable in only one store in Aranyaprathet. Yesterday, she also asked for a coconut. Finding these two items took me all over Aranyaprathet. I have really become a Thai driver, quite capable of parking a car in the middle of a main street, and a Thai pedestrian, making my way between weaving traffic.

22 October 1982

Today has been a bit stressful. The 15-year-old girl, whom we have all striven to help with her advanced rheumatic heart disease, died. Her death was gradual over several hours and attended by the chanting of Buddhist priests.

24 October 1982

For the first time this tour, I am seated at a comfortable desk with suitable light and proper height of chair. I have no excuse for poor handwriting. I am in Hua Hin, a three-hour bus ride from Bangkok. I left Aran this morning at 5:30 and arrived here about 2:00. I really miss you here, for this is a beautiful beach with fine white sand, and the waters of the Gulf of Thailand are warm and smooth.

I will stay here till Tuesday, then return to Bangkok. I really needed a day or two of rest and to be by myself.

Yesterday was the day of the great race. I had heard Chris Feld say she was going to enter, but thought she would have to walk part of the way. We agreed to go as partners. There were between 300 and 500 runners. I thought I would do well to run a block. However, when the starting gun went off, there was a great surge of enthusiasm. Chris and I did quite well, running about 75 percent of the 3.2 km, and walking the rest. Father Pierre, with whom I have formed a warm friendship, greeted me with the statement, "You nearly won." Actually, there were a few who came in after we did.

25 October 1982

Hua Hin—and it is raining, just perfect weather for alternate napping, reading and writing. My trip here commenced when I awakened yesterday at 4:30, a few minutes before my alarm was due to sound. Stumbling around our quiet and darkened house, I performed my morning ablutions. Wanda, the cat, who does not rank high in my affection, spoiled my attempt to be quiet. Crisscrossing in front of my feet, she caused me to stumble and step on her. I'm sure my housemates awakened and concluded I had kicked her a mighty blow.

In the dark of predawn, I walked to the train station. There in its patch of light, the two-car train was preparing for departure. Shortly after departure, the light of dawn revealed beautiful panoramas of rural Thailand. There were frequent stops at small stations. The train became more crowded, and soon a young Thai mother and bright-eyed one-year-old child were sitting across from me.

At each station, peasant hucksters boarded and made a quick pass through the train, selling a variety of Thai foods. I purchased three boiled eggs and an orange soda for breakfast. The egg had been boiled to the consistency of a rubber ball.

The beauty of this early morning journey was marred as we entered Bangkok, for here the tracks lead through the poorer section of the city, and the filth was incredible. Arriving at the Bangkok station, I proceeded to the information desk, where an English-speaking taxi driver waylaid me. With only a little bargaining, I yielded and he took me to North Station, just in time to catch the Hua Hin bus.

28 October 1982

Sweating and hot and just a shade exasperated, I am sitting in the North bus station (Ma Chit) in Bangkok, waiting for the 10:30 A.M. departure to Aranyaprathet. I had breakfast with Susan Walker at the Trocadero this morning, and then engaged a taxi. The driver was a nice older man. He drove in a most leisurely fashion, and assured me he was letting me off at the right station. It turned out to be an Orange Crush bus station, which really wasn't too bad since the Air Con station was only a block away. However, a not so helpful information attendant pointed me 180 degrees in the wrong direction, so I ended up walking several blocks. My two bags are heavily laden with red tape forms from Susan to Becky, and goodies for the team—wine, cheese, ham and bread.

I shall be quite happy to get back to Aran and its relative peace and cleanliness in comparison to the noise and carbon monoxide of Bangkok. Last evening, I had dinner by myself at La Paloma, a nearby French restaurant.

31 October 1982

Last night I again put on a pot roast dinner. However, the evening was somewhat overshadowed by melancholy. On Friday night there was a hassle between the TF 80 commander and Tiger Man and two of our Khmer workers.

Today is Loy Kratong day and the big party sponsored by TF 80. ARC has fairly well decided to boycott the party in protest. As in so many such situations, there is considerable question about what good or harm this may do.

We were encouraged to dress Thai-style for the party. Accordingly, yesterday I went shopping for a Thai shirt. One can buy any number of U.S.-style shirts in Aran with a choice of USC, Notre Dame or New York University emblazoned across the chest. Finally, in the depths of the day market, I found a store that had Thai shirts. I had great difficulty being sure I was buying a man's shirt and not a woman's blouse. Through a combination of sign language and getting the saleslady to do the Loy Kratong dance in the aisle I managed.

1 November 1982

The party itself was very nice, although interrupted by torrential rain. It was another example of how rain here only seems to delay activities, whereas at home it would destroy such a party.

My major assignment this week is OPD; however, Dave, the internist, continues intermittently sick, and I had to cover Medicine and Surgery today as well. It was a fairly tough day. Claire, the new Belgian nurse, is a flutist and quite interested in the recorder. We started working on some of the duet music I brought along.

3 November 1982

My letter-writing program is a shambles. Evening activities have been frequent—chess games intervene and now Ping-Pong. Working OPD, I must leave at 7:00 A.M. For the first time over here I am having diarrhea. It just started last night. I hope it doesn't get bad.

This Saturday ARC is putting on an all-Volag party for 200 people, and I am supposed to provide popcorn and peanuts.

I am working very hard this week and find OPD to be the most challenging, as usual. I have been here long enough now to feel free about offering suggestions. Becky, the medical coordinator, will probably be glad to see me leave. Last day of work scheduled for 14 November.

3 November—later

I continue with cramping and diarrhea. My weight is down to 150. I am working quite hard during the day. There are some major differences in my eating: there are rarely seconds, virtually no fat, less sugar, and only an occasional dessert—ice cream. No doubt a healthier diet than at home.

Tonight I go to the Deli restaurant to talk to some medical students and residents regarding my view of family practice. The intermittent arrival of mail here makes the world you are living in seem even farther away. It is hard for me to visualize taking up life at home after 1 December, but I suppose I will adjust again.

4 November 1982

We had a very interesting day in the OPD. I saw my first case of Stevens-Johnson syndrome, an extreme inflammation of the skin and mucous membranes. Also a young Khmer lady came in with two unimpressive skin lesions, one on the left leg and one on the elbow. The Khmer diagnoser had detected anesthesia in these lesions and was already suspecting leprosy. This was a great teaching situation, so we gathered several other Khmer diagnosticians together and demonstrated that the lady's lesions were indeed anesthetic. It is almost certain: the diagnosis of leprosy is correct.

5 November 1982

Came home late from Nong Samet today to find lots of mail had arrived, for which I am very grateful. I spent a delightful half hour reading letters and drinking coffee.

The latest creature anecdote: We have a pop-up electric toaster, very modern. This morning, when I put the toast in and pressed the lever down, a lizard popped out of the toaster. Yesterday, while standing in the latrine, I spied a long, skinny tail protruding from the wall. I only splashed my shoes a little bit as I hastened out the door and around the latrine, where I found this tail belonged to a fair-sized lizard, not a snake.

7 November 1982

Today is Sunday, a day off. Dave, internist; Dim, his Thai girlfriend; Claire, Belgian nurse; our Thai driver and I went to Sakeo Falls, about 20 km beyond the town of Sakeo. We traveled in a small Toyota pickup. The falls are not large but form a beautiful scene, with a large and deep enough pool at the bottom for swimming. The water was cool but quite pleasant. We had lunch and then hiked around a bit in search of monkeys reported to be nearby. We did see one snake scurry away. Our Thai driver and the Thai girl were not too comfortable about this exploring. He kept talking about tigers.

9 November 1982

Some days over here commence with a negative ambience, and this was one of them. I got up late. I forgot the radio. I misplaced my pack and spent an hour wondering what would be the consequences if it had walked away. I had to go to the bank and thus stayed late in Aran. While waiting for the bank to open, I went to the PO to check the general delivery. The clerk was in the process of sorting mail. He had a bundle of letters tied with 12 pieces of common string. With the patience of the East, he untied each of them, whereas a Westerner would have cut them. There was no mail for me here, but Susan later brought some with her from Bangkok.

Reentry

The intensity of life for a farang in a refugee setting is such that it is common to develop a mental set of two worlds. There is the world of comfort, status and conformity from which we came, and there is the world of Khmers, Thais, exotic foods, crowded days, distant artillery and bright colors. The latter is also the world of *mai pen rai,* the Thai saying that means "never mind." It is in common use for trivial events such as accidentally bumping into somebody, and to more serious events such as a fender-bender accident.

Reentry is the mental and physical phenomenon necessary for the farang to readjust from the world of *mai pen rai* to the sophisticated world of his origin. For me, that readjustment commenced gradually as my departure date of 14 November approached. There was no letup in activities. On my last day, I worked at Nong Samet until 1:00 P.M. and then hastened by jeep to Aranyaprathet.

The air-conditioned bus to Bangkok takes four hours. One was ready to leave just as I arrived at the station, and as a consequence I boarded without anything to read. It was just as well, for I spent the hours studying my Thai fellow passengers and enjoying the passing vistas. Night fell as we came to the outskirts of Bangkok, and we were soon in the clutch of traffic. The flashing lights, the horns, the odor of engine exhausts, all were sensory confirmation that I was on my way.

"Running errands" is a common activity for farangs in Bangkok. Some farangs become expert in using the municipal bus system. I generally favored the *tuk tuks.* In 36 hours I had my fill of Bangkok.

The first leg of my flight was from Bangkok to Hong Kong and scheduled on China Airways. American chauvinism makes one dubious of foreign carriers, but these airlines have counteracted this tendency very well. The airbus we boarded was immaculate. The seating arrangements were comfortable and the service impeccable. The creature comforts of a comfortable seat, a good meal and air-conditioning made Aranyaprathet seem farther and farther away.

An overnight stay in Hong Kong was occupied mostly with travel arrangements and a few hours' sleep in a modern hotel. A midnight snack at an Orange Julius and a hurried breakfast at McDonald's no doubt contributed to progress in readjusting.

The flight across the Pacific is a blur in my mind, a mix of meals and short periods of dozing. Customs procedures at San Francisco were handled in a friendly manner, and soon I was out in the airport encumbered by my heavy baggage. With great difficulty, I finally arrived at the sole elevator that takes one from the ground-floor arrival area to the first-floor departure area. Imagine my chagrin to see a sign, "Temporarily Out of Order." I struggled up the escalators.

Sitting, waiting for the Seattle plane, I thought about reentry and realized that very quickly I had accepted as reality this other world. It was the world in which I spoke a language in common use, where there is no time for *mai pen rai*. Soon I would arrive in Seattle to be absorbed into the warmth of family and friends. The physical effects of jet lag remain to be dealt with. I have changed in my thoughts and values, but I will once again fit in this modern world, yet I shall not forget Aranyaprathet.

Chicken-on-a-Stick, Sick-on-a-Stick

13 June 1983

ARC has gone first class in its travel arrangements—well almost. We do travel economy class but now we go on regular commercial flights. Gone are the intriguing, small-hour departures from Oakland. Now I depart from Seattle. The flight to Hong Kong was routine. The flight from Hong Kong was only two hours and went very well, as did customs—they didn't even open my bags. Wichai, the driver, was waiting for me. Susan Walker had given him an identification picture of me, but he laughed and said he only needed to look for his father.

16 June 1983

The conversation could have taken place in a VFW or American Legion club in the U.S. We were sitting around the table in ARC House 2 after dinner when the ladies started telling war stories. It concerned a trip to Nong Samet during the bad days when they found themselves beneath the apogee of shells from the Vietnamese and shells from the Thai, and their conflicting emotions when they found the bunker filled with Vietnamese refugees and no room for farangs. These are brave ladies I serve with.

16 June—later

Today was my first day of work. I spent most of the day visiting the various centers of the camp, greeting my Khmer friends. Their happy smiles and warm welcome confirm the rightness of my decision to come.

18 June 1983

Yesterday was my first full day of work. On arrival, I found the surgery in a state of activity. A two-year-old had just arrived with an accidental gunshot wound to the head. It was a hopeless case. LyRath did the few measures that could be done very well and was very good in dealing with the parents.

21 June 1983

We are seeing a great deal of tragic injuries and disease. The worst are the infants with malnutrition. Some of them respond to medical care, but some seem to have lost too much and their little flames flicker and go out.

Life here is filled with contrasts. The other day I hitched a ride from Khao-I-Dang in a huge water truck. The driver, a replica of U.S. truck drivers, had fixed his cab up nicely with flowers and cushions and Buddhist symbols. His very fine stereo tape deck played some beautiful Thai music as we rolled along, passing oxcarts and heavily laden pedestrians.

My theory for staying well here is to eat well, drink lots of potable water and walk a lot. Every morning I get out of the van about 2 km from camp and walk in. The Khmers who are hacking little garden plots out of the jungle have become accustomed to this strange white man carrying his little pack and trudging down the road. We exchange good mornings, each in our own tongue.

23 June 1983

Today is my last day as pediatrician. Tomorrow, Mary O'Conner returns, and I will take care of surgery, obstetrics, and serve as bike-riding consultant. Making rounds on about 40 little ones each day and accepting about one death per day is a bit tough. I would not care for this over the long haul.

25 June 1983

Last week was tough. Peds was quite demanding. Thursday at noon and yesterday at noon, we received major casualties from land mines. One had a chest wound, and LyRath and I put in a chest tube. The trip in the ambulance is really indescribable. With three severe casualties, there is hardly room to turn around. Each has one or more IVs. The heat and noise in that little aluminum box are punishing. One can only imagine what the poor Khmer wounded are experiencing with each jarring lurch. I try to go on the serious runs—not that I am really better prepared to handle the problems, but I still am not comfortable seeing young women doing such tough duty. I really admire the women farangs of the border camps. They truly have great courage and dedication.

On Thursday evening, I ran into Anne Armstrong in Aranyaprathet. She offered me a ride home. Later that evening, we had dinner at the night market. She left alone driving an IRC van. Near the railroad crossing, her car was struck by machine gun fire. She sustained a grazing wound to the forehead and a shallow puncture wound to the buttocks. She was able to continue driving to IRC house. At the Aranyaprathet hospital, her wounds were found to be minor, but she was nevertheless sent to Bangkok yesterday.

Tomorrow evening, I am going to put on a pot roast dinner. This afternoon, I plan to go to KID to visit OPD 4, where I am told some of Peggy's Khmer colleagues are working. Monday evening I hope to have the first meeting of the Aran symphony. (Larry Li on the mandolin, Claire and I on the recorder.) So you see, my social life does not suffer.

26 June 1983

Sunday, and I work this morning. This evening I put on a pot roast dinner. I just put 5 kg of meat on to slowly cook. I refer to it as beef, but my suspicion is that it is water buffalo. This will be a celebration of Becky and Supot's wedding, and I will get some flower leis for them.

Last evening, I went to the Catholic Church service with Bernadette. The service started with the singing of "Amazing Grace," a cappella. There was prayer, a sharing of concerns and communion. The theme was taken from St. Paul's writings, "Show your love by your service to your fellows." The sharing of concerns in this setting was very meaningful. I believe I may go again.

27 June 1983

Oh me, I was determined to get to bed early tonight. The big pot roast dinner came off excellently. All 15 of the team showed up, and we had a good time together. The menu was pot roast with potatoes, carrots and onions, and gravy (best I ever made), green salad (cucumbers and tomatoes), and fruit salad (pineapple, banana, papaya and grapes). I gave Becky a towel that said, "Make love, not chicken soup."

29 June 1983

I don't know if I am more tired from my work during the day or play during the evening. Today was quite pleasant at Nong Samet, with no tragic cases to handle. The rainy season has set in. I now have my bike in full operation. In the morning, I make surgery rounds and then help in the Vietnamese clinic. After lunch, I ride my bike to OPD l, spend half the afternoon there, and then go to OPD 2 for the second half. Back to the hospital, I make evening rounds before heading for home. Today I had to use my yellow poncho to keep from getting totally drenched, and I form quite an apparition for the Khmers as I ride the muddy roads and compete with myriad other cyclists for the smoothest sections of the rutted roads. I am followed by the muted, good-natured laughter of the street-side merchants and the occasional friendly call of "Papa."

3 July 1983

Today is Sunday and my day off. I got up at the usual time and went to breakfast at Kim Kim's. I had orange juice, coffee, a waffle, and scrambled eggs and topped off with a scoop of chocolate ice cream. I had determined not to fill my letters with accounts of gustatory delights, but this was such a good menu I could not pass it up.

Friday night was exciting. As with most tales, it requires a bit of background. Jill Butler had invited me to dinner at the Christian Outreach center. IRC is promoting a 4th of July party and had asked all American Volags to contribute money and talent. As you know, I have little of the former and less of the latter. The meeting was to be Friday evening. I proceeded to Jill's, where I enjoyed a delicious dinner featuring pork cutlets. After dinner we sat and talked for a while, and then Jill suggested we might "go out for a drink." I twitched a little, realizing I was late for my IRC meeting. Jill dropped me off at our house about 9:00. I picked up Vicki Florine (nurse), and we went to IRC house. There they were in the throes of trying to learn to sing the Thai national anthem in Thai. The only thing worse was when they practiced the "Star-Spangled Banner."

I felt an insect land on my left shoulder. With my right hand I reached up to crush it. I felt a sharp sting at the base of my middle finger. Seated next to me was a Thai woman, who identified the insect as a bee. Not having my first aid kit, I moved quickly to get Vicki to come with me back to our house. A young IRC man sensed the urgency and insisted on coming with us. We drove to our house and soon were seated at the table with adrenaline syringe ready. Ten minutes passed without symptoms, and it became apparent that the stinging insect was benign for me. We finished the evening with a trip to Kim Kim's for ice cream. While we were there, the rest of the ARC team, concerned about me, came to the house to check on me. When they learned we had gone for ice cream, they of course assumed I had chosen a novel way to excuse myself from a frustrating meeting.

Yesterday was a demanding day. Saturday is the toughest workday of the week. Half of the team goes out and attempts to operate all the services. On arrival, I found they had just admitted a Khmer woman with snakebite. She stepped on a small snake about five hours previously and suffered a bite on the great toe with two very small fang marks. She was cardiovascular stable, and there was only a slight amount of local swelling. They killed the snake and brought it in. The head was badly mutilated, but we could identify the fangs.

We recently received a current protocol on management of snakebite. While this lady did not appear to be seriously bitten, I decided to test our readiness. Theoretically, the ambulance was supposed to have antivenom available. I talked with our Thai ambulance driver, and together we searched the first aid equipment to no avail. The driver suggested that the Thai OPD might have antivenom and went off to talk with them. He soon returned, rather apprehensive, saying the Thai doctor at OPD did not have antivenom, but thought the patient should go to Khao-I-Dang.

The art of diplomacy is the avoidance of confrontation. I thought that if I brought the patient to see the Thai doctor, we might confer as colleagues. We bundled the lady into our truck and brought her to the Thai OPD. The young Thai doctor agreed that she did not require antivenom, but insisted she should have a cortisone preparation. This is specifically negated in the current protocol. I tried to explain this to my young colleague, but alas, my diplomacy failed, and we were in confrontation. There are few things in this tropical land that can be called cold, but his response to my parting handshake and the expression on his face certainly qualified. So much for diplomacy.

In the examining room, I observed as the Khmer medic took the history from an ailing Khmer mother. My mind was not on their conversation, for I was watching her active two-year-old boy, the victim of some military action. His left arm terminated in a stump, two inches from his shoulder. Interested in the contents of an envelope on the bed, he pulled it toward him with his agile feet and toes. He used his mouth and good right arm and hand to empty the contents. Later, as he was leaving, instead of putting on his flip-flops, he tucked them between his cocked head and raised left arm stump, leaving his good right arm free to investigate various items as he walked down the hall, oblivious to his handicap.

On this hot afternoon I arrived on my bike at OPD 1 simultaneously with the arrival of a patient "sick-on-a-stick." This is the local expression for the native ambulance service. A long pole borne on the shoulders of two to four men, in the center of which a suspended hammock supports the sick one—this is the basic transport for the very sick. It was apparent this lady was very sick, and I immediately ordered her shifted to our OPD truck. I drove rapidly to the hospital. While the patient was off-loaded, I went to the surgery to check on the condition of a fresh mine injury. On return to the medicine ward, I found the staff engaged in CPR on the patient we had brought in. Despite suction, assisted ventilation, IV therapy and cardiac compression, there was no response. After 15 minutes, drenched with perspiration and frustrated by death, we discontinued.

Apparently Khmer custom calls for the body to be transported wrapped in a grass mat. With plenty of help, we moved the body back to the OPD truck and slowly drove to a small hut near the village market. In this crowded neighborhood, word had spread quickly of the death of this mother, friend and neighbor. Instead of the usual cacophony of village life, there was silence. The lady's daughter rushed to the back of the truck and by herself succeeded in lifting out the grass-mat-enveloped body. It was obviously a physical impossibility for her to carry this load, and so I took it from her. It was indeed a load and much farther to her home than I expected. The body slipped back and forth within the grass mat, and I feared I would drop her. With what seemed to be my last reserve of energy, I deposited her on the bamboo platform in her humble little home. As I left, the moaning dirge of death began to fill the air.

Fortunately it was the end of our workday. I returned to the hospital physically, mentally and emotionally spent.

Therapy for the preceding can be the ride home through the beautiful Thailand countryside, with my good friend Ellie Valleroy at the wheel and a stop at a roadside stand for a cold Pepsi.

6 July 1983

This week I am the internist. It comes at a busy time on the medicine service, with a broad cross-section of major diseases. For some reason, there has been a marked increase in poisoning. We have several cases of undiagnosed disease progressing to inevitable death, despite all our efforts. We even have a full-fledged diabetic. In a world where I seldom see anyone within 10 years of my age, I am pleased to have several patients older than I am.

7 July 1983

The young Cambodians who are our colleagues in providing medical care are a picked lot. A minimal knowledge of English is necessary for them to start their medical training. As a result, most of them are at least high school graduates, an attainment far above the average for Khmers. They share the Khmer traits of friendliness, sense of humor and sensitivity. These qualities, accompanied by superior intelligence, make for great companions.

Virac Mak is one of these. With broad shoulders, tapering down to slim hips, his outstanding physical characteristic is a wide, beautiful smile. Good humor marks his demeanor, and every morning he appears clean and shining, his clothes pressed and spotless.

A week ago word reached us that Virac was sick, his blood smear positive for malaria. I was asked to make a house call. With one of Virac's Khmer friends as guide, I walked across the hot barren space that had once been the infamous NW 82—site of incarceration of hundreds of Vietnamese. We entered a warren of small Cambodian-style thatch-and-bamboo huts. In the shaded porch of one of these, Virac lay in a hammock, his beautiful Khmer wife and children gathered around. Virac's usual look of handsome virile health had faded away and was replaced by pallor and thinness, the result of malaria as well as nausea and vomiting caused by the medication. I was of course intent upon his illness and made arrangements for intravenous fluids and medications. After this was accomplished, we sat and talked. I studied this small hut, its crude bamboo furnishings and the dirt floor. What a testimony to the courage and dedication of this young family that every morning Virac leaves here dressed so clean and neat and ready to treat his people.

15 July 1983
Pattaya

My bus leaves at 12:30, and I have a few minutes to write. This 24-hour escape from reality turned out quite well. Pattaya is located on the ocean, and the beach is beautiful. However, to my surprise, there were very few swimmers. The Royal Gardens Hotel is in the medium price range and of course has a swimming pool. There were a few people in the pool, but most were ensconced on lounges at poolside taking the sun. I do not believe that bikinis can get any smaller. My route to and from my room led me by the pool, so I had ample opportunity to observe.

The town was crowded with tourists—English, German, and Arabs. I got into a conversation with a friendly young Arab man who thought very highly of the U.S. I had a snack with him, and it was interesting to learn a little about him and his country. Adjacent to the hotel lobby was a Mr. Donut, so you can well imagine that I made up for my donut deficiency. My room had a very nice walk-in shower, and I must have used it 10 times. Even in this warm land, hot water is really enjoyable.

Brother Bob's Tuberculosis Treatment Program

Tuberculosis, widespread in the refugee population, is a difficult disease to treat on the border. Untreated, it is chronic and almost always progressive. Treatment protocols require consistent long-term medication under close observation, requirements not easily met in this situation. Interruptions or premature cessation of treatment can result in worsening of the disease. For several years, it was felt that treatment of tuberculosis on the border was not feasible.

Brother Bob Maat is a 29-year-old Jesuit Brother. Of average size, his most striking physical characteristics are his bushy auburn hair and beard, bright blue piercing eyes, broad shoulders and an almost ascetic thinness. Bob does not wear his religion on his sleeve, but those who know him have seen flashes of the sternness of an Old Testament prophet, mixed with the love and compassion of the New Testament.

Struggling with the ravages of this disease, compounded by the intricacies of international politics and diplomacy, Bob has succeeded in establishing a treatment center for tuberculosis at Nong Samet. Only patients with laboratory proven tuberculosis are considered for this program. Once the disease is proven, the patient is interviewed by Bob. Aided by his command of the Khmer language, Bob assesses the commitment of the patient to long-term treatment, usually nine months in duration. In essence, a contract is forged between Bob and the Khmer in which the Khmer pledges to follow the treatment protocol, knowing that any lapse will result in cessation of treatment.

Recently Bob asked me to see some patients in consultation. It had been a busy and distracting morning on the medicine ward. After lunch, I mounted my trusty bicycle and made my way along the crowded roads of the camp to the TB treatment center.

Most Western-dominated treatment facilities in the refugee camps tend to have an aura of frantic effort, to keep up with the tide of demand for care and treatment. Not so the TB treatment center. This large bamboo structure is cool as it is in the shade of overtowering trees. A palpable quality of peace was present in the single large room. At one end, Ahn, Bob's assistant, was taking the history of a Khmer family. At the other end, Bob was at his little desk, seated on a well-worn block of wood similar to a chopping block. He was talking with a patient. The X-rays and charts of the patients I was to see were on a nearby bed.

Bob presented the patients. I reviewed the charts, examined the patients and looked at the X-rays. The problems presented consisted of questions of continuation of treatment, possible presence of other disease or complications. The records would do credit to any medical institution in which I have worked. The patients, by every expression and action, gave evidence of understanding and appreciation for the care they were receiving. In two hours, I saw seven patients with Bob.

Besides his theological education, Bob is a trained physician's assistant. After seeing the patients, we talked for a few moments. I asked Bob if he ever considered undertaking medical school. The words had scarcely left my mouth when I realized that 10 years of medical education could scarcely improve upon the reality of what this young man has accomplished here.

Many people have asked me why I return to this scene repeatedly. Like many such questions, there is no single, simple answer. Certainly one of the reasons is the opportunity to have experiences such as that afternoon. Brother Bob will probably never attain world fame, but there are hundreds of Khmers who will live longer, more comfortable lives because of his efforts, and likewise many, myself included, who will catch a vision of what a dedicated and talented man can do.

17 July 1983

I returned from Pattaya late yesterday afternoon. I brought loaves of French bread, sliced ham and cheese. This disappeared rapidly. Maribeth Brown (health education) asked me to teach a three-hour course on medication and drug therapy for next Wednesday. I spent the evening studying this. The *Merck Manual* is coming in very handy.

20 July 1983

Today was a break in our rainy weather, and the sunshine was welcome. At the end of the day, an ambulance transport came, and I was quite willing to go. We had two sick ones, an older woman and a young Khmer girl, perhaps 15. This girl had just arrived from Cambodia, where she had been treated for TB. Arriving here, she was found to have a large accumulation of pus in her chest. This was tapped and arrangements made for transfer.

In the clanking confines of the ambulance, bouncing over the rough Nong Samet roads, her beautiful Khmer face expressed apprehension. I took her hand and looking into those wide bright eyes said, "OK." A beautiful smile replaced her expression of anxiety, and she said, "OK." Later, on the smooth road, she stood with me and looked out the little window. We saw the little rice fields in infinite shades of green. Water lay in pools, and there were water buffalo and Thai peasants working and enjoying their land. Her expression became wistful, and I thought I could sense her longing for freedom in her own land.

25 July 1983

Here I am at Phanat Nikhom, trying to get organized in this different living situation. The major difference I sense thus far is that the mosquitoes are fierce. Screen doors, mosquito coils and repellent are really in.

The bus trip down yesterday was interesting. There were few people on the bus. One was a large man, who did not appear to be Thai. Suddenly he stood up, came across the aisle and sat next to me. With rather belligerent tone he demanded, "Where you born?" "America," I replied. With a look of pure malice he said, "I hate Americans, I Vietnamese, Americans kill many Vietnamese, I hate Americans." With this he glowered fiercely and went back to his seat.

Arriving in Chonburi, the bus boy suddenly pointed at another bus headed in the opposite direction. With great horn blowing, arm waving and shouting, he grabbed my bag and indicated I should follow him. I jumped off our slowly moving bus and ran after the bus boy, who handed me my bag and indicated I should run and jump on the other bus, which was slowly moving in the opposite direction. Despite my thongs, I made it fine. This bus was crowded, but fortunately I spied a farang woman. She works for Save the Children and is well acquainted in Phanat Nikhom. She assured me I was on the right bus and helped me to get on a *tuk tuk,* which brought me here.

25 July—later

I have completed my first day at Phanat Nikhom and have indeed seen a lot of my friends from OPD 23 and NW 82. There were heartwarming reunions, for all of these people either have definite dates for departure or are close.

The housing arrangements are adequate. The schedule calls for departure from the house at 7:30 A.M. On arrival at camp, we go to the restaurant, which is superb. The houses of the camps here are made of asbestos boards, not nearly as picturesque as Nong Samet or KID. The atmosphere here is much lighter than Nong Samet, since we are on the transit side, and all the Khmers and Vietnamese know they are leaving. I saw 40 patients in the OPD—most with minor complaints.

26 July 1983

The maid here fixes dinner each evening. Last night we had a curry, a boiled vegetable and of course rice.

Mosquitoes are really fierce here. Last night I climbed into bed having forgotten to put on repellent. After a number of low-level attacks, I got up and put the repellent on.

Robin is the nurse supervisor here. She is making a serious study of Buddhism. The Buddhist equivalent of Lent occurs at this time, and there are many celebrations. Sunday evening she asked me if I would like to go to the nearby wat. We arrived just at the time of the ritual walk three times around the temple. Armed with three incense sticks, we walked around the temple "thinking good thoughts."

26 July 1983

To son and family:

I am spending a few days in Phanat Nikhom. This is a transit camp; in contrast to Nong Samet and Khao-I-Dang, the people here are en route to definite expatriation. I work in the OPD; again in contrast, their medical problems are more mundane. Another fascinating feature is that there are sizable numbers of Vietnamese, Laotians, Hmong, and Yao. As a result, I am usually surrounded by three or four interpreters. It has also been my pleasure to greet a number of Khmers with whom I had worked on previous tours at Nong Samet or KID. Now we all hope that they will find happiness in their adopted countries.

My responsibilities in Nong Samet require me to move from clinic to clinic, and I persuaded ARC to purchase a bicycle for my use. The roads are narrow and rough and often crowded with other cyclists, pedestrians, geese, chickens, pigs and the occasional car or truck. To ride down the main street of the market section is always an adventure. This bicycle is also a therapeutic vehicle, for when I have been stressed at the hospital I often escape to take a short ride on narrow trails through the nearby jungle. I of course keep a sharp eye out for snakes, small animal life and interesting geology.

28 July 1983

Each day here I have seen 40–50 patients in the OPD. The system is different here from Nong Samet. The Khmer health workers serve only as interpreters. As a result, a farang doctor or nurse sees every patient. I must say I prefer the NS philosophy that considers delivery of health care as a Khmer operation, with farangs serving only as consultants. Tonight I am going to stay at the camp, primarily for the experience. There is a very good Khmer restaurant there and plenty of beds in the OPD.

28 July—later

As often happens with good ideas, my idea of spending the night at Phanat Nikhom camp has turned into more than I bargained for. As a result of combined staff illness and holidays, there is no nurse to pull night duty tonight, so I am it—along with three interpreters. The Khmer interpreter's name is Yada, and he is a longtime favorite medic from NS. He will try to handle most of the patients and only call me for the most serious ones. We shall see.

29 July 1983

To Peggy:

RE staying overnight in camp: I spent the evening sitting in a circle with six health workers—Khmer, Lao and VN, and all eager to practice their English. Once during the evening, I took a walk around camp. The houses here are constructed of asbestos paneling, and to Western eyes are completely lacking in the attraction of the bamboo-and-thatch huts in KID and NS. At night, their incongruity is hidden, and the small islands of orange that glow from their kerosene lamps lend beauty to a scene drab in the daytime. Scattered throughout the camp are street-lights. Once again, this Western soul was humbled to find that refugee families were gathered in the cone of light shed by these tree lamps, the children doing schoolwork, the older ones sewing and handcraft.

I am told that night duty can be rough here, but for me it was quiet, and I had a good sleep. The local Khmers bathe in the pour-on shower just outside the OPD. With my *pakima* for modesty's sake, I also bathed there, to the delight of the Khmers. They complained of the cold water, but I found it quite comfortable.

Right now, I am sitting in the Khmer restaurant drinking some of that good coffee I'm sure you remember. Work starts soon, breakfast awaits. I must make my morning report to the arriving crew. I will report on the six health workers all suffering from dehydration, whom I treated last evening with Sprite.

30 July 1983

My morning walk is already over, and I am sitting on the steps of the ARC house. With good reason, there is an accentuated effort at Phanat Nikhom to teach refugees about American idioms. Hearing this makes one aware of how important idiomatic expressions are to our everyday conversation. For instance, how confusing to a refugee would be the expression, "I'm all packed, including the kitchen sink." In return, the Khmers have taught us some of their sayings. One I am trying to remember: "A man who speaks without thinking is like a man who fires a gun without aiming."

30 July—later

Yesterday, 700 refugees in transit arrived from KID (to Phanat Nikhom). It was an emotional experience to see the expressions of hope and fear on their faces as they conclude the first tangible step on their way to a new life.

31 July 1983

My tour at Phanat Nikhom was enjoyable and satisfying. There is a psychiatric nurse there who became my particular friend. It was only after I got to know her a bit that I discovered she is a Catholic nun. It was really enjoyable to discuss the psych factors playing on both the refugees and the farangs.

4 August 1983

I am sitting at our kitchen table. Maribeth and I bought chicken-on-a-stick, corn and cauliflower. I am in charge of Surgery at present, and with LyRath gone it is much more of a job.

Each late afternoon this week, I have had an ambulance run. The passenger compartment of the ambulance comprises a small cube about six feet in each dimension. There are four stretchers suspended from the walls with a narrow aisle between. On a recent trip, I accompanied a young woman having problems with a miscarriage and two mothers with babes in arms in respiratory distress. Shortly after departure it was apparent that one of the mothers was becoming sick from the lurching ambulance. I took the baby in my arms and had her lie down on the stretcher. This six-month infant possessed beautiful dark eyes. As he lay in my arms, he studied me, and slowly his features changed as he prepared to cry. The natural thing to do was sing him a lullaby, and so I did throughout the trip. Each time I stopped, his little mouth seemed to move as if he were saying, "Sing some more"—or was it "please stop"?

10 August 1983

I am sitting in the phone center on the main street, awaiting completion of a call to you. This has been a very busy day for me. Hal, the pediatrician, is taking two days off, and I am filling in. We are in the middle of the worst pneumonia epidemic I have seen. I think we have at least 20 infants with malaria, malnutrition and the occasional meningitis. I have always said that pediatricians here have the toughest job.

This Saturday evening, I will be putting on a chicken and mashed potato dinner. I am more in the mood for it than I was a week ago. I hope I can find some good potatoes. This may be my last letter to you of this tour. I look forward with anticipation to the visit here by you and Peggy. I'm sure the joy you will bring to the Khmers alone will make the trip worthwhile.

8 September 1983

My tooth has continued to give me intermittent hours of severe pain. Tomorrow morning is decision time. Perhaps I should have deferred writing until this chapter is over.

I am physically and psychologically ready to go home. I in no way regret coming here this tour, but have second thoughts about the wisdom of extending. I was greeted on return with warm hugs and handshakes. I had dinner with Becky, Susan, and Steve Miles [ARC volunteer physician] last night. Next week I will probably spend in Dang Rek with the Vietnamese. Their abrupt move there has cast a pall over Nong Samet. Today was very quiet, with few patients appearing. The ground where their tents stood has been bulldozed, but bits of debris remain to testify to the madness of their situation.

Tonight I made my dinner of ham, cheese and rye bread, which I had brought from Bangkok. There followed a good nap terminated by toothache. Some aspirin and a shower took care of that. I then cleaned up my room. I will try to write a few more times, but don't be surprised if I fail. I look forward to seeing you soon.

Tour V

Life as "Papa"

12 March 1984

We arrived at the Bangkok airport on time, well rested after one over-night at Taipei. After getting settled at the Hotel Trocadero, I went for a little walk. It was warm, and the noise, fumes and interesting sights have not changed. Life in Bangkok for an administrator does not have the physical and emotional stresses of life in the refugee camps. Rather it has the frustrations of unending demands, of phone calls made difficult by busy signals or wrong numbers and of impossible requests by personnel from the field. And by the agony of being at the point where what one feels should be done for the refugees meets in unfair conflict with the forces of diplomacy, politics and financial reality. Becky Parks has found that an early-morning run in Lumpini Park is an appropriate therapy. It was my pleasure to join her.

The park is a few kilometers away and our 6:30 venture starts with bargaining with a *tuk tuk* driver. The freshness of dawn still lies on the park, but there are a surprising number of people present. There are various group activities, some doing aerobics and some doing a version of Thai dancing—slowly and gracefully shifting from one posture to another. On the broad pathways there are many walkers interspersed with the occasional runner.

I started out running with Becky. She soon drew away, and I ran by myself. Our path led along the shore of a beautiful lagoon dotted with little islands and in the center a beautiful fountain. I encountered many runners—mostly Thai, a few Caucasians. There are many factors that make up community of spirit, and in this situation age is a major one. The young runners passed me without a change in expression, but the few runners of my age group I encountered, almost without exception, held eye contact and smiled. They seemed to say, "I know about your aches and pains, the breath comes hard, the heart beats fast. But isn't it wonderful that we are able to do this at our age?" We meet at the gate, breathless and perspired. During our little exercise time, the morning traffic of Bangkok has developed to its usual blue smoke and roar. We bargain for the short ride back to the hotel. A quick shower and we are better prepared to meet again the world of frustrations.

14 March 1984

Yesterday I left Bangkok; Ellie Valleroy and I traveled by ICRC van, which was crowded, hot and bumpy, but safe. We arrived in Aranyaprathet about 4 P.M., by which time there was a 2 kg weight on both my eyelids. As soon as possible, I made my way to House 4, where I will stay at least temporarily, about two blocks from the day market.

I looked around the place a little and then I crashed. I awoke at 8:30, hungry and alone in this dark house. My imperative was to go to eat. The truck assigned to this residence was available but had a flat front tire. Wandering around in the dark, I managed to get it jacked up but had to give up when I could not find a wrench for the wheel studs. I walked to the day market and had a rather unimaginative meal of hamburger and French fries, being even a little more disillusioned when they poured my pineapple juice from a Del Monte can.

At Kim Kim's, it was different. They immediately greeted me with my "usual"—one scoop of chocolate ice cream, a cup of coffee and shy smiles. I made my way home safely and crashed. I awakened this morning at 6:30, so perhaps I am past the 3:00 A.M. wide-eyed stares. I am taking the day off for settling in. I presented the maid with a huge pile of clothing for washing.

Notes on Returning

Aranyaprathet remains essentially unchanged. The hundreds of little shops still display mounds of fruits and vegetables, piles of utensils, showcases filled with the latest electronic equipment. The night market awakens every day as darkness falls. Traffic roars, and the mangy dogs still patrol the streets.

At Nong Samet, it is different. The entire camp, including the medical buildings, is gone—leaving flattened areas with only scraps of bamboo and protruding bits of broken furniture, as markers of lives begun, pain suffered and lives departed. It is a sad and haunting scene. About 2 km away is the new Nong Samet. The hospital building is U-shaped, more spacious and well lighted. There is a road in front of the camp, along which we can walk but must not leave to enter the camp. And so, no coffee shop, no restaurants, no market street to ride through as in the old days.

Some of the patients I recognize from previous tours, but many are new. At present, there are many with malnutrition and diarrhea, and there are many IV bags hanging in the Peds [Pediatrics] ward. The sad, steady stream of mine injuries and gunshot wounds continues, and the ambulance runs regularly.

The prediction that this would be a season of intense military activity does not seem to be valid at this time. It has been very quiet, for which we are grateful. The Khmers remain kind and warmhearted and much in need of our help and encouragement, making our work here most gratifying.

16 March 1984

Yesterday was my first day of work, and it was hot—106° Fahrenheit. The new camp is beautiful as far as the buildings are concerned, but does not have the charm of the old one. No coffee shop, no streets to ride down. I saw most of my old Khmer friends, many of whom look thinner and more stressed. I was promptly scheduled for an ambulance transfer—a young Khmer man with a foot blown off by a mine. KID appeared much the same; however, the Buy-Me Girls are not seen—except for one little girl who made a half-hearted approach with some paintings.

Later in the morning, I worked in OPD with Ellie, who is certainly one of the strongest and most liked of the personnel here. The afternoon started with another ambulance run, this time with six passengers. Two boys had superficial wounds, the result of playing with a hand grenade, and a girl with asthma. The rest were accompanying family. At KID, I ran into LyRath, who is thinner but still smiling. His situation is now critical with TF 80 searching for "illegals." Last evening, I had the house to myself, bought chicken-on-a-stick, rice and pineapple, and ate at home. Helen Murphy and I are writing to the Canadian embassy, hoping to mobilize some help for LyRath.

17 March 1984

I have Saturday and Sunday off—yielding to a proposed trade that will require I work 13 days straight—not so good. Last night I ate solo dinner at the Deli, which is again open to the public. Later I went to UNBRO [United Nations Border Relief Operation], where Hans, a TB physician, and another fellow put on slides of their recent trip to Vietnam.

18 March 1984

Yesterday I went to Dang Rek, the border camp for VN, with Dominique—legal, with a pass. Physical conditions for the VN there are much improved, but they remain hopelessly hopeful, and besiege any visitor with questions about their fate.

Tomorrow I start a long stretch of hard work. For a week, I will be the internist. Tim Mastro, the regular internist, is on vacation.

20 March 1984

The roosters crow, the birds chirp and the ants crawl—another day starts. Two items I have forgotten to mention: Saturday afternoon I decided to go to the barbershop. Growing a beard is unpleasant for the first week, for during that time you merely look unshaven. By Saturday, my beard was well started, and I decided to have it professionally trimmed. The smiling barber seemed to understand. He sat me on his chair and laid me back in a most comfortable position. He then disappeared, and of course I fell asleep. I awoke to the first rasp of his razor; he had not understood, and his first swathe took care of my beard. Now I must start all over again.

Also on Saturday I discovered what had happened to my other suntan shirt. My longtime VN friend at Dang Rek was wearing it; I had forgotten that, before leaving last time, I had left him some clothes.

Yesterday was moderately busy. There are a number of empty beds on Adult Medicine, but nevertheless rounds took up a lot of time. I am again impressed with how well the Khmers do in taking care of these patients. I worked in OPD in the afternoon and finished up the day arranging for the transfer of a 17-year-old boy with hemoglobin of 2.6.

Marc and Nancy Knopp invited me to dinner for Monday night. They wanted to hear more about Vietnam. They served refried bean burritos—very good. It was a nice evening and home early to bed. It cools off fairly well by midnight.

21 March 1984

I am now in a schedule. My watch alarm is set for 5:30. I don't always hear it or respond promptly. I am first up in this house. I put coffee water on and two eggs to boil and then proceed to the bathroom. As I come out, the coffee water is hot and while dressing I drink that. I eat, clean up my mess and go back to my room and write you a letter. I then either walk or ride to House 1, stopping at the mailbox by House 21 en route. I arrive at House 1 in time to leave with Bob.

The day at Nong Samet starts slowly, with quick rounds of all wards to see if there are any special problems. Then I sit with the Khmers in soft conversation. By 9:00, full rounds commence. There are always a few patients who have made an excellent response and a few whose condition is unchanged or worse. These are frustrating, since often the diagnosis is unknown. By the end of rounds, I have usually reached the end of my energies and retreat to the lounge for cold water and snack a little from my lunch. I buy a Thai lunch every day—10 baht for rice, a few strips of chicken and an orange. In the afternoon, I see new patients, special problems or go to OPD. By the end of the day, I am sodden, tired and sleepy. A nice shower and I'm ready to go again.

23 March 1984

It rained again last night. These are called mango rains—necessary to the ripening of mangoes. I didn't realize they are also eaten green— taste and texture much like an apple. The rains turn out to be a mixed blessing. I went to bed early but was attacked by a horde of varying insects. I finally had to get up, shake out my bedding and install my mosquito net.

25 March 1984

Friday night I went to dinner at House 3 with Helen Murphy and her friend Jean, a French family practitioner from the suburbs of Paris. Our dinner on the verandah was interrupted by thunder, lightning and a rainstorm. We had a delightful meal and a fine time talking around the table.

I am doing a fair amount of driving these days and am accustomed to the left-hand drive. The antics of the opposing drivers are still amusing, challenging and occasionally frightening.

I bought a hammock and at noontime can usually take a short nap. I have recovered from the fatigue of the first few days here and feel very well.

26 March 1984

Yesterday was Sunday, and I worked. We have four infants in advanced stages of malnutrition, and the probabilities are that all will die. One of them appeared to be moribund yesterday, and I stayed late in the afternoon, but the flickering flame continued. In the meanwhile, an infant who seemed to be doing all right suddenly died. We tried resuscitation without response. And so it was a tough day.

I decided to stay at House 4, perhaps primarily to avoid repacking. The other reasons were the advantage of a smaller house and fewer housemates. I also consider the highway between House 2 and House 1 to be more dangerous for walking and bike riding.

On return from camp, I took a nap and then prepared dinner—an omelet with ham and tomatoes, boiled-fried potatoes with onions, and a large fruit salad. Marike [Keuning Landstrom, ARC volunteer from Holland] plays the soprano recorder. Susan Zainer was here, and with the three of us the German pieces sounded better. We still need an alto. If I were rich, I would have you and Peggy come for a concert. In the evening, we all went to the Catholic service. Father Pierre, of whom I shall write further, spoke very feelingly of the thought that compassion may be the most important service we render here.

27 March 1984

The wild boar has a curved tooth that protrudes from its lips. As the boar gets older, the tooth loosens, and eventually, in rooting out trees and roots, the tooth is left impaled. If a Khmer finds this tooth, he will make a necklace of it, and it is his belief that as long as he wears it neither bullet nor sharp-edged knife will harm him. Of course, entrepreneurs are aware of this belief, and make fake boars' teeth from ivory, bone or plastic; this explains why occasionally we see wounded Khmers wearing the tooth necklace.

There is also a very rare vine called *Wah Trai,* which grows in Cambodia and bears the same properties. It is very expensive, costing 30,000 baht for about 20 cm of vine, dried and fragmented. Believing Khmers who can afford it carry a vial of this and hold a piece of the vine between their lips for protection at times of danger.

I will keep my eye out for a boar's tooth or some of that vine. Actually, it remains very quiet here, although there is a report of some action at one of the border camps.

Yesterday I bought a bicycle, 1,300 baht, equipped with light, bell and lock. One of the advantages of living here is that there is almost always a car available, but it is nice to be independent. All goes well here; the rains have ceased and it is very hot again, but I remain in good health.

28 March 1984

My new bike is working out well. I ride it to House 1 in the morning, and it is most convenient at the end of the day to ride it home, shopping en route. Every day I hang my hammock in the lounge and have a half-hour nap after lunch.

I am getting accustomed to going barefoot. Last night I got all the way into the car before I realized I didn't have any shoes on—a real barefoot doctor.

30 March 1984

This has been a hard week in Peds. The two senior medics and the head nurse have been sick, and Lisa has been on vacation, leaving me without a farang nurse. The ward is now full and soon will need to go to two per bed. I make rounds from 9:00 to noon, and am ready for lunch and a nap by the time they are over. The hammock I bought is proving to be an excellent investment. Thus far my knot-tying has been good. Paul has had his hammock collapse twice. In the afternoon, I see outpatients and new admissions and try to prepare the night staff for the problems of the night.

31 March 1984

Saturday, and my first day off in two weeks. Yesterday was a bit easier in camp, with Lisa's return. At noon, I took a baby with rapidly progressive pneumonia to KID. Once ensconced in the hot little aluminum box, which comprises the ambulance, there is little one can do. The mother sat on the only seat while I stood. She held the febrile child in her lap; there were two fans made of woven reed material. I used these to fan mother and child. As my arms grew tired, my Western mind sought some better means of cooling this child. There is one window high on one side of the ambulance, and I found that by holding the fans in a certain position I could direct the wind of our passing to the mother and child. I failed to notice that while I was working this out the mother was digging out of her bag several items of clothing, which she draped over the baby to protect him from the wind this strange Western doctor was directing toward them. And so once again East meets West.

2 April 1984

A chunk of cheese, some dried-out bread, pineapple and a cup of Swiss Miss cocoa make a fine breakfast. Yesterday was the big race. I teamed up with Helen Murphy, and we came in last. I thought I was doing her a favor, but in truth I had a hard time keeping up with her. There was a party after the race, but the lure of the shower was too much for me, and I went home. In the evening, I went to the Catholic Mass again. Father Pierre is one of few ministers/priests whose life seems to approach the words he speaks. I wish I had the energy and time to attempt a story of his life—40 years in the slums of India and now this.

Today it is back to the little ones. I will also cover Surgery. We have had no deaths recently, but this cannot last. Yesterday, we admitted a little boy with malnutrition who, sitting on the bed in yoga position, covered with flies, would make a cover for *Time*.

3 April 1984

You may on occasion have wondered about my relationships with the young ladies I work with over here. Have no fears. I am strictly "Papa" as evidenced by the following story.

Last evening, as I prepared to go out to do some mail business, M'Liz [Mary Elizabeth Ross, public health nurse] came out of her room and announced she was sick and had a temperature of 101.6. I asked if I could help in any way, and she replied, "Would it be too embarrassing for you to stop at a store and buy a box of sanitary napkins?" I, of course, agreed and asked how I would ask for them. She replied, "Oh, don't worry, you will find them on the counter; they will have a picture of a woman running on the beach."

I stopped at the first store, since it was late. Thai store attendants are usually not all that attentive, but the little Thai lady in the store immediately followed me as I entered the store. I wandered through the store; she followed, mumbling Thai words, no doubt meaning, "Can I help you find something?" Under these circumstances, pantomime is usually my forte, but I could not figure out a way to do this. Finally, I spotted the lady on the beach and grabbed the box. The young lady looked at the box, looked at me, and with incredulous expression again spoke in Thai, no doubt saying, "Are you sure this is what you want?" I nodded my head and proceeded to the man at the cash register. While he made change, she placed my purchase in a brown paper bag rather than the usual plastic sack. As I left, there was considerable conversation and laughter going on.

Such is life as "Papa."

4 April 1984

Late yesterday, we received a critically ill infant, and I went on the transfer. We were stopped on the road by a heavily armed KPNLF [Khmer People's National Liberation Front] group of soldiers, who insisted on searching the ambulance. With those young boys waving around their rocket launchers, it was not a good scene. Later I learned that someone has stolen the head of their Buddha statue, and they are searching for it. I understand this is not an unusual situation, and wars have been started over kidnapped Buddha heads.

Since it was relatively late when I got back to Aranyaprathet, I went to Ploen's and had a hamburger and French fries. My appetite and digestive system seem to thrive on scrambled eggs for breakfast, rice for lunch and American food for dinner—with generous amounts of pineapple thrown in. Despite the heat, I don't think I am losing weight as rapidly this trip.

6 April 1984

A job for you, Gwen. Khmer babies often wear necklaces with tubes of lead. Would you please call the medical library at Eastside Hospital and tell them of my situation. I would like to know if there have been any medical articles written about lead poisoning in Khmer or other Third World children. The ladies at the library are accustomed to peculiar requests from me and are always helpful. Lead poisoning can be a potent cause of anemia—a common problem here.

7 April 1984

For the first time in several weeks, I did not get a letter written this morning. I guess I can blame it on taking M'Liz to dinner last night. She has been sick and depressed about certain aspects of her work. I told her that, with the agreement we would not talk about work, I would take her out to dinner. We went to Noye's and had the fried stuffed squid. Later we went to Valentine's, a nice and proper "nightclub," where I drank coffee and M'Liz drank orange pop. They had a series of Thai girls singing Thai songs and then a Thai man guitarist who was quite good. John Schuster joined us, and we requested "Take Me Home, Country Roads." In a sense, it was ludicrous, but it brought down the house. We stopped at Kim Kim's on the way home, and I think M'Liz felt better after her evening with Papa.

We have had no deaths on the Peds ward recently, but it cannot last, for we have a half-dozen advanced malnutrition cases, which are drifting despite our best efforts.

I have tried my best to maneuver a change in my vacation schedule but to no avail, so tomorrow I will go to Bangkok. I will see the ODP section at the embassy. A chunk of filling came out of one of my teeth, and I will go to a dentist. You know how I like that. Ah well, that experience will no doubt make a subject for a letter.

8 April 1984

I am sitting in the air-conditioned bus headed for Bangkok as I start this letter. Who knows where I shall finish it. This is the most comfortable bus I have been in; air-conditioning is working and a comfortable seat. I hope the driver is as good.

9 April 1984

Herewith is what transpired at the dentist's. I was referred to Dr. Ridge, a Thai woman who appears to be about 50 years old and is managing director of the clinic. She turned me over to a young male dentist. The office and equipment are impressive. Like at home, he immediately took X-rays. He concluded I would need a root canal. This was done with dispatch, and I thought I was ready to go, but I suddenly realized that he was scaling and cleaning my teeth. He found another cavity and believe it or not drilled it out without anesthetic. He filled it temporarily and recommends if I have pain that I return to him or to a U.S. dentist for root canal. His office was nicely air-conditioned, but I was nevertheless quite ready to leave after 2½ hours. One of the young lady assistants walked me about three blocks to the river, where I promptly caught a boat going to the Oriental Hotel dock. A much nicer way to travel.

At the Oriental, I felt justified in having a nice lunch—croissant with ham and cheese grilled, and a plate of tropical fruit. It was 5:00 P.M. when I got back to the hotel—naptime.

11 April 1984

I overslept yesterday morning and did not get started on my errands until 9:00 A.M. I engaged a taxi driver at the Trocadero and started out. First I went to Central Department Store, where I bought some ham and cheese to bring to Aran. One of the Khmer nurses had given me 500 baht to buy him a Casio watch like mine.

After bank and embassy errands, we went to Siam Square, where I squandered taxi time while I had spaghetti and salad bar at the Pizza Hut and coffee and a doughnut at the Dunkin' Donuts. We finally arrived at the bus station, just in time for the bus. I was really hot and tired, and my tooth with the temporary filling was really aching. The bus trip seemed unending, requiring a full hour to get out of Bangkok traffic, taking a total of five hours and twenty minutes.

By the time I arrived home, my toothache had declined, and I took the car and delivered mail I had picked up in Bangkok. I stopped at Kim Kim's and had a BLT and lemonade. Walking to the night market, I found the jewelry store where I had bought my watch, and wonder of wonders they had one that I bought for 450 baht.

I am currently reading a thick paperback having to do with the history of India since WW II. Of course there is a great deal about Gandhi. He was a great believer in natural medicine and every day took a salt-and-water enema. It was a mark of friendship for him to offer to administer such to a guest. I am a great admirer of his courage, principles and philosophy, but can't quite go along with this.

I don't think I have written about the dedication of the hospital. The hospital and OPDs are new buildings, and it is considered appropriate to have them blessed by the monks. On Saturday, I drove to their temple. While waiting for them, I wandered around the grounds and was impressed with the aura of peacefulness. We transported 20 monks. The auxiliary bishop, about 40 years old, rode in front with me. Like many people here, he was impressed with my age. Buddha, he said, advises that we spend the first stage of our life for our family and should spend this second stage working for the people of the world. He invited me to come to the temple to get my "mind cleansed." I'm not sure what he meant by that.

It is getting very hot again. I will pump up the tires on my bike, go to the PO, then take a nap. If my tooth continues to give me trouble, I will have it extracted.

12 April 1984

We had a staff meeting last evening. Afterward, I took Candace Vanderbeek to dinner at the Deli. At noon yesterday, I was in town and ran into my friend Jean Rismondo—the French physician. He asked me to join him and several MSF nurses for lunch. It was a most welcome chance to exercise my French. I had quite a time explaining the recent theft of the head of the Buddha. This was even more difficult when I used the expression "this caused the Nong Samet Khmers much loss of face." I have also made a little progress with the Thai language. On occasion, I can count to 20.

Yesterday, the ants in my bed got just too numerous, and I went to the store for ant spray. That was difficult, but I managed and the spray was effective.

13 April 1984

We had a session of recorder playing last evening. We play mostly German pieces but spent some time on Vivaldi. Prior to the music, I put on a simple little dinner—grilled cheese-ham-onion sandwiches and a huge fruit salad. It was made of sliced pineapple, cantaloupe (a new find at the market), papaya and bananas, to which I added four scoops of strawberry ice cream. I must say it was good.

On the ward, we have a child who typifies marasmus. Skin almost black, wizened face, pipe-stem arms, he would sit for hours in yoga position staring with dull expression, totally uninterested in life around him. Yesterday, as we made rounds, we looked across the aisle and saw a beautiful sight. The lady in the next bed was beating a Cambodian rhythm on an empty IV bottle, and our little child, sitting in his usual position, was making those delicate and graceful hand motions that are part of the Khmer dance culture. Along with this, he has started to eat. He will live.

15 April 1984

This is the Khmer–Thai New Year, a happy, water-throwing time. Only the very sick appear at the hospital. Lisa [nurse] asked for extra days off, and so I have worked both Saturday and Sunday.

On Friday morning, after a bad night with my tooth aching, I therefore determined to get it extracted and walked over to the dental clinic at Nong Samet. In short, after four ampoules of zylocaine failed to relieve the pain, they determined that I must have an abscess that was making the zylocaine ineffective. Perhaps tomorrow I will go to KID and have the oral surgeon there do the extraction under general anesthesia.

Saturday morning, I worked as usual at the hospital. The ICRC delegate brought me a pass to Dang Rek, and at noon I set out. The route passes Kilo 6, so of course I had to stop for a coffee shake and lunch.

The route to Dang Rek offers many choices in turns to take, but Red's friend, Fagin, must have been watching for me, because I made no mistakes. I was surprised and overwhelmed at the warmth of my welcome at Dang Rek. It turns out that this was a special New Year's celebration in which the Vietnamese, perhaps for the first time, joined with the Khmers. They had invited farangs who were important to them. It was indeed warming, humbling and delightful to be *waied* and hugged by so many. The celebration started with a Buddhist service followed by a Khmer dance entertainment.

16 April 1984

It is 7:00 A.M., and I am sitting in the courtyard of House 1 waiting. As you probably have heard, the border has broken out into fighting. It started in the north and south camps, and Ban Sangue was attacked yesterday, with a reported 50 killed or wounded and 31,000 Khmers on the roads or in ditches. Ban Sangue is between us and Dang Rek, and of course we worry about our VN brothers, who are often the target of such attacks. There is an UNBRO meeting at 8:00 this morning. They will tell us if we will be allowed to go to camp. The mood here is somber and restless.

17 April 1984—11:00 A.M.

I am sitting in the farang lounge at Nong Samet, having just had a dough-nut and coffee. There is now a Thai bakery that produces excellent bread and doughnuts. It is difficult to suffer here gastronomically anyway. How mixed up my letters must be. I can just see you looking from one to the next, trying to figure out what happened when. This morning I dashed off an aerogram to you, now this jumbled account. There was shelling not far from here earlier, but all is quiet. A number of our patients packed up and left, and it is relatively quiet medical-wise at present.

17 April—later

The Khmers were anxious today but no unusual incidents. We received two babies in terminal condition. The Khmers tend not to come to the hospital when the situation is tense.

I hope you have not been worrying too much about the fighting over here. With radio communication, ICRC and UNBRO really keep up with things, and they are being almost too cautious. Remember that what really happens here often bears little resemblance to what is reported in the newspapers.

18 April 1984

The situation remains tense here but thus far no action at Nong Samet. UNBRO and ICRC have made excellent preparations for evacuation. The team seems quite composed. I have not felt any apprehension.

I have toyed with calling you to reassure you but still hoping to be able to call and tell you that it's all over with—my tooth that is. Last evening, Mary Dunbar, a real Irish woman, asked how my tooth was doing. She insisted on sending over a bottle of Irish whiskey, which she said I should gargle over my tooth and then swallow it. And so I did last night, and I did sleep well. You don't need to worry: the others depend upon my sobriety to provide driving in the evening.

Since we are on restricted access to camp, we are required to keep the numbers of farang down, and so today it was my turn to leave at 1:00 P.M. I came here to KID to make arrangements for tooth extraction.

19 April 1984

I almost got my tooth pulled yesterday. It seems that they are afraid of medical-legal entanglements should some complication of surgery or anesthesia occur. Currently, I am having very little toothache, so I shall await developments. If it starts again, I will go to Bangkok. I do not wish to take that time out until the situation settles at Nong Samet. Yesterday was very quiet along the border.

22 April 1984

Today is Easter Sunday, and I have the day off. I got up in time to see the workers off to camp. I spent a couple of hours getting our car and bike relocated and hauling water for our house. I then took a super nap in the hammock. It was very hot this morning. Our house is on stilts, so we have a perfect place to sling hammocks. I then went for a bike ride and lunch. Another nap attack occurred and then I went to House 2, and Susan and I worked some more on Vivaldi. This afternoon, we have had the granddaddy of summer storms, with winds, intense rain and thunder and lightning you wouldn't believe. Ah, but it is cool and nice.

It has been militarily and dentally quiet for the past two days. Yesterday was a long, hard, hot day of work. We have a new crop of infants with malnutrition. We also had a hassle with a drunken KPNLF soldier, who had suffered minor injuries in a fall from a motorcycle. He refused to give up his sidearm at first, but eventually the MPs persuaded him.

Last night Kirk from UNBRO put on a folk dancing session. The beginner square dance tape is great. With a square made up of five women and three men, representing U.S., Israel, Sweden and Switzerland, we managed to learn one dance; it was fun.

25 April 1984

Becky and her husband, Supot, came from Bangkok yesterday bearing letters. We had a staff meeting, and then all had dinner at the Bamboo. Afterward, I had a pleasant hour of reading letters and thus to bed late again. This afternoon, I was very sleepy and determined that I would go home directly after work and eat a quick snack and go to bed very early.

On arrival home, I found that Marike had made a pot of chicken stew—delicious. A nice shower, followed by this good meal, and thoughts of going to bed had fled. Instead, Marike, her husband, Stig Landstrom, M'Liz and I went bike riding, about 20 km, and ended up at Kim Kim's.

26 April 1984

On arrival at camp, there is usually a short period of getting the Khmers organized, then rounds start. We are running about 35 inpatients. Rounds take about two hours. The first segment of patients gets our full attention, but as time goes by, I begin to lose energy, and the last few patients get less attention. As a result, we start rounds in different places every day so that no segment is always first. After rounds, I disappear to the lounge for coffee and readjustment. The Khmers go to their lounge to eat the fruit I bring every day. Usually there are several patients to go over thoroughly with the medic in charge, and the morning is over. The demands of the afternoon vary from very busy to slow. Yesterday, I sat on the bench at the entrance and suddenly became aware that along side of me there was an infant, largely hidden by a covering *kroma* (Khmer for *pakima*). At first I thought the child was dead, but there was the slightest respiratory excursion and tremor of tongue. An IV had been started, but there was no sign of mother or attending Khmer. This infant represented the most advanced state of malnutrition I have ever seen.

28 April 1984

This limited access to camp really makes for longer days. Bob, who does security, likes to have one car stay at camp until he is ready to close the camp, and usually I am the one who stays. Also, it turns out that I drive both ways each day, and that is a bit tiring.

Military-wise, it has been very quiet the past few days. We had several heavy rains, and there is much talk that this is an early rainy season and the VN will be forced to withdraw prematurely. I doubt it, but who knows. My health remains excellent, with no toothache at all. This seems to be the season for stinging insects, and I have had a few skin infections but nothing bad.

I have worked out a slide sorter of sorts—two Polaris cases, emptied, one on top of the other, a lamp in the bottom and a sheet of plastic across the top. My initial review indicates my slides of Vietnam are of good quality, and my housemates are very interested in them. So I guess I will proceed to try to put on a show.

29 April 1984

Something about the weather here has really brought out the insects. There is a type of grasshopper—large, about three inches long. They move through the air by a combination of jump and fly. They do not seem to have any form of radar and as a consequence strike against walls, ceiling or furniture at full tilt. Their thuds are heard continuously through the evening. However, they do not seem to be even slightly stunned by these collisions.

30 April 1984

Yesterday (Sunday) I was on the work schedule. I brought the little tape recorder I had bought. During rounds, I wore it on my belt and got a very good recording of the sounds of making rounds. Now if I could bottle some of the smells.

In the evening, after a simple dinner at home—leftover chicken and pineapple—I went to the Protestant Sunday evening service. Unfortunately, they sang only one song and then put on a long (45 minute) videotape sermon—legalistic explanation of the authority granted one by salvation. Not my cup of tea. I think I will stick with the Catholics.

Peace

"Peace, an idea whose time has come." Peace, let it begin with me!

"Samalot, peace will not come until I can look at you and see not a brown man, not a Muslim, but only see my brother. Likewise, peace will not come until you can look at me and not see a white man, a Christian, but see me as your brother."

The background of this little sermon commenced in Nong Samet a year ago, where, while working with Vietnamese refugees, I met Abdullah, a Muslim who served as translator. In subsequent months, Abdullah made his way through the maze of administrative steps necessary for expatriation of refugees. My next contact with Abdullah was a phone call from him announcing he was established in a little apartment in south Seattle. As the months passed, it seemed to me that Abdullah was making all the proper moves to establish himself in his newly adopted land. He became active in the local mosque, and on hearing that I was headed back to the border camps, persuaded his fellow Muslims to contribute to a fund to be given to Muslims in the Dang Rek camp.

Abdullah and the leader of the mosque came to me with $356 collected from their congregation to help their fellow Muslims, still held in the confines of Dang Rek camp just inside Cambodia. I explained to these gentlemen that a pass for me to get to Dang Rek might be difficult. Also, that as anxious as I was to deliver this money to the Muslims, I would not do so illegally, and it was possible I would have to bring the money back to them.

On arrival at the border camp of Nong Samet, I talked with the delegate of the International Committee of the Red Cross. He explained to me that no matter how great the individual need, it is illegal to pass money to a person in the refugee border camp. This nice Swiss gentleman was eager to help and said he would discuss it further with his colleagues in the delegation. The result of their deliberations was that the money could be passed, but the recipient, Samalot, chief of the Muslims, would need to pledge that this money would be used for the mutual good of the other religious denominations, Buddhist and Catholic, also. A party, some special food, or possibly some playground equipment all were suggested.

I felt this was reasonable and agreed that Samalot should be approached. It was a great disappointment to learn that the Muslim leader objected strenuously to this stipulation and sent a message to me to take the money back to America. I determined to go to Dang Rek and talk with Samalot.

And so I delivered the little sermon to Samalot, but it was for naught. He put his hand upon my shoulder and said, "It is not necessary for you to tell me these things. We have just held a meeting and have decided we are all refugees, and whether Christians, Buddhists or Muslims, we are brothers. We will accept the money."

There Is Hope

Of the thousands who have suffered as a result of the political and diplomatic machinations of the superpowers in Southeast Asia, the Vietnamese boat and land people may have suffered the most. My contact with them commenced in 1982 when they were incarcerated in the infamous NW 82 at Nong Samet. In theory, they were segregated in this indescribably crowded enclosure to protect them from the hatred of the Khmers—hatred which extends back through the centuries.

In 1983, the Vietnamese were abruptly moved to Dang Rek, a camp in the process of being constructed in a valley bordered by the Khao-I-Dang Mountains. In the haste of moving, they were placed in tents on marshy ground. It was during the early days of this sojourn that I shared their life for two weeks. Eventually, as the new camp was completed, the Vietnamese were moved to more comfortable quarters.

April 14–17, 1984, were the New Year's holidays for Thai and Khmer, but not for the Vietnamese. To my surprise, I received an invitation to attend a New Year's celebration at Dang Rek, and the all-important pass allowing me through the military checkpoints. The reception at Dang Rek by my friends was so warm and friendly it was overwhelming. I sensed a different feeling in the air. Several Vietnamese told me they were pleased to join the Khmers in their happy celebration. This coming from a people whose tradition was hatred and segregation was indeed different.

It became apparent that this particular celebration was to honor farangs who had worked at Dang Rek. The first regimen was a Buddhist service. About 100 refugees, Khmers and Vietnamese intermingled, formed an aisle through which we passed with murmurs of welcome, smiling and much bowing and *waiing*. The Buddhist service, largely chanting, even though unintelligible to this Western mind, was inspiring.

We next moved to a large bamboo hut where seats had been arranged, and we were served tea and small bits of Cambodian desserts and fruits. In front, a Cambodian band, largely a variety of drums, beat out the unique rhythms of this country. Soon a group of Khmer girls, perhaps 6–12 years old, did their graceful national dance. The final presentation was a young Khmer woman, formerly official dancer for Sihanouk, doing the flower dance. In one hand, she held a bowl filled with flower petals. With infinite grace, she made her steps through the crowd placing flower petals on the heads of the guests.

It was a scene and experience of beauty and peace augmented by the realization that the audience was made up of Khmers and Vietnamese, once formidable enemies, and a scattering of us farangs who had come to serve. Our efforts to provide sustenance and medical care may have been of help to these people, but certainly there was more than one farang who realized that this experience may well have blessed us far more than anything we have been able to do for these people.

1 May 1984

At two years of age, Soon was an unusually long and lanky Cambodian infant. His measurements put him in the 80th percentile, height for weight, but this was deceptive because a significant part of his weight was made up of edema of the legs and arms.

He and his family lived the life of peasants in present-day Cambodia. About six weeks ago, he had measles; following this, his cough continued, and he refused to eat. Repeated trips to the local healer, a Krou Khmer, were not effective. Someone told his parents that at the border camps there were hospitals and American doctors who often can help. Thus the little family made its way to Nong Samet.

Lethargy is one of the classic signs of kwashiorkor, and Soon demonstrated this to the extreme. He was not only not interested in food, he responded to unpleasant examinations with only the weakest cry and with no physical resistance.

On presentation at Peds, we recognized him as a severe case, a challenge. That is, to our Western eyes he was a challenge. It is difficult to mobilize our Khmer health workers to work with this problem. To succeed, one must continually ply such an infant with feedings. Signs of success are difficult to see.

For days we worked with this child, enlisting the aid of the maternal-child health group and encouraging the Khmers to talk with the parents over and over again about the need for repeated feeding of small amounts. Several days ago, it appeared that we had passed a milestone. For the first time, Soon took some rice in his hand and ate a few grains.

It was for naught, and he lapsed back into the dull stare and lack of response of kwashiorkor.

2 May 1984

This afternoon, it was apparent that Soon was dying. His pale skin, stretched taut over the cheekbones, barely perceptible breathing and the tiniest pulse in his neck were the only signs of a life that would soon end. For many Khmers, there is merit, if one must die, that death should occur in their own home. I turned to my faithful medic, Saeroeun, and asked him, "Do you think these parents know their child is dying?" "I don't know," was his reply. "Saeroeun, I believe they need to be told that Soon is dying and that if they wish they may take him home. They must be told this with compassion."

There followed a long conversation between Saeroeun and the father, holding his son in his arms. Finally Saeroeun turned to me and said, "The father says that to them it is not important that he dies at home. The father tells me that they were living in Cambodia a month ago when Soon became ill. Repeated trips to the Krou Khmer were not availing, and the child became sicker. Someone told the father that at the border camps there were American doctors who can help. The father wishes to thank you and the Khmer medics for all of the effort in trying to help this child."

In my frustration and disappointment at the outcome of this effort, these were healing words for me. As I held the hands of this father and mother, I realized again that the Khmers have done far more for me than I have done for them.

The military situation remains questionable here. It is quiet, but many rumors float around. Each morning we listen to our radio handsets and try to interpret the meaning of the short staccato conversations. "Dancing on the tabletop" means small arms fire, a term we haven't heard for several weeks. Driving to camp, we study the military traffic. Trucks loaded with young Thai soldiers—are they smiling or are they grim?

At the last checkpoint, they have a number system from 0 to 4 posted; 0 is quiet and 4 is take cover. For days it has been 0. On occasion, the Thai soldier will say, "Good luck." What does that mean? Like many things, this has become an accepted way of life, and our security people must work continuously to make us follow the precautions that one day may be necessary.

Work in Peds goes reasonably well. We are being flooded by malnutrition cases. In the middle of this, we had a case of meningitis, possibly polio, who died abruptly yesterday. Our resuscitation efforts were unavailing.

4 May 1984

It is 1:30 A.M., and I am in the Admissions ward at KID. I am sitting on a bench and a wiggling table is my writing platform. It wiggles because a Khmer mother sits to my right, patiently guarding her nine-month-old baby as he explores the top of the table. Farther to my right, an ancient Khmer woman struggles with her asthma. Her patient husband sits and stares. A sleepy French physician enters and administers to the ailing lady.

I arrived at KID about 5:30 P.M., tired and worn from my day at Nong Samet and wondering if it would not be reasonable for me to just go back to Aran to a refreshing shower and the comfort of my little room. These thoughts were dispelled by the warm welcome of Jean, the French pediatrician soon leaving, Claude, his new replacement, and the nurses, Marie, Bénédicte and Élisabeth.

I came here to observe the French medical group Médicins Sans Frontières, in action and to experience a Khmer refugee camp at night. As dusk came on, I performed a few errands, including a nice encounter with my longtime friend LyRath.

My appetite was ready for the chicken, rice and pineapple I had brought, but my French friends said it was not necessary for me to have brought anything, for they have a Khmer cook who prepares a meal for them. A series of patients presented themselves, and the French physicians were busy. I became hungrier. The French nurse was searching through various books for the treatment protocol for a rare tropical disease, and I helped her with that. Bénédicte, French midwife, came bearing a dead snake in a paper bag, and I accompanied her on a search for some formalin as a preservative. We finally found some in the anesthesia department of the Red Cross surgery, bought at the price of a serious lecture by the anesthetist about the need to conserve this precious liquid. We returned to Admissions, where the snake joined several of its kind, pickled in clear pop bottles. This collection is kept to aid in snake identification when snakebite victims come in. One bottle was labeled Malaysian pit viper, poisonous, and I am sure this was my old acquaintance of two years ago.

Finally we sat down to eat. Augmented by the food I had brought, it was a fine meal with plenty to share with the Khmer staff.

After dinner, it being about 10 o'clock, Jean asked me if I wished to go with him in the ambulance to see some patients. This Khmer camp had been upset on the previous night by a band of Khmer robbers, and rumors were that the robbers were again active. As a result, the Khmers were huddling in their huts, and the sick ones sent word of their illness but refused to leave their homes. Sitting in the back of the ambulance, I indeed experienced KID at night. The roads, so crowded in daytime with walking traffic, were empty. A few tiny glows of soft kerosene lamplight shone, but most of the houses were dark and quiet,

Our first call was at the TB hospital, where an older Khmer man, probably with only a few days left, received the concerned care of my friend Jean. Soft and gentle with the patient, his eyes sparkled in the dim light, intensified by the blackness of his full beard, when he demanded appropriate service by the Khmer health worker for their brother Khmer, I was most impressed. Our next call took us to a district control office, where one patient received, as was appropriate, the KID equivalent of "take two aspirins and see me in the office in the morning." In this case it was two paracetamol tablets and advice to go to the outpatient clinic in the morning. The other patient we took to the hospital.

It was 3:00 A.M. by the time I finished treating this patient, and who should appear but the irrepressible Jean in search of a bakery. Off we went. We wheeled through the narrow streets and our search was rewarded. In a little smoke-blackened room, there was a Khmer family making their version of doughnuts by the dim light of kerosene lamps. The man manipulated the dough with movements no doubt handed down from his ancestors. The wife and son sat at either side of a hibachi-heated wok and gracefully tipped the doughnuts as they floated in the hot grease.

Back to the hospital, and again horizontal under my restructured mosquito net, I fell asleep. Fully intending to greet the dawn, I awakened much later to the sound of babies crying and monks chanting. I got up and put on my soggy, malodorous clothing. Café au lait and fresh Khmer bread, and I was ready to go home.

7 May 1984

Monday morning and I must confess I am not in the mood to go to work. Nothing serious, it's just because of too many social activities. I could feel much more virtuous if I could plead tired from overwork.

Tim is pressuring me to take a few days off, and I may do so.

8 May 1984

The recorder session, a quartet, went well. We had leftovers for dinner. With Marike's help, I made a macaroni casserole (macaroni, cut-up beef, cheese, tomato sauce) cooked in a rigged-up double boiler, and another fruit salad.

Ah me, I am at a loss for further things to write about. There is always the weather. For the past week it has been delightful. It is hot during the daytime but cools at evening and by morning is just right. This has been overall a wonderful tour marked by great contrast—some tough times on Peds and some great times, the duress of the hot weather and the greater creature comforts of Aranyaprathet.

9 May 1984

I took yesterday off and spent most of the day working on the slides. Finally, I have them sorted and arranged for showing. There must have been 300 of them, of which I have picked out about 80. I found it intriguing to see those scenes of my first travel to Asia, not realizing at the time that it was the start of an important part of our lives.

I also wrote letters to the American embassy about Hung and Sieu, Vietnamese interpreters at Dang Rek. Besides that, a little reading and a nap or two—it was a good day. Today I am quite ready to go back to work.

10 May 1984

Yesterday was a long hot day but quite pleasant. I was the only doctor in camp, so I was kept quite busy.

For lunch, I usually buy a 10-baht packet, which contains rice, some strips of chicken, a few slices of cucumber and some sauce. This is about twice what I can eat. Late in the afternoon, I often pick out one of the Khmers who had worked particularly hard or perhaps seems down. I take him into our lounge and present him with the remainder of my lunch, make him a cup of coffee, and we talk. It is a good time for both of us. Yesterday, I chose an older Khmer who does not work for us but is often around and frequently helps with carrying boxes. When I presented him with the lunch, he asked, "Would you mind if I took this home to my son?" I thought it was beautiful, and it made my day.

12 May 1984

We are back on regular schedule—no restricted access. During the restriction we had no X-ray service, no OHI [Operation Handicap International, prostheses] no education and minimal MCH [maternal-child health] activity. As a result, only the minimums of acute care were carried out. Now we can get back to what we came for. During this time, a few of us worked most every day, but some of the rest of the team had many days off. We are all anxious to get back with it.

Yesterday I went home early. I ran some errands and started a nap at 5:30 P.M. I got up at 8:30. Jack Moore's good-bye dinner was under way at the Bamboo, and I put in an appearance. Following a dose of Kim Kim's medicine, I returned home. This is the time of year when young men go to become monks, and the air has been full of throbbing drums, chanting and Thai music. This has continued through the night, and I awakened several times to it but no loss of sleep.

I remain in excellent health and spirits and ready to make these last two weeks count. Today I will again be pediatrician, surgeon and internist.

13 May 1984

The potatoes are nearly boiled and ready for mashing, and I must make the gravy. The chicken is stewed and the salad made, the table set. It is Sunday evening, and I have spent the day alternately sleeping, reading and preparing dinner. It was not all smooth, for I ran out of propane just when I started the potatoes and had to go get a new tank.

My tooth has given me a few low-grade painful hours. The Indian dentist at KID says he has had good experience at the Aran Hospital, and would be glad to see me through extraction there. It would be the simplest answer and I may do it.

16 May 1984

I took today off as a vacation day. I had no particular reason for this except, not having used all my vacation days from last month, I felt that the luxury of a day here alone would be a nice thing. I awakened at my usual time, performed my ablutions and then relished lying in bed, drifting off to sleep to the sound of the others headed off to work. Robert, family physician, and his wife, Dorice, nurse, have arrived. He will take over from Tim on 1 June. I don't believe I told you that Tim is going to work for UNBRO as border control medical coordinator.

I have tentative plans to get my tooth extracted either Friday or Monday. I will be glad when that is over.

16 May—later

Footwear has been somewhat of a problem. I brought with me two pairs of flip-flops, a pair of ventilated summer shoes, my running shoes and my substantial walking shoes.

For the first few weeks, I wore my running shoes every day to camp and there changed to flip-flops. I felt that, if some disturbance occurred at camp and I had to walk any great distance, the running shoes would serve me best. The running shoes deteriorated to unwearable, and about the same time the pair of flip-flops I left at camp walked away.

It is customary here on arrival at a house to leave one's shoes or sandals at the door. Several weeks ago, I wore my summer shoes to a party. There were many pairs of shoes and sandals at the doorstep of the house where the party was held, and mine joined them. Later, when I was ready to leave, amongst all that collection of footgear, I could only find one of my shoes. I was convinced that an amputee must have walked off with one of my shoes, but the people of the house were convinced a dog had walked off with it. Why did the dog pick *my* shoe?

By now I was reduced to wearing my one pair of flip-flops, and now they are worn through. The ground at the hospital is gravel on the surface, and the sharp stones go right through the soles. The most popular footwear here is a plastic sandal called "speed car" (like a scuff), and it is favored by Khmer and farang alike. Today, I spent an hour searching the markets of Aran and finally found a pair of "speed cars" that fit. Some days the problems we face really are mundane.

17 May 1984

I'm in a time when "the best laid plans of mice and men" applies to my efforts. We had the slide show yesterday evening. I have spent several hours making sure that the slides were in order, proper side presenting and upright. In the middle of the show, one of them got jammed and caused some short in the changing mechanism. We finished the show by hand exchange, but now I must figure some way to get this borrowed projector fixed. Nevertheless, the slides were well received.

As I wrote recently, I had arrangements made to have my tooth extraction at Aran Hospital tomorrow. Yesterday, I received word from the dentist that he has made arrangements for it to be done this morning. I am of course restricted to nothing by mouth since last night at midnight. Some mornings I have difficulty with what to have for breakfast, but of course this morning I am really hungry.

17 May—later

Yippee and hot dog, it is so good to feel good again.

I awakened at my usual time this morning, aware that I should be at KID at 8:20, in time for surgery at 8:30. Indeed, I forgot that this is the land of *mai pen rai* [never mind]. The ARC people were aware of my appointment and had set aside a car to leave early for my convenience. Righteously, nothing passed my lips except four tabs of penicillin and a sip of water. Never did thoughts of breakfast seem more appealing.

Unfortunately, my special car had to stop at Task Force 80 to pick up a pass for the bicycle we were transporting for the education department. Next, at our first stop at a military checkpoint, we found ourselves behind a long line of vehicles awaiting the right to pass. It was obvious I would not be on time.

Arriving at KID at 8:40, I was prepared to be greeted by an irate anesthesiologist and dental surgeon. But I had forgotten *mai pen rai*. The anesthesiologist was just finishing her coffee, and the dental surgeon was nowhere to be seen. Preoperative physical consisted of the question, "Are you in good shape?" The dental surgeon still had not shown, so I left the surgical suite and walked the hot dusty road to his clinic, only to find him getting into his car en route to our appointment. He brushed aside my talk about being late, and in his kind Indian manner assured me that it was all simple, no problem to pull two teeth instead of one. The expensive root canal, gold crown upper molar, which opposed the offending tooth, was chronically infected and would serve no purpose. I was in agreement.

Soon I found myself on the surgery table. For the patient here, the clothes one comes in are the ones one is operated on in. Hot, perspired and physically taxed by my arrangements to get the show on the road, I was aware of a blood pressure cuff applied to my arm, a distant intravenous needle prick and then growing lassitude. I am an expert at falling asleep, but that was the best.

Dim awareness of being carried on a stretcher was my next sensation. Next I sensed I was in a storage room, a kind and attentive Khmer medic sitting next to me. Slowly I realized the left side of my face hurt, and there was an uncomfortable pad between my jaws on the left side. The feel of a needle in my buttock followed and then several hours of oblivion, intermittently mixed with trying to sit up, blurred vision and dizziness. By 11:30 A.M., I was able to sit up and drink some warm water. The pad between my jaws came out, the anesthetist came in to check me and told me I could leave at any time.

I gathered myself together and made my way along the hot dusty roads of KID to the gate, where I sat listlessly awaiting some kind soul to offer a ride to Aran. After an hour of this, my throat was sore, my head aching and I wondered about my independence, for several of the ARC people had offered to baby-sit me through this. Then came an MSF car, with my French physician friend Avery at the wheel. One look was all he needed. Quickly he helped me into the back of the truck, where there was a nice padded seat on which to lie down.

By the time we arrived at House 1, I was somewhat improved. After a short rest, I proceeded on my bike to Kim Kim's for a double chocolate ice cream treatment and then home at last. Four penicillin tablets, two aspirin tablets and two hours of sleep wrought wonders, and I was well.

And so ends my dental adventure. M'Liz put on dinner last night. She made a wok full of fried chicken with carrots, onions, also mashed potatoes and a green salad. The food was wonderful, particularly since it contained a spice that I remember from the France of my boyhood and which I have never been able to identify. It is called *herbes de Provence,* and you must buy some.

Even better than the food was the company of Father Pierre. What a privilege to hear his beautiful blessing over the food, and after dinner to listen to tales of his life experience.

I slept well through the night. This morning, I am generally stiff and sore in all muscles, and have a slight sore throat but no jaw pain.

Late yesterday afternoon, I bought some flowers, which I took to the anesthesiologist who took care of me. She told me the anesthesia went well—atropine, pentothal and halothane through a tube in the nose. The latter explains my sore throat and slight hoarseness.

19 May 1984

I think I wrote that the borrowed projector broke down in midshow. Stig, who is an electronics expert, was able to fix it, thank goodness. The IRC group has asked for another showing, which will be on Wednesday.

I have only a few days left here now and obligations are piling up. It will be a busy time, but I will have extra hours since it now takes less time for me to brush my teeth.

| *Departure*

Leaving Aranyaprathet and Nong Samet is inevitably a time of mental, emotional and physical stress, resistant to the best of plans and intentions. The separation starts about two weeks prior to departure. Dates of departure are frequent subjects for conversation amongst farangs, and the standard observation when that date approaches is "But you just arrived. How do you feel about going home?" The Khmers also keep track of departure dates; when they speak of it, they often grasp your arm and want to know "will you come back?"

Saying good-bye is not my forte, and I have often wished it would be possible to abruptly and in secret sneak away. Such is impossible in the close-knit society of this refugee operation.

The last week of my tour was very busy, with every evening committed and the days filled with the routine work and a list of special things to accomplish before leaving. One evening was devoted to a good-bye dinner hosted by House 3. Evening functions here usually start about 8:00. On a routine day, a farang returns to Aran about 6:00. Tired, sometimes emotionally drained, sweaty and often dirt encrusted, the standard goal is a shower. In my case, I would ride my bike from House 1, stopping along the way for shopping or talking with friends encountered en route.

A cool shower, clean clothing and sometimes a short nap are great therapy for the after-work letdown, eradicating the wish that there was no activity for the evening. Arrival for dinner is never prompt, but the practical philosophy of *mai pen rai* of this society is quite compatible with the usual menu. The average dinner consists of rice, a chicken curry, mixed vegetables and a variety of fruits. Guests arrive at varying degrees of lateness, and while some are relaxing after eating, others are just starting.

Departure dinners often have a slightly melancholy ambience. No speeches are made. Indeed, often the reason for the dinner is not mentioned, for leaving this situation is such a mix of anticipation and grief, of satisfaction over what has been done and guilt over leaving when there is so much left to be done. Friday was to be my last day, and my plan was to make pediatric rounds and then go to the outpatient and public health clinics to say good-bye to farangs and Khmers. I was in good shape physically and emotionally. As rounds were ending, the farang laboratory technician approached; even from a distance, I could detect that he bore serious news. "Situation 1 at Ban Sangue and nearby Nong Chan," he reported. We had been at Situation 1 a number of times in the past month, but the past two weeks had been at peaceful Situation 0. A small thing, but somehow it pressed an emotional trigger in me, for one of my major reasons for coming to Nong Samet at this time was to share with the Khmers the expected military action. Now after what seemed to be peace brought on by the approaching rainy season, I must leave the Khmers again threatened.

Saeroeun has been senior medic on Peds. In his late twenties, married and a father, he is a good medic. He stands out from other Khmer medics by his avowed goal to return to Cambodia and to again spend his life raising rice. Most of our Khmer health workers hold as their highest hope expatriation to the U.S., which they envision as a magic land of milk and honey, of total health and happiness, despite all our talking. But not Saeroeun, who with an infectious grin says, "I only want to go back to Cambodia and be a rice farmer," an occupation well suited to his spare but strong physique.

I took Saeroeun back to the empty doctors' room to do a last bit of business and tried to say good-bye. It was too much for me, and I knew I could not go through with my planned good-byes.

There was an available truck in front of the hospital. I ran to it and took off in a cloud of dust, driving the familiar road to the military gate post. I came here to the border camp for the fifth time with the thought that this would probably be my last tour. But on that melancholy drive back to Aranyaprathet, I realized that if the Khmers remain in their incarceration and if my health allows, I shall return.

Tour VI

Bittersweet New Year

5 March 1985

Every seat on the 747 was taken. The Chinese flight crew did a wonderful job of keeping us well fed, and the 13-hour flight passed easily with a good book to read and short naps. I even got my exercise thanks to the Chinese lady who sat next to me, who must have a small bladder. We landed at the Taiwan Airport in darkness. Besides the large number of Chinese passengers, there was an Elks tour group of 57 people, most of them middle-aged and older, all well dressed, a number grossly overweight, and a few with physical disabilities. I inferred that most of them were recently retired and reasonably well-to-do. These are, I think, the new ambassadors of the U.S., replacing the rich of 50 years ago and the hippies of 25 years ago. It sounds self-righteous, but their complaints and queries about waiting in line, do we get breakfast, and how far do we have to walk, tempted me to shout, "Don't sweat the small stuff."

We proceeded to the new and somewhat luxurious Chiang Kai-shek Hotel, where I slept very well. After an early-morning breakfast, we reboarded our plane and were fed another breakfast en route to Hong Kong and a delightful shrimp curry lunch on the Hong Kong–Bangkok segment of our flight.

I was met at the airport by Supot, the Thai husband of Becky Parks, field director. With my trusted friend Supot at the wheel and a marked feeling of déjà vu, my main reaction was that the traffic was not nearly as heavy as I remembered. It turns out that it was a Buddhist holiday.

The Trocadero Hotel is the country headquarters of ARC, and the hotel staff greeted me as an old friend. I passed the afternoon sleeping and running errands. In the evening, I went to dinner with Becky and then crashed on my bed at 9:30, only to awaken at 2:30 A.M. with the wide-awake blind stares that most travelers experience at some time or another.

8 March 1985

When I am not otherwise occupied, I think of all the letters I should be writing. I left Bangkok by taxi yesterday morning at 5 o'clock. It was my best trip from Bangkok to Aranyaprathet. The early morning was beautiful; it was cool and there was little traffic. I went directly to House 1, where they had left the Rover for my use and directions to settle in to House 2. This is a familiar house to me, and the other occupants—Bernadette, Maribeth and Patty Anderson—friends from before. The house is spotless and well organized. The only disadvantage for me is the distance to town.

I immediately headed to town and bought a bicycle (1,300 baht). I spent the balance of the day alternately napping and unpacking.

10 March 1985

ARC is a much larger organization now with six houses. As a result, days can go by without seeing some of the other folk. I put on a "cheese dream" plus ham supper last night but could host only about a third of the team.

This is a hard time to be working here. We have 60 Peds patients, average 10 deliveries per day and Adult Medicine also is very heavy. The only service that is down is surgery—we see no war-wounded now.

11 March 1985

You may have noted I have written less about eating than in former tours. For some reason, my eating pattern has been different. I have not been to the night market yet. I have eaten at Delegation [ICRC's restaurant] once and have snacked at Kim Kim's. Tonight I made a pan full of fried preboiled potatoes with onions and topped with several slices of cheese. Bernie and I polished that off quite happily.

This evening I went to a meeting at IRC; two recruiters for their effort in the Sudan were there. It sounded like tough duty, and probably I did well to return to Thailand.

We periodically hear distant artillery fire but otherwise are not aware of military activity.

14 March 1985

Man, do I feel well today. During the night before last, I awakened with abdominal cramping followed by diarrhea, which lasted throughout yesterday. Today I am fine. Last evening was the weekly staff meeting, which seemed to go on forever. One problem is that MSF is going on strike—refusing to staff Peds, Admissions and Adult Medicine at night until the Thais have provided better night security. There have been many robberies and violence in KID in recent weeks. We are sympathetic with MSF, but unfortunately it is the Khmers who pay, and we are seeking some alternative action.

I don't think I wrote about going to Catholic Mass Sunday evening. Father Pierre was in his usual good form and embarrassed me by his overcomplimentary remarks about my service here.

15 March 1985

We hear reports about Vietnamese activity but some distance from us. A recent picture in a Thai newspaper showed Tim Mastro [internist during Dr. Braile's Tour V and now UNBRO medical coordinator] and Sheryl Keller, Peggy's friend, helping with wounded.

16 March 1985

Yesterday, it cooled off with a rather stiff wind blowing most of the day. I heard rain during the night. Now during my early morning quiet hour it is cool. The only sounds I hear are the strains of Handel, a distant rooster greeting the dawn, and the rumble of traffic on the highway.

Last night, ARC held its welcoming dinner for Coo Walawal and me. She is a Thai TB nurse who will follow Bob in managing the TB ward. We ate at the Bamboo and had the usual fare.

Bob Maat is staying in our house for the last few weeks of his tour—a real honor and privilege for us. He moved out of House 1 because of repeated robberies. Yesterday, I saw Helen Murphy for the first time. She looks great but has found her job very stressful. Before going to dinner last evening, I made a house call on Donna Lazorik, a friend of Peggy's who heads up MCH and has been sick for the past week—probably giardia plus some kind of flu. I regret her illness but did enjoy making the house call. We remain very busy in Peds. Yesterday, there were five transfers to MSF at KID and one death from pneumonia.

17 March 1985

Sunday, and a day off. The heat has moderated, and last night, sleeping under a sheet, I was just on the edge of being cold, but not enough to get up to get a blanket.

There are many rumors of an imminent move from Bang Phu (adjacent to KID) to Top Seam. This is about 3 km from Red Hill and not far from Nong Samet. (Pouen, chief of Peds, a solid fellow, says he is not sure he could stand another move.) It would be tough for the Khmers but most likely an improvement over the present situation. There is something basically unhealthy physically and mentally about our present situation. The *Bangkok Post* has articles about the Thai army going on the offensive, but locally we see no signs of this, and all is quiet. It seems likely that if any action occurs it will be in Surin Province. Tonight we are having a house dinner for Bob.

18 March 1985

Yesterday, I spent the morning shopping and visiting. I checked on Donna, who is better but not well yet. The afternoon I spent alternately cooking and sleeping. Neang, our maid, is most helpful, doing vegetables and fruit preparation. We had scalloped potatoes, cauliflower and fruit salad. We had a lemon meringue pie for dessert. Besides our house people, Ellie and Tim Mastro came. It was a fine time. Bob Maat gave a beautiful blessing. I feel ready to go back to work today.

20 March 1985

Yesterday was a busy day. We continue to receive many very sick babies. The situation is made worse by the MSF strike. Last night, I had dinner with Helen Murphy. She is right in the middle of the local and international politics of this place and is under considerable strain.

I have found another recorder player. Gloria is a family nurse practitioner working in OPD. She plays the saxophone at home but years ago played the recorder. We shall see. Meanwhile, I practice my limited repertoire.

25 March 1985

Yesterday was Sunday, and I worked until 1:00 P.M. I then went to KID for lunch with LyRath. During the months that LyRath existed as an illegal at KID, he lost weight and had a harried and anxious appearance. But now, being legal and having a rice card, LyRath appears healthy, and his charm and confidence have returned. We had lunch in the Khmer training center, empty on Sunday and very much LyRath's domain, since he is the lead Khmer in the Education department. Wonder of wonders and what an honor, LyRath had his whole family there. I was so happy to greet his wife, to admire their little girl, to renew acquaintance with his brother and to hug his mother. This lady, younger than I, has a grace and nobility forged by sorrows and anxieties that have failed to daunt her spirit. It was a wonderful time for me.

26 March 1985

Chris being on vacation, this is a busy week for me. Making rounds on about 70 sick infants is only possible with the help of the Khmer medics. There has been a gradual shift in the incidence of disease. We are seeing fewer measles or pneumonia now and more diarrhea, dehydration and malnutrition. As in all societies, there are all degrees of intelligence and dedication. Thus we often see families who show every evidence of being well organized, making the most of what they have. At the other end of the spectrum are those who seem to have been defeated by it all. Yesterday, we received a 14-month-old infant who, except for a soft tissue infection over his right chest, gave evidence of excellent infant care. He was started on intensive medication, but in three hours his condition had worsened markedly. Despite a rapid transfer to KID, he died within a half hour of arrival at the hospital there. We also received an 18-month-old child, whose malnutrition had resulted in matchstick arms and hands, a grossly enlarged head and thorax, and all of his bones clearly visible through his stretched tight skin. Strangely enough, his father and mother appeared in good health and had no explanation for why their child's condition had so declined in the past six months. He will live, though, for he is not lethargic and eats continually, unlike many with malnutrition.

27 March 1985

Last night, I was invited to a good-bye party for Michelle, a nurse in OPD, combined with an early good-bye for Eileen LaForte. It started with a wine and cheese session at House 6 (only a taste of wine for me). I devoted most of my attention to a variety of cheeses and, wonder of wonders, a delicious pâté. Sheryl Keller was there and told us tales of her war experiences on the Tatum-Surin front. How does it happen that I miss all this action? We went to Delegation for dinner, where I had a simple Thai dinner of lemon grass soup and rice, while the others had chicken and steaks. Have I really gone Asian?

28 March 1985

Adjacent to the platform area of our hospital is a fish farm operated by YWAM [Youth With a Mission]. It is a man-made pond, about one acre in size. Barred to public access, but open to ARC personnel, it constitutes an escape from the pressures of our work. Just off the shore and accessible by a flimsy walkway, there is a gazebo built on stilts. There I escape for lunch most every day. Through some vagary of geography, there is almost always a breeze blowing through this structure. While seated there, through all of my senses there is the awareness of life here on the border. In the waters below, one hears the quacking of ducks and the occasional splash of a rising fish. In the distance, a monk chants an ancient ritual in front of an electronic microphone. The gazebo shudders and creaks with periodic gusts of the wind. From the hospital, there is a constant murmur of mothers talking and infants crying. One hears the dull boom of artillery in the far distance. In one direction, one sees the ascending rocks and forests of Khao-I-Dang Mountain, scene of so many tragedies, and in the other direction, the barbed wire enclosures of Bang Phu, now called Site 7. The warm wind occasionally brings fetid odors of tightly packed human habitation. These sensations are the essence of life here. While I observe this, a myriad of tiny ants, which share the gazebo, are crawling up my legs, periodically stinging lightly—a fitting price for enjoying this scene.

29 March 1985

On arrival at camp in the morning, I meet with the night medic, who reports on new admissions, deaths and very sick patients. Rounds start shortly thereafter and last until about noon. At lunchtime, I usually retreat to the gazebo for some alone time. At 1:00, we make second rounds on all patients we have identified as 3 or 4-plus on a sick scale of 0 to 4. Some of these we transfer to KID. This is also education time, either bedside teaching or class. At 4:00 P.M., disengagement commences. Inevitably by 4:30 or so, one or two additional patients are found who are more seriously ill, and agonizing decisions are made about keeping or transferring them.

I continue in excellent health, which I attribute to my bicycle and the fact that rice and pineapple form such a large part of my diet.

31 March 1985

Yesterday turned out to be a rather ironic, comical day. On arrival at camp, I was informed that an infant had been admitted with classical signs of meningitis. The medic was performing the spinal tap, which went in routine fashion. My first job in the morning is to check the accounting of drugs and medications used from the night box. Accordingly, as soon as the spinal tap was completed, I pushed aside the sponges that had been left on top of the table we use both for writing and also procedures. Unfortunately, the spinal needle just used was hidden in the sponges and I was fairly stuck. This is a classic accident in medical procedures, easily avoided by routinely covering the used needle with its plastic container. After cleaning the small wound, I called the nurses and medics together and talked with them about this lapse in proper procedure. We then waited for the lab report, which indeed showed white blood cells and gram negative cocci, either hemophilus influenza or meningococcus. There followed a conference with the farang staff, and now for four days I am taking rifampin, an antibiotic. The funny thing is, rifampin causes one to pass red urine and in some cases perspiration is also red. Thus far, I do indeed pass beautiful red urine but no red sweat. (I write this to you now only because by the time you receive this, you will know that all is well.)

3 April 1985

Here I am, back at House 4. You may recall that I had asked to be here originally, but when I arrived there was room at House 2 only, and of course I was quite happy there. Paul, field director, has asked me if I would be willing to move to House 4 to "sort of lend a bit of maturity and peacefulness." I don't know about that, but since geographically this is the best house, and since I try to help in any way I can, here I am. My housemates are Philomena, nurse epidemiologist; Marie Chavez, OPD nurse; and Gloria, OPD nurse. Gloria is about to move to IRC. This house is probably the least fancy that ARC rents, and my little room is quite crude, but I'm sure I will get along here, and of course will enjoy the proximity to the market.

On Monday, it appeared that things were quieting in Peds, and we even had a few extra beds. But it was only temporary, for yesterday we received a flood of extra patients—pneumonia and malnutrition. We try many different systems for dealing with malnutrition, but have yet to find a really good protocol.

Well, I'm off to another day of work. The Khmers are all preoccupied with approaching New Year's. UNBRO is making plans to help them to celebrate this—I hope it works out.

5 April 1985

Due to the vagaries of the mail, I haven't had any letters for a number of days. Perhaps it is the reason that life in the U.S. seems very distant, and my mind is occupied with the plans and activities of life here. I am again impressed with the fact that each morning we appear at House 1, freshly clean and energetic. There follow the physical and emotional demands of the day, enacted in an atmosphere of dust, heat, noise and odors. By evening, we return tired, perspired and emptied. A shower has marvelous redeeming qualities, and there is enough energy to perform the evening activities, but on most evenings bed calls at an early hour.

My inner time clock is working well now. I set the alarm every night but awaken at 4:45 and turn it off. I so enjoy the early-morning hour all by my lonesome. As I sit here writing, there is the continuous trill of crickets and the raucous crowing of at least a hundred roosters vying for broadcast time, with the occasional basso grunt of some nearby pig.

Tonight, I will put on a small house dinner—back to fried boiled potatoes, onions, cheese and bits of ham. The potatoes are boiling. I must go check them, and I must drink some extra water, for I sense I am dehydrated.

6 April 1985

Chris asked if I would switch working schedules; as a result, I will work today and be off tomorrow. In the past, I have often found such changes do not work out well for me, and I am suspicious about this one. I was really ready for a day off. However, it will allow me to leave for Bangkok tomorrow morning in the cool of the day. It has been hot and humid all this week, and everyone seems rather tired. The Khmers are occupied with their observation of the forthcoming New Year's. Arrangements between TF 80 and UNBRO to allow them extra food for their celebration are very complicated, so there is a fair amount of tension in the air. I hope it all works out so they have a good time. You recall their custom of pouring water on one another as part of the celebration. Part of the concern is lack of sufficient water to observe this.

7 April 1985

This morning, I arose at 4:00, and with great stealth dressed and made my departure, my goal the 5:00 A.M. bus to Bangkok. The street in our immediate area was bare beneath the full moon. My route led me through the day market. Here, as in similar markets all over the world, there was much good-natured activity. The farmers had already arrived with their trucks laden with produce for the day. Frugal housewives and buyers for the countless restaurants and food peddlers were already making their way through the piles of fruit and vegetables. This bearded stranger, carrying his overnight satchel, was the object of much staring and the occasional query, "Benai?"—Thai for "Where are you going?"—to which I answered, "Bangkok."

There is a small restaurant adjacent to the bus office, and after purchasing my ticket, I proceeded there for breakfast—noodle soup with bits of chicken. There followed a pleasant bus ride, alternating reading, dozing and kaleidoscopic views of rural and urban Thailand responding to the dawn of another day.

Arriving at the Bangkok bus station, I was hungry, strangely enough, for some noodle soup. Fending off the taxi hucksters, I made my way to an open-air restaurant, where I again ordered noodle soup and studied my map.

Again I was determined to make my way by city bus rather than succumb to the expense and convenience of the taxi hucksters. My memory and my reading of the map told me that a #2 would take me directly to my intended hotel. Wonder of wonders, the designated bus arrived promptly, and for 5 baht I rode in air-conditioned comfort to the Victory Hotel.

The Victory, a few blocks from the Trocadero, costs about the same. There is a difference: a wonderful bathtub and shower, hot water, all the switches working, and a delightfully quiet air conditioner. While I am normally gregarious, this opportunity to be alone and totally comfortable is a nice antidote to the stresses of Site 7.

9 April 1985

Adventures in Thailand are sometimes born of mundane desires. Yesterday afternoon was spent in this cool and comfortable room, writing letters, reading, showering and napping. When I awakened, the thought in my mind was that I should find and sample the new and first McDonald's, recently opened in Bangkok. Such adventures do not start easily. The Thai girls at the reception desk no doubt have been asked for help in finding many strange things, but this must have been a first for them. With much giggling and enthusiastic consultation, they finally understood my request and told me to go to the President Hotel, a structure I could find on my street map.

Leaving the hotel in the early evening, I fended off the insistent taxi drivers, and lo and behold, almost as if specially bidden, a bus with the proper number designation pulled to the curb. I boarded, stood in the aisle, and soon a Thai gentleman seated nearby engaged me in conversation with the ubiquitous query, "Where are you going?"

"To the President Hotel," I replied.

"Oh," he said, "I will go with you, and we will drink whiskey together."

Unfortunately, this is one view some Thais have of visiting Americans. I told him I did not care for whiskey. It served a purpose, though, for he identified the proper bus stop for me.

Except for the cacophony of Thai language and the prevalence of Thai faces, this could well have been a McDonald's in the U.S. In order to scientifically test their product, I ordered just what I have partaken of many times at home: two hamburgers, milk and small fries. The hamburgers were smaller than the U.S. version, and the first one, although wrapped in a hamburger covering, was actually a cheeseburger. The second one was a plain hamburger, and its flavor and consistency were a true replica of the American product. The food was good, so good that I ordered a third and a cup of coffee, also excellent.

Before leaving, I went back to the counter and asked to speak to the manager. It was as if I had pressed a fire alarm bell. All activity stopped in our area, and I could hear the words "American" and "manager" passed along in apprehension. Soon a young and capable Thai man approached and in impeccable English introduced himself as the manager. Shaking his hand, I told him that I merely wished to congratulate him on the quality of service and product. His worried expression changed to one of those beautiful Thai smiles, and he thanked me profusely.

Well satisfied with my repast, I returned to the street, and confident of my map reading, boarded a bus for the return trip. It was indeed a nice and inexpensive evening.

I am well rested and frightfully clean from many showers and baths, ready for the heat, dust and challenges of Bang Phu.

10 April 1985

On Tuesday, I packed my bags at the Victory Hotel and went to the dentist at 1:00 P.M. With a very effective zylocaine block, it was a painless but a very long session. I was really tired and wrung out upon leaving the dentist, so I checked in a nearby hotel, unwilling to face a long hot bus ride.

I got up at 4:00 A.M. and took a taxi to the North bus station. There I found that contrary to my information, the first bus to Aran was at 6:00, not 5:00 A.M. Once again, the advantage of early bus rides was confirmed. I spent the time happily reading and dozing.

I spent the balance of the day napping and shopping and went to bed early in preparation for the early start today. I got up at 4:00 this morning to pick up Eileen at House 6 and drive her to the bus station. She has been one of the most-liked members of the team here and will be sorely missed.

This has been a very hot spell, and even as I write at this early morning hour I am wet with perspiration, and so—off for another day.

12 April 1985

Yesterday was not a happy day at Site 7. Early on, Bernie had a woman in labor—persistent dystocia [difficult or slow labor]. The eventual delivery was traumatic, and the baby was dead. The mother had eclampsia, and she died several hours later despite all our efforts. She was a Thai woman married to a Khmer; she had chosen life in the camps. The husband was distraught, and his crying and moaning after the death made it very hard on all of us.

While all of this was going on, someone reached through the bamboo of our staff room and stole Amy Casey's purse—70 baht, passes, passport copy, etc. One of the passes was for the ARC contribution to Khmer New Year's—a truckload of ice and ice cream. Paul says that unless the Khmers find the pass there will be no ice or ice cream. A sad time for all, and yet one of those events that's an inevitable result of this whole sad situation.

13 April 1985

Today is Saturday, the big day of New Year's and my day off. Most everybody is going out to camp, day off or no, but I am happily staying at home. I find the bittersweet irony of such celebrations hard to take, and a day here at home alone hard to pass up. I am preparing a beef pot roast dinner for tonight, and have the roast simmering on the stove, with odors of garlic, *herbes de Provence* and hot peppers filling the air.

As a result of the holidays, our census at the hospital is down. We have had a run of food poisoning, marked by nausea, vomiting and diarrhea related to Khmer noodles. These are made from rice flour, which is mixed with water and allowed to sit, ferment and incubate for 24–48 hours and then pressed through a round-holed sieve to attain the noodle shape. The MCH people and Khmer administration have tried to teach cleanliness in preparation of this traditional dish, but it's an uphill battle. Yesterday, Mr. Teuton, chief of the camp, put on his customary New Year's lunch for the Volags. What did he serve but Khmer noodles. It took some courage, but we all ate of it, and I haven't heard of any ill effects.

Time to go shopping. There is supposed to be a great water battle in Aran at noon. I'll go prepared with my wallet wrapped in plastic and a water pistol. Happy Year of the Ox.

14 April 1985

At noon yesterday, I took a bike ride through town. The farmers market was like running a gauntlet. The Thais respect age, and many of the water throwers approached gently and poured water on my back apologetically. However, when I laughed and squirted them with my squirt gun, they quickly realized that I was with it, and I was soon thoroughly doused. Uptown, a parade was starting. Accompanied by the exotic throbbing of the drums, the marchers were doing the exquisite movements of native dance. It was great to see the joy and happiness on the faces of the people. These customs may seem strange and meaningless, but in an area where there has been so much hurt and deprivation, it was wonderful to see such pure happiness in the smiling faces.

This is Sunday and I work. It is still holiday time, and barring the unusual probably will be quiet. I am scheduled to go to Bangkok 26–27 April for final dental appointment. Will try to phone then.

15 April 1985

The halfway mark of this tour, a time to take an accounting. My little room is cluttered, evidence of the fact that I've been using my time and energies in other ways. Physically, I am in good shape, although the continual heat is exhausting. It is reassuring that the Thai copymart man says this is the hottest hot season he can remember. Professionally, I think things go well, although with frequent deaths on the Peds ward one continually questions, could we have done better?

My work at camp yesterday was demanding and ended in midafternoon with transferring two infants to KID. On return to Aran, I went to the UNBRO pharmacy to get my Japanese B encephalitis shot. ARC was scheduled to provide nursing personnel for this, but Donna was sick again, so I filled in. I will need another dose next Sunday.

16 April 1985

We stood around the bed of this little girl and pondered the reasons for the course of her illness. We talked about the role of her health prior to the onset of her illness, the decision not to send her to KID for more sophisticated treatment, the rationale for the choice of medication, our individual responsibilities, and how we had fulfilled them. It was a satisfying time, for this charming, plump and bright-eyed three-year-old had recovered from a severe pneumonia, which four days ago threatened her life. Her initial good health, her good fortune in having an infection responsive to our medication, the loving and intelligent care of her mother, and the faithful attendance of the Khmer medical staff were all recognized.

It was a healing time for us. Several beds away was an undernourished infant irrevocably dying with no spark of response to our efforts. This scene, so often repeated, not only causes sadness in the hearts of the medical staff, but raises paralyzing doubts about our efforts and capabilities. The little girl, who was recovering, smiling, bright-eyed and active, was therapy for us, and we were grateful.

17 April 1985

Last night, Tim Mastro came to visit. There is great concern about the measles and malnutrition problem on Site 7, and we talked until late about possible causes and remedies. Unfortunately, I'm coming down with a super cold, and so today will be a difficult day.

We still have problems getting our Khmer medics to accept malnutrition as a worthy condition to treat, and many of the infants who are admitted are also burdened with some other debilitating condition. Somewhere in the bottom of my pack, I shall have to find a supply of energy to really get things going.

It is now 8:30 P.M. I worked hard today despite the fact I am in the throes of one of my super colds. The one I had a week ago was a minor warm-up for this one, which is complete with screwdriver in the nose. I would happily take tomorrow off, but not only is Chris away, but I will be the only doctor in camp. I am grateful for the supply of handkerchiefs I brought along.

Tonight after work, I bought chicken-on-a-stick, rice and French bread. On arrival home, I found that John had made chicken soup, which they call Jewish penicillin. I was in bed by 6:30 but am awake now. Shall I go to Kim Kim's? You guess.

18 April 1985

I did indeed ride my trusty bike to Kim Kim's last evening and had a banana split. Back to bed, I slept super well and awakened at 10 minutes before the alarm went off, feeling like my cold was gone. I do feel better and quite able to face the day.

Yesterday, Dr. Everte came to visit. He is a young multilingual physician from Holland who has spent the past year with MSF doing pediatrics, and has largely provided care for the patients we have transferred from Site 7 to KID. I have always encouraged such visits, since I am sure that better understanding of our mutual problems helps ultimately in better care of the Khmers. We made rounds together, and I served him a nice lunch out in the gazebo, where we discussed life, medicine and philosophy.

The rules we operate under require that we do not transfer to KID after 2:00 P.M., except for emergencies. Fortunately, we had a good case to demonstrate to Dr. Everte. This one-year-old was admitted in the morning with the diagnosis of acute bronchopneumonia. He was started on IV antibiotics and his condition was considered 2+ sick on a scale of 1 to 4+. By 1:00 P.M., his condition had worsened, and we had added aminophyllin and decadron for his increased bronchospasm. His respiratory rate increased to 72 by 3:00 P.M., and his lips were becoming blue. By this time, we were all in agreement that transfer to KID, where oxygen is available, was indicated. My friend now understands better why we often appear at KID at 4:00 P.M. bearing in our arms desperately sick children.

Actually, the MSF personnel have been very good about accepting our late arrivals. The problem is that here, as in many human organizations, the rules are often made by people in high office who rarely experience the stresses of bedside care on the border.

20 April 1985

Saturday morning. It has been a long hard week and somewhere I must find the energy to work today. That sounds pretty down, but I really don't mean it that way, for always there is that extra bit of energy brought by some little experience or exchange.

Last night Betsy Grieg, who replaced Eileen as education coordinator, and I tried duets. She is just a beginner on the flute. Talk about the blind leading the blind. We tried simple rounds such as "Row, Row, Row Your Boat." It was fun, but we finally quit when smiling and patient Donna looked like she was getting seasick.

21 April 1985

Yesterday's letter started with my wondering where I would find the energy to get through the day. As it turned out, it was a very good day with good and satisfying experiences and plenty of energy to complete the day's demands.

We still see lots of pneumonia, but not in the overwhelming numbers of a month ago. We are seeing more diarrhea and dehydration and a fair amount of meningitis. The new system that I instituted to put all the malnutrition cases in one section seems to be working well, and after some ranting and raving on my part, the medics and nurses seem to be improving in their attention to these poor little thin babies.

This coming week, I will work Monday to Thursday, and Friday morning early will go to Bangkok to have my gold crown inserted (in my tooth, not on my head).

22 April 1985

I did not sleep well last night. There were many flying insects and much itching. But that wasn't all. There were four rats in my room. I could hear them scurrying about in the corners and crannies. Then suddenly, as if in organized play, they would run onto the grass mat in the center of the room chasing one another. Just before my alarm went off, one of them ran across my forehead. Today I lay the law down; either the rats go or I go. I am careful to keep no food in my room. Perhaps we should get some cats.

Yesterday Amy and I went to Site 2, a large evacuation center now housing Khmers evacuated from four border camps. Carved out of the forests near the Dong Rek Mountains, it is a much more pleasant scene than our Site 7. Driving through the camp, searching for the Vietnamese section, we saw all kinds of activity—houses being constructed, newly arriving Khmers carrying their bundles, pots and pans, and a thriving market. The Vietnamese once again are crowded in a small enclave, still under blue plastic. Our friends Sieu and Hung, Vietnamese translators from Dang Rek, were happy to see us. They look surprisingly well and bear their troubles bravely. Both have been declined by the authorities for expatriation, which is particularly sad since all the others we know have gone. They put on a nice lunch for us, and except for the heat, it was a good visit. Sadly, there is little we can do for these young men.

23 April 1985

Yesterday, I bought some rat poison. Early in the evening, the rats were back, but by bedtime there was no sign of them, so I assume these little pink pellets did their business.

We had a very sad and upsetting death yesterday. This child had been with us for about 10 days. With congenital heart disease, complicated by pneumonia, we were pleased to see original response to treatment, but two days ago it began to fade again. Despite the care of a loving mother and combined efforts of Western and Eastern healers, the child died about noon. Suddenly the child's grandmother appeared at the bedside. With frantic gestures and wailing, she expressed all the anguish of loss. Then her anguish turned to anger, directed at the mother and then at the health worker; the poor little mother huddled in her misery. It went on and on. Such experiences of course touch our vulnerability, for in the face of death, we all have pangs of futility and feelings of guilt, which commence with thoughts of "what if we had . . . ?"

Sorry to burden you with a sad tale, but it is part of life here. I slept well last night, and am now refreshed and ready to face the new day, as are all the roosters I hear crowing in the nearby farmyards.

The big measles vaccination campaign starts tomorrow. The MCH, under the leadership of Donna and Phil, have worked hard on this. I hope it goes well.

24 April 1985

Yesterday, I left camp early and had time to purchase two lengths of steel and a piece of chain to connect them. Finding these and indicating to the Thais what I wanted was difficult. Hung over a beam by the connecting chain, these can be beaten with a piece of pipe, making a loud clanging sound. My idea is that once every hour these will be clanged. At this time, every mother whose child has malnutrition or dehydration is to give food or drink to her child, and every child with pneumonia is to receive chest physiotherapy (clapping on the back over the lungs). We shall see how that works. The staff is eager to try it.

25 April 1985

The first day of the measles vaccination program went very well. Their goal is 10,000 vaccinations, and they did 2,000 yesterday and have four more days to go. There is a bit of bribery involved, for a validated vaccination card is now necessary for admission to special feeding programs. I can accept that without qualms, having seen so many deaths from post-measles sequelae.

My rat poison campaign seems to have worked—no more nighttime marauders and good sleeping at night. The preliminary rains of the rainy season have started, and it is definitely cooler at night.

26 April 1985

I had a quick bowl of noodle soup before boarding the bus to Bangkok. On arrival, I was hungry again and had another. I arrived at the dental office in good time. The fitting of the crown went very well, and I am happy to have that over with. Like dentists the world over, she could not resist picking around my remaining teeth, but did not come up with any new work to be done.

On Thursday, I had one of those experiences that fits in with the description of life here as being like climbing—from the valley to the summit and back down again. One of our trucks pulled up in front of the Pediatrics ward, and the nurse jumped out carrying a beautiful six-year-old boy. He was unconscious, not breathing and had a heart rate of 30. Between me and our medics, we did a credible job of resuscitation; within a few minutes, his cardiorespiratory state was stabilized. Soon thereafter he regained consciousness. A little later, I went to a meeting and on return found his body wrapped in funeral fashion. The medic reported that he had been behaving normally. Lying on the bed, he asked his mother to lie down beside him. His mother told him that she would sit beside him. He turned on his side and died abruptly. He had post-measles pneumonia and probably died from cardiac arrhythmia. Resuscitation this time was fruitless.

28 April 1985

Yesterday evening, after talking with you, I made my way by bus to Convent Road. Lois Visscher was out to dinner, but she returned shortly. We had a very nice visit.

After visiting Lois, I was ready to eat. Having eaten American-style for several meals, I was ready for some simple Thai food. I came upon one of those sidewalk cafés, cooking on a cart, and had my usual noodle soup, only this time it was quite spicy. Later, I had to put out the fire with a *nam sodá* [soda water].

I was in bed by 10:00, thinking that perhaps I would awaken early. I actually awakened at 7:00. and got up in leisurely fashion. My trip home to Aran was quite pleasant and uneventful. Arriving at 3:00 P.M., I promptly took a nice nap. Now I have showered, cleaned up my room and will go to church this evening.

30 April 1985

The Peds ward at Site 7 is divided into four rows, A, B, C, and D. Each row is in the charge of one medic. We have five medics. Pouen is the senior medic. We have arranged the staff along the lines of a residency, with Pouen as chief resident and the others as junior residents under him. Chris and I serve as consultants.

On arrival at camp, I make rounds with the night staff, seeing the new admissions and the seriously ill. In the meanwhile, Chris checks the medical supplies, accounting for those used and those on hand. Making rounds on 40–60 patients is a big job. I usually do two rows, Chris does one row, and the chief makes rounds with one of his juniors. At the conclusion, I go down the rows I have not rounded on, checking on any problems they have found. The rounds are a combination of consultation and teaching, for we definitely emphasize that the medic is in charge. Usually there is at least one patient who presents a problem worthy of 15–30 minutes of teaching. By the end of rounds, I have a list of the patients who will require special attention later. This fills the morning hours.

The afternoon is spent seeing new admissions and usually a class teaching situation. By about 4:30, disengagement tasks occupy us and we leave, hoping all our little charges will greet us in the morning.

Last night I fixed dinner—fried boiled potatoes topped with ham, a layer of tomatoes and cheese. After dinner, John and I went to Kim Kim's, where—over a scoop of chocolate—he shellacked me in chess.

1 May 1985

Each morning, I leave home on my bike and make my way to the market, where I buy fruit for the Khmers. From there, I choose a route that takes me along a road that borders a large pond in front of a school. There I usually pause in solitude and ponder the day ahead. Yesterday, there was a Thai fisherman standing in my usual spot. He had a net draped over his shoulder. Wading into the water, he draped the net over his arm and hurled it. After a few moments, he gathered it in, finding a few sardine-size fish enmeshed in the filigree. These joined the few he had in the bottom of his pail. He seemed quite content, and I think we both sensed kindred souls as we exchanged a few words, each in his own tongue.

3 May 1985

Last night, there was a welcoming dinner for Betsy and John held at the Bamboo. The food was particularly good, and everyone was in good humor. It was a good time, but it did keep me up later than usual. To-night is practice for "Showers of Blessings," and tomorrow I have the day off. In the evening we will present our song. One of the Protestant organizations, CAMA [Compassion and Mercy Associates], has a Casio keyboard, and a nice young lady from that group has agreed to accompany us.

Pouen is our chief medic on Peds. About thirty years old, married, two children and his wife at the end of her third pregnancy, he is senior to all the medics in camp. Even for a Khmer, he is small in stature, with not a single extra ounce of weight on his small frame. He has been through all the experiences of his people in the past several years. His face often reflects his past and the stresses of today, but periodically he breaks into a smile, his eyes glistening, and he comes up with some comic-philosophical thought. For instance, once when I bewailed my inability to speak Khmer he pointed out, "But Papa, you are not doing bad, you have learned one Khmer word for each of your trips here. Keep coming."

Pouen's youngest child has been sick, and yesterday I made a house call at his home. His hut is one of a dozen small structures in a row. Constructed of bamboo and thatch, they have one room about 10 by 16 feet.

To refugees and farang health workers alike, blue plastic tarp is a ubiquitous reminder of what these people have endured. It has been said that UN agencies have used enough blue plastic tarp to make a continuous strip three meters wide extending for 700 kilometers. This is the material that provides temporary shelter for these people when they are moved to a new camp under emergency conditions. As more permanent structures are built, the blue plastic finds its way into the walls of the structure. Thus the door to Pouen's little home is made of bamboo, lined with blue plastic; but the irony is that the protruding edges of plastic have been carefully scalloped so that this symbol of their trials is evidence of Khmers' attempt to inject some beauty into their lives.

4 May 1985

Today is Saturday and my day off. Yesterday, UNBRO came around asking for volunteers to help in the census at Site 2. Looking forward to a day of rest, I declined, but now it is early in the morning, and I decided to go after all if they can get me a pass. We shall see.

Maly, 2½-year-old daughter of Pouen, failed to respond to treatment at home, so I decided to take her to KID. By late afternoon, she was doing better.

Yesterday's letter ended with the description of the outside of Pouen's house; I will carry on from there.

Entering this little house through the low doorway, I was greeted by Pouen's wife, Nery. She is a beautiful Khmer woman, slight of frame and obviously at the end of her pregnancy. Our little patient looked sick, but on exam appeared to have a well-localized pneumonia. She tolerated examination without fuss, and it seemed probable she will respond to treatment.

After I examined the child, Nery and I sat for a few minutes and talked, over a cup of lukewarm tea. This is the common drink offered to farangs in Khmer homes. It is their subtle way of assuring their guest that the water has been boiled. This small, dirt-floored room contains a bamboo sleeping platform. In one corner near the window is Pouen's desk, with a number of medical books on a shelf and nearby a kerosene lantern. Some neatly stacked clothes and a few pots and pans represent their worldly goods. It seemed a sparse and humble site of family living, but the room was filled with love and a sense that in this room and others like it, this family has found the strength to survive and the courage to continue. Like many of my experiences in medicine, I left feeling that I had received more than I had given.

8 May 1985

Pouen's child did well at KID, and they came back to Site 7 yesterday.

On Saturday evening, we did "Showers of Blessings." There were eight of us from ARC and the three Apostle sisters plus the accompanist. Father Pierre spoke on the importance of love that farangs can bring to the Khmers. He enjoyed the song, and I ended up happy to have accomplished this and grateful to my colleagues.

Our new housemate, Marie, is a nurse from Belgium who speaks only a little English, so I am having an intense opportunity to speak French.

It is indeed getting close to time for me to leave; a pair of my socks has holes in them, and my oldest suntan shirt is missing two buttons, and the threads on the pockets have given way. The Khmers love to point out these defects and point out I need a woman to take care of me.

Two nights ago, I was awakened by a nearby explosion followed by sounds of small arms fire. I got up and went to the living room, where I found Philomena O'Dea, an MCH nurse here, staring out the window. There were two more explosions, which sounded like grenades. In hushed tones, we discussed the possibilities. A Vietnamese incursion? A band of marauders? Accompanying the sounds of explosions and small arms fire, there was rattling and tapping, suggestive of men keeping contact with one another. It quieted down, and we agreed we would do best to go back to bed. Before sleep would come, I heard Phil tapping at my door and whispering my name. She thought she had seen a man climbing a tree adjacent to the house. There was another explosion, more popping and tapping sounds. Standing at the window, we could not detect any intruder. I did notice that the once-full moon was distorted and very orange in color, gradually becoming its normal brightness. The sounds disappeared, and I voiced the possibility that this might be some tribal rite or tradition. We went back to bed, and in the morning I learned that there had been an eclipse of the moon, and many Thais believe that one must make noise to persuade the moonlight to return.

9 May 1985

I have reached that time in this tour when I am torn by the desire to return to life in the U.S. and appalled at the speed with which these last days are passing.

Yesterday, it was hot all day long, but it has rained during the night, and it promises to be cool today. There has been a marked decrease in the severity of illness we are seeing, and consequently we are having far fewer deaths. This is the last day of Chris's vacation, and about a week from now my replacement will arrive. He has just finished a pediatric residency, so there will no doubt be big changes in the Pediatrics department. It will be an interesting experience to "orient" him.

I remain grateful for health, the opportunity to work over here, and the support of family and friends.

13 May 1985

To visit another border camp here is not a simple matter. First, one must arrange a day off. Next, arrangements must be made for a truck to be available. Lastly, a pass from Col. Praneth, the Thai military commander, must be obtained.

Bill Holmes and I approached these hurdles with the Eastern philosophy of karma, which I think translates similar to "que será, será" and our local saying of "let 'er go how she looks." To our happy surprise, it went through like clockwork.

As a result, we found ourselves on Friday making the 50 km drive to Site 2. Bill has done one year of internship and then interrupted his educational path to spend a year in foreign service and travel. We had lots to talk about.

Site 2 is located at the base of the Dong Rek Mountains and was chosen for the location of a large border camp because it is not readily accessible to the Vietnamese army in Cambodia. The approach road is narrow and bumpy. There are many possible turnoffs, so it was with happy surprise that we spotted blue plastic through the trees, indicating we had arrived.

There is a large Vietnamese refugee compound here, and we quickly found my old friends Sieu and Hung. Hung has hopes of expatriation to the U.S., and Sieu is pondering acceptance of the opportunity to go to Denmark.

I'll finish this tomorrow. I am working on a paper, "Family Practitioner as Pediatrician on the Border," and have spent considerable time on it the past few days. Last night, I went to the Protestant church service (YWAM and Christian Missionary Alliance), where there was wonderful singing of the old hymns. I missed you and Peggy.

14 May 1985

Site 2 continued: Sieu is very apprehensive about going to Denmark. He has relatives in Canada and the U.S. but none in Europe, and he knows very little about Denmark. I have tried to reassure him; while I think it would be best for him to accept this opportunity, I do not wish to force his decision.

Bill and I walked about the camp and visited the three hospitals. Staffed primarily by MSF, they have some different ideas about treatment, but there are few differences in the patients. In the pediatric wards, I saw the same thin little faces, distended abdomens and swollen limbs I am so familiar with.

Site 2 has a thriving market. We stopped at a little restaurant and had coffee, where I again enjoyed watching the cook prepare coffee by pouring boiling water through a long narrow cloth sock.

We parted from my friends Sieu and Hung with considerable sadness, for we knew this could well be our last contact.

Our trip home during that hot afternoon was interrupted by a stop at Kilo 6 (AKA Curry House), where I enjoyed a refreshing cold café smoothie.

16 May 1985

I will leave here Wednesday or Thursday of next week, depending on the arrival of my replacement. I am trying to figure out the mode of my departure. You know how little I like good-byes—nothing would please me more than to be able to slip away unnoticed. And what to do about parting gifts, party, etc., for the Khmers? I could use some advice from you.

Yesterday started out poorly but ended well. On departure, the chain on the sprocket of my bike came off. The maid and I worked on it for some time before we got it back on. It lasted long enough to get to House 1 and came off again. En route to camp (I hear artillery fire in the distance, the house shakes, first in some time), we dropped the bike off at the bike repair shop.

It was very hot all day. Our little patients were all doing well, and the Khmer medics several times demonstrated the marvel of their wisdom. There was one little girl admitted with mild dehydration, secondary to vomiting, and diarrhea. The mother gave promise of causing us trouble. Since the girl had not vomited for several hours, the medic decided to rely on oral rehydration. When the mother realized this, she angrily packed up her belongings, tore up her chart and stalked out. They have strong belief in the power of IVs.

17 May 1985

Amy is sick again. I drove her home from camp early in the afternoon and stayed home the balance of the day. After delivering her to House 3 and the car to House 1, it started to rain heavily, and I was soaked by the time I reached home on my bicycle. I had a nice snack followed by an even nicer nap and then went to the staff meeting; it was raining again. Two soakings in one day is a little much. It is raining again this morning, and I shall have to figure some maneuver for getting to House 1. I am reluctant to leave my bicycle in the stable.

19 May 1985—Sunday

This has been my day off and I have been busy—busy enough that I have delayed writing until this late hour of 6:30. You know it does not take long to go from the vertical position to the horizontal, and vice versa, but when you do it many times a day, it takes up your time.

I started the day early, 5:30, for a dawn bike ride with Betsy. We went out to the farmyard to commune with the ancient lady herding her ducks, then explored some little alleyways where the real Thais live, and then out to the final gate, where a Thai soldier indicated we could not go farther.

I returned to the house, took the car and picked up Amy. We went to Kim Kim's for breakfast, where we were joined by a French man of my age. We had a good time talking, but it was not exactly breakfast conversation, as he is a sanitary engineer and described with professional expertise the faults of the latrines at Site 7, something I am quite familiar with. I then took Amy to the Bangkok bus. I will see her no more this trip, but she may visit in Seattle this summer.

On return to the house, I began my yo-yo activity—a few moments of preliminary packing alternating with naps.

20 May 1985—5:30 a.m.

Last night continued busy. I went to the Catholic service and then to Kim Kim's with Bernie. I arose this morning at 4:30 to take Phil to the bus station. A beautiful dawn promises another hot day, and I have much to do. Tonight is a good-bye dinner for me and Fred and a welcome dinner for Susan and Rosa.

21 May 1985

The good-bye dinner last evening was at Noi's Squid restaurant. It was a nice affair and the food was good. Assuming that my travel plans hold firm, I will fly from Bangkok on Monday and arrive in Los Angeles on Tuesday, 28 May.

My replacement, Randy, arrived yesterday. This is his first overseas trip, and I will no doubt be doing much talking today. Hopefully, jet lag will not overtake him tomorrow, and I can spend the day visiting and taking pictures. I will borrow a camera.

En route home

Departure from Aranyaprathet is made easier by leaving early in the morning. The taxi came for me at 5:00. My lady housemates all insisted on getting up, and in the cool of the dawn, with daylight just commencing, I rode those familiar streets again. The trip to Bangkok was uneventful.

In Bangkok, I had some departure business to do and repacking. On Saturday, I went on a bus and riverboat tour to Ayutthaya, ancient capital of Thailand. The ruins were interesting. The nineteenth-century summer palace was particularly enjoyable, bringing visions of the musical *The King and I*. Most fascinating was the discourse by the young tour guide on the history of Thailand and on Buddhism. He stressed two main aspects: the belief that in this life the evil acts we perpetrate against our fellows will return to us, and the state of reincarnation is dependent on the type of life we live in our present life. This may well be an oversimplification, but certainly worth considering.

As I write this, our plane is approaching Los Angeles. Mentally somewhat foggy from this long flight, I nevertheless have some final thoughts.

I am happy to return to this land and the people I hold dear.

I am grateful to my wife, Gwen, and family, who not only allowed me to make this trip but also supported me in many ways.

Despite the stresses, disappointments and occasional failures, I still look upon this effort as worthwhile.

To those who wonder if I will go again, I respond positively. Granted all the various factors necessary to make it possible are present, I will return again sometime in the future.

Refugees fleeing the violence with only what can be carried, their old lives gone.
Source: Jim Hubbard

A new wave of refugees arrives at the Thai–Cambodian border camps.
Source: ARC staff archives

Khao-I-Dang Holding Center—From 1975 to 1992, more than 235,000 Cambodian refugees were resettled overseas, including 150,000 in the United States. Most passed through the gates of Khao-I-Dang.
Source: ARC staff archives

The Acute Adult Medicine Ward at Khao-I-Dang, Papa Louis's first ARC worksite on the border.
Source: Jim Hubbard

Families find space at Khao-I-Dang to set up shelter.
Source: ARC staff archives

Haing Ngor (fourth from left) hangs a new sign identifying the Acute Adult Medicine Ward where staffing was provided by ARC personnel and Kampuchean (Cambodian) volunteers.
Source: ARC staff archives

A refugee child explores the world outside his shelter, a typical scene in the early days of camp life at Khao-I-Dang.
Source: Jim Hubbard

The hospital at Nong Samet where Papa Louis served as physician, teacher, wise elder and friend.
Source:
Steve Miles, M.D.

Inside the Acute Adult Medicine Ward at Khao-I-Dang, a woman helps care for a family member, a common practice in camp hospitals.
Source:
Jim Hubbard

Task Force 80, the Thai paramilitary security force operating in the camps (center) came to be feared for their sometimes abusive practices.
Source: Doug Hulcher

The opening of a new TB clinic at Nong Samet (also known as Rithisen). Happy to have access to lifesaving treatment, refugees celebrate with a party. Treatment protocols begun here were copied at sites all along the border. A top ARC-trained Khmer medic from this clinic, Sok Thim, continues to run a large TB treatment program in Cambodia today.
Source: ARC staff archives

Papa Louis walking with a Khmer child. Children were drawn to him, finding comfort, laughter and learning in even brief, shared moments
Source: Braile family photo

Dr. Braile teaching by doing. Khmer medics observe a procedure as they strive to develop their skills and abilities to provide health care to people in the camps
Source: Braile family photo

Outpatient Clinic at Site 2 refugee camp on the Thai–Cambodian border. An ARC-trained medic examines a child as her mother anxiously watches.
Source: Doug Hulcher

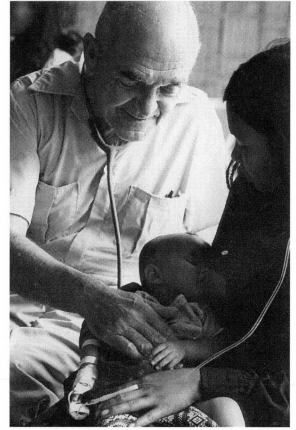

Papa Louis with a Cambodian mother and child, hands touching in healing and hope.
Source: Doug Hulcher

New arrivals at Nong Samet, awaiting the first step in the long process of admittance and adjustment to camp life. *Source: ARC staff archives*

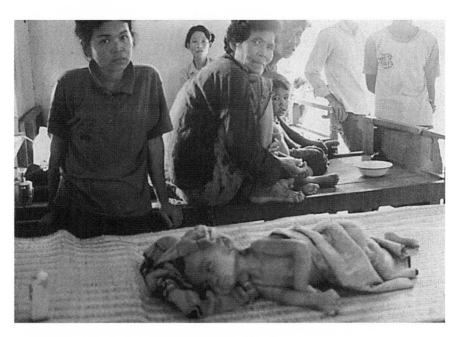

Pediatric Ward at Banteay Meanchey Provincial Hospital where Papa Louis worked inside Cambodia. *Source: Karen Johnson Elshazly*

Papa Louis at Nong Samet holding twin babies named Good Luck and Bad Luck, though both babies had good luck to be in Papa Louis's care on that day.

Source: ARC staff archives

Of Time, Place and Person

Editor's note: Dr. Braile retired from his medical practice on 1 June 1986. He left for his seventh tour with ARC in Thailand in September.

4 September 1986

We arrived in Taipei on time and in good shape. The layover there was just one hour, long enough to accomplish the paperwork and for me to shave and freshen up. On the three-hour flight to Bangkok, they served us yet another meal. By chance, I was seated next to a young French woman, who seemed to enjoy speaking her native language with this old one. The time went by quickly. The Bangkok airport was nearly empty, and only a few people from the plane were staying in Bangkok. As a result, baggage claim was quick, and the customs man took one look at my balding pate and waved me through to the smiling Supot, ARC driver extraordinaire. By 1:00 A.M., we were checked into the Hotel Trocadero, which seems somewhat refurbished since my last tour.

5 September 1986

At 4:30 A.M., I awakened from a good sleep distinctly aware there would be no more sleep for me for a while. It's time to leave Bangkok and head for the border. After 36 hours in Bangkok, I find myself concerned with trivialities. This little hotel room has an air conditioner unit. It keeps the room pleasantly cool, but at the price of an irritating noise. Making the choice between a clammy warmth or the assault on my ears is difficult. Life at the border is indeed simpler. Such a trivial matter to write about, but it is part of the answer to that oft spoken question—why do I go to Thailand? On the border there are fewer choices to make.

7 September 1986

Our trip from Bangkok to Aranyaprathet was by taxi and without incident. In Bangkok, we had been told there were rooms available in Ta Phraya and in House 1 and House 2 in Aran. They would prefer I stay in Aran, but it would be all right if I chose to live in Ta Phraya. Ron Roddy went to House 2 and I stayed at House 1. This house has a transient ambience, and the maid has not been known for her diligence.

On Saturday, orientation at camp was preceded by a visit to Khao-I-Dang. LyRath and family were just informed of acceptance by Canada, so it was a joyous reunion. At Site 2, it was one reunion after another—Khmers and farangs.

Today is Sunday and I arranged to visit Ta Phraya. Apparently there has been a contest regarding my choice of domicile. Chris Feld greeted me. Together with Arlys and Kathy, we went to Fargo's Restaurant for an American breakfast. Then Chris and I went for a long bike ride. The roads were perfect, little traffic, and they led between rice paddies and through little hamlets. We saw water buffalo, and we ended up in a dense rain. On our return, Sharon Brown appeared; she teaches music to the Khmers—her instrument is a recorder.

I just had a great nap in this beautiful room. This house is a jewel: a comfortable bed, a soft pillow, a reading light, and a kitchen that one can cook in. The only thing lacking is a writing desk and a chess player, and for that I have Elmer (computerized chess game).

You guessed it: I will move to Ta Phraya. This little village has adapted itself to farang presence. I am told there is even a replica of Kim Kim's. There is a real advantage to living in Ta Phraya: the transit time to camp is one-half hour versus one to one and a half hours from Aran.

10 September 1986

On return from camp, my routine is to shower and shave, and then think about eating. Last night I went to the market and bought some chicken-on-a-stick. Bob, Bernie and Chris went to Aran, so Arlys and I had dinner together. Three times a week the maid buys the makings for salad. She shreds up a dishpan full of cabbage, and another dishpan holds chopped onions, mint leaves, tomatoes, peppers and cucumbers.

One makes a salad according to taste. I should mention that the maid has been instructed in treating the salad vegetables with a solution of potassium permanganate. The people here have followed this procedure for some time and have not suffered any GI distress. So we had chicken-on-a-stick, sticky rice and salad—pretty good fare, I would say. By 7:30, I was ready for bed. I fell asleep to the throb of rain on the roof and the bass rumbling of bullfrogs.

11 September 1986

Ampil is a small camp located in what is called Site 2 North. (We are Site 2 South.) Yesterday afternoon, shortly after we left our camp, a Khmer woman, six months pregnant, walked on the rice field and stepped on a mine, suffering loss of left lower leg and left hand and multiple soft tissue wounds. This incident is the cause of great concern. As a result, we were on limited access today. Since I am not yet on the emergency team, I had the day off. They are sweeping the camp area. Because such mines are now made of plastic, the electronic instruments used to detect metal are not effective, and the area is swept by Khmers rolling rocks in front of them.

There is much discussion about who might have placed this mine. The rice field, site of rice distribution, is packed with humanity every Tuesday, so it is unlikely that this mine has been left over from previous military action. Ampil has been the area in which there is much dispute between various Khmer factions, and it seems possible that this was fratricide.

A Year of Peace

In 1979–80, several thousand Khmers, fleeing the chaos and devastation of their homeland, found refuge in a border camp near the village of Nong Samet. Situated precisely on the Thai–Cambodian border, this population was exposed to the stresses of nearby warfare; the threat of onslaught was frequently present. During the last week of 1984 and in early 1985, full-scale warfare came to Nong Samet, and evacuation to a temporary site at Bang Phu adjacent to Khao-I-Dang was necessary.

Disruption of families, loss of homes and fear took their toll. Nong Samet was an idyllic setting in the forest. Bang Phu was an old, over-used section of Khao-I-Dang. As always happens when refugees are sub-jected to such pressures, disease and malnutrition followed. At Bang Phu, a measles epidemic occurred soon after the Khmers arrived, and this was followed by pneumonia in epidemic numbers. Many infants and children died as a result.

The most frustrating and sad problem we farang medical workers faced was malnutrition. Words and even photos of these wasted chil-dren do not convey the pathos of seeing the Khmer mothers bringing in these dying children. Even more frustrating was the all but impossible task of trying to get our Khmer health workers to accept malnutrition as a treatable condition and one worthy of the intensive effort necessary to treat it. This was the situation during my last tour.

In August 1985, the Thai government moved the Bang Phu resi-dents 40 km north of Khao-I-Dang and only 2 km from the border. This camp is called Site 2. While fighting continued around them, this past year has been one of relative peace within the camp. Now some of the causes of malnutrition have been dealt with. Distribution of food by UN agencies has improved. Public health and maternal child health or-ganizations have succeeded in improving sanitation and in identifying children in early stages of malnutrition. Mothers have been educated in techniques of feeding and provided with appropriate foods.

On my first visit to Pediatrics, I found that there were fewer children with the malnutrition diagnosis, and those present were not nearly as severe. Dr. Fern Houck, a family practitioner, has worked on the ward for the past six months. She has the enthusiasm of youth, excellent edu-cation and experience, and a determination to serve the Khmers. She has accomplished much during her tour—most outstanding is the establish-ment of a feeding center for children with malnutrition. As a result, now in contrast to the hopelessness of former years, there are Khmer health workers interested in treatment and prevention of malnutrition.

The progress I have mentioned is no doubt the result of efforts by volunteer health workers. It is also the result of more than a year of relative peace. We are indeed making some progress in the treatment of the body. Would that we could make similar progress in healing the mind and heart.

13 September 1986

Yesterday was my first day of managing Peds on my own, and I found it a good day. Site 2 South is a marked improvement over Bang Phu. The Khmer population there has been spared any military activity and it shows in the hospital. At Bang Phu, our census ran 80–100 on Peds. Now it is 30–40, and no deaths thus far this month. We are seeing a fair amount of asthma, bronchiolitis and otitis media. There is still a "D" row for malnutrition, but I have not seen any of the moving skeleton types of previous years.

It was a hot day, though, and by the end I was ready to go home. However, on the way home Bob suggested a scenic drive. The girls were all in favor, so of course I went along. Seated on the spare tire in Bob's jeep, I was bounced around. We rode up into the Dong Rek Mountains, and in the fading light of dusk the mountains, the little farms, the rice fields and the Thai villagers were glorious. Returning to Ta Phraya, we bought Thai food to go and had a very nice "family dinner."

16 September 1986

I used to bring fruit to camp every day, but the Khmers are fairly well fed now, and it is not as necessary and no one else does it. Next Sunday I start four days off. I will go to Bangkok and possibly a one-night trip to Pattaya or Hua Hin. I should like to try wind surfing.

17 September 1986

Yesterday was a busy day for me since Hal, a surgeon, is on vacation. In addition, we had a visiting consultant on Pediatrics. In Surgery, we had a girl with an infection involving her whole forearm. In the afternoon, we had a young man with a fracture of forearm.

Hal is 65 years old—imagine that, older than I am. He has spent his professional life in Hawaii and is now doing his second overseas tour.

17 September—later

At noon today, I managed to obtain use of a car, and Chris and I drove to Site 2 North to visit the orphanage where Sharon Brown is teaching recorder. Sharon is working in education with COERR [Catholic Office for Emergency Relief and Refugees]. She speaks Khmer fluently and obviously has her students in the palm of her hand. They are just beginning on the recorder, but by next week will have passed me. Trills and flourishes seem to come naturally to them. Sharon had insisted I bring my recorder and we tried a duet, "Lo We Walk a Narrow Way." This didn't go well. When she saw I had a copy of "Jesu, Joy of Man's Desiring," she insisted I play that. Fortunately, I have been playing that recently and it went quite well. The orphans even clapped when it was over.

22 September 1986

A Trip to Bangkok

ARC regulations provide for and encourage a four-day vacation each month. This is a form of burnout insurance. After three weeks here, burnout seems an unlikely possibility for me, but nevertheless, I am sitting in a bus that will take me to Aranyaprathet, where I will catch the bus to Bangkok.

The bus to Bangkok is a blue air-conditioned model and relatively comfortable, except the seats are of Thai dimensions. I feel what minorities have sensed in our country, for the seat beside me remains empty until every other seat is filled. A good book, a nap, people watching and the occasional glance out the window make the trip (4½ hours) pass quite rapidly—until we reach the outskirts of Bangkok, where the last hour seems like eternity, until I reach my hotel at last.

The Victory Hotel is listed as first class, a step down from luxury class and a step up from economy. The little room they assign me has all I need: relative quiet, a comfortable bed and lots of hot water. A nap was first on my agenda.

I awakened from my nap with a hunger for pizza, available at a Pizza Hut. The Pizza Hut is busy, and a very efficient Thai waitress asks a

Nordic-appearing man if I may share his table. He accedes readily. For a few minutes, we sit in silence. Feeling uncomfortable with this, I introduce myself, and there follows a wonderful conversation that makes this trip to Bangkok worthwhile. This middle-aged man is from Munich, Germany, a businessman who travels the world. In a short period of time, we cover history, geography, race relations and ecology. His convictions are much the same as mine. The most interesting thing he told me was that one time he listened to a tape of one of Hitler's orations, and despite his modern concepts of one world, it affected him to the extent of "goose bumps." There is a lesson there for us Americans, for we too have gifted orators who can appeal to our baser natures. My German friend and I parted with a handshake, and we both uttered the blessed word "Peace."

23 September 1986

Fern is still here in Bangkok. We ate dinner here, for this hotel restaurant specializes in Japanese cuisine. I had rice and chicken and a big plate of pineapple. Fern is Jewish and a vegetarian. She is also an excellent physician and has done much for the Khmers. We had lots to talk about—future plans for Peds, where is ARC going, etc.

24 September 1986

Last evening, Susan Walker took me to dinner at the Wall, a continental-type restaurant near the Trocadero. The food was excellent. I was particularly anxious to learn about Susan's knowledge of Cambodia. I had thought she was acquainted with Michael Vickery, but I was in error in that regard. Her trip to Cambodia was restricted to Phnom Penh and a small village about 30 km away. This trip was made with the help of Nancy Smith, who works with American Friends Service Committee (AFSC). Subsequently, Nancy Smith visited our ARC hospital and talked with our medics. She came away from there very discouraged, for she felt that their training and medical capabilities were so superior to that of Khmer health workers in Cambodia that the government there will never allow them back. To top that off, tonight Lisa told me that there has been a change in visa regulations, and that to obtain a visa to go to Cambodia now one must go to a country that recognizes the present Cambodian government—Russia, Vietnam or India. It appears that I will not be making that trip.

Lisa came by shortly after I arrived here. Her pregnancy goes well. It is Thai custom that friends, men and women, affectionately pat her growing belly; she says that takes a little getting used to.

25 September 1986

Early afternoon and I am back in Ta Phraya. My excuse for poor handwriting is gone, for I have found a nice table and stool. Ah well, I can still blame the heat and my perspiration, which makes my arm and hand stick to the paper.

29 September 1986

I write by candlelight—romantic, yes? My wristwatch plays its little wakeup tune, but I have been up for about one hour. I was awakened by the flashes of lightning and the booming of approaching thunder. Now it is directly overhead, and rain is drumming on the roof.

The electricity was on when I got up, and a large frog sat immobile on the floor of our bathroom, presumably watching my early morning procedures. Suddenly, the electricity failed and the bathroom was a black void. The occasional flash of lightning helped me to move about, and I was able to wash and brush my teeth without stepping on my friend. In the kitchen, I lit a candle and managed to make my breakfast and prepare my lunch. Now, as light begins to show through the windows, I write.

Thus far, I don't think I have outlined our daily schedule. On arrival at camp, I proceed to the Peds ward and check with the night medic. There follows a quiet time until about 9:00 A.M., when the rest of the farangs arrive and the Khmers are ready to start rounds. Rounds are divided between myself, the farang nurse and the Khmer medic chief. The Khmer medic presents his cases, and I listen, observe and occasionally try by questioning to direct. Our time with this group may end before too long, and it is important to prepare them to manage on their own.

The rumor is strong that KID closes in December, and who knows what will happen to the rumors of Site 2.

The farangs eat lunch in the health office. After lunch, I usually take a short nap and spend the afternoon teaching and seeing new patients. By 4:00 P.M., departure procedures begin, largely connected with being sure no one is left behind. We usually leave between 4:30 and 5:30.

Evening activities I will write about at a later date. Now I must make my last-minute preparations for the day. I like to be ready to go on time and not keep the others waiting.

A morning like this makes me realize the distance that separates us and the difference in our lives. I miss you.

30 September 1986

I go to Bangkok early tomorrow morning to hear Michael Vickery talk. Bob Medrala is a member of the Press Club and has invited me as his guest. It is a hurried one-night trip, but perhaps less worthwhile since I have pretty well decided not to try the Cambodian venture.

In my account of a day's schedule I think I left off with leaving camp. We usually arrive home about 5:00 P.M. I take a shower, which is becoming progressively colder, and shave. Then there is the question of dinner. There are three basic choices—to eat out, to make dinner at home, or to go out and buy on the street and bring it home. When we choose the last option, I often buy chicken-on-a-stick and sticky rice. Of course, often when we have not gone out, I make my way in the darkened streets to Fargo's for one scoop of chocolate and a cup of coffee. At first, they confused this with one scoop of chocolate and one scoop of coffee ice cream.

1 October 1986

Here I am in the bus station, Dolt pack on my back, slightly perspired from walking here from House 1. Even at this hour the streets were not deserted. Motorcycles put-putted by, and at one time I was surrounded by a pack of dogs, who promptly dispersed when I bent over to pick up a stone.

Arriving at House 1, I found Mary Beth, a young nurse with a sweetly soft Boston accent, and her boyfriend, Bob, getting ready for dinner. Bob is one of those delightful young Americans who, with no real background in education, came to Thailand and found himself a job teaching Khmers for COERR. He is considered to be an excellent teacher who teaches with his heart. With the spontaneity so much a part of life here, and so compatible with my concept of fullness of life, we picked up Father Jean and Andrea.

Father Jean, about 50 years old, is French and Swiss and speaks the three languages of Switzerland. He has spent 11 years working in Calcutta. Andrea is Jewish. The good Father said he is reluctant to baptize the Khmers because he feels it is better for them to remain good Buddhists than try to accept a foreign religion—irrevocably related to the hope that in so doing it might work to improve their earthly situation. This I took to be a remarkable observation from a man of the cloth and marks a radical difference from the forceful evangelization of former years.

It was a happy and inspiring time for all of us, so separate in age and background, but united in the hope to help these people.

The Thai prime minister has just announced that KID will close, but no date was given. Some Khmers, legals, will go to third countries, the balance to border camps.

2 October 1986

I shall write a future letter on Prof. Michael Vickery's talk. The trip back to Aran in the bus seemed relatively short thanks to a 1½-hour nap and a good book. On arrival at House 1, I found David about to leave for Ta Phraya. Right now I am sitting in his car while he talks with TF 80.

3 October 1986

One of the bright and dedicated medic students died in his sleep two days ago—a sad time for all.

4 October 1986

| *Armpit to Armpit, Buttock to Buttock*

Today is Saturday, my day off, and I decided to go to KID to see my friend LyRath. LyRath and I became friends during my first tour in 1981, and I have vicariously shared his physical and mental suffering as he worked his way toward expatriation to a third country. LyRath is in KID and leaves for Phanat Nikhom in one week, in transit to Canada. I went to rejoice with him and to say good-bye.

KID is about one-third of the distance between Ta Phraya and Aran, so I decided to go on into Aran and do some shopping. Back down on the highway, I waved down the bus. In Thailand this is literally true, for one leans over and waves one's arm just over the pavement. For one patron the bus only slows, not stops, and one swings into the open door like a fireman. The only problem was there was scarcely room in the bus to accept another passenger, at least that was my Western judgment. Nevertheless, we stopped periodically, and gradually I was pushed and packed to the middle aisle, where I hung on to the overhead handrail, pressed on all sides by perspiring humanity. After a while, the fare taker made his way between us sardines, and with careful movements we late arrivals extracted our pocketbooks and paid our fares.

It was a relief to arrive in Aran, and I didn't even mind the flooding that had left the streets with six inches of water. Refreshing to the feet at least. I had a nice lunch, did my shopping and made my way toward the bus stop. En route, I encountered a bus that I thought might be headed for Ta Phraya, so I entered this nearly empty bus. To my questioning "Ta Phraya?" the bus driver nodded, so I made myself comfortable. We were parked in the sun, and remained immobile for half an hour—more next letter.

5 October 1986

When the bus started, I quickly realized that instead of heading for Ta Phraya, it was headed to Bangkok. I disembarked in a hurry, but had a quarter-mile walk in the hot sun.

At the bus stop there was a crowd waiting. Soon a little red truck went by slowly, driven by a Thai man and accompanied by his young son, who was leaning out the window and calling out what sounded like Ta Phraya. The car stopped at the nearby refreshment stand, and the boy got out to buy some candies. Several girls from the waiting crowd got into the back of the truck and, weary from my attempts to get home, I decided to investigate. To my question "Ta Phraya?" the father nodded and indicated I should get in the front seat. Not knowing the custom, I tried to offer him some money, but the son smiled, shook his head, and said "Free." It was a nice ride out to Ta Phraya. En route, I pondered whether I should try to pay. The quotation "It's better to give than to receive" came to my mind. It occurred to me that this saying implies that there is some merit in receiving as well. And so, when we arrived at Ta Phraya, I shook hands with father and son and did my best to express my thanks.

My letter writing has been somewhat interrupted by other demands. I am working with Bob and Vince (adult medicine, young, good head and heart) on developing a fellowship position in Pediatrics. This is designed along the line of programs in U.S. universities. The idea in this case is intensive study of malnutrition by the Khmer Fellow and the farang. It is requiring considerable study and writing—more later. In the meanwhile, if you happen to see articles in medical magazines or newspapers on nutrition/malnutrition, I could use some. We have an excellent book we are studying.

10 October 1986

Bob and Bernadette have gone to Aran, Arlys is in Bangkok seeing Chris off, and I have the house to myself. The electricity has been off in Ta Phraya for several hours, and it is very dark except for the glow of many candles and lamps in the Thai shops. It is kind of nice, for the blare of loud radios and TVs is absent. Even the motorcycles are subdued.

I had to get up early yesterday morning to make a hurried trip with Bob into KID to check on a patient. In the ward there, I saw many Khmers in various stages of recovery from grievous war wounds. The mayhem goes on in areas away from us.

On arrival at camp, I did my usual morning chores and then made arrangements for transportation to KID for LyRath's good-bye party. I had a nice long visit with LyRath, his brother and Lisa. Since staff meeting was to be at our house in Ta Phraya, I decided to take the bus rather than call for transport. I went down to the highway and waited. It was hot, and finally I went across the road to the "Fly Palace" and bought some Orange Crush. I returned to my waiting position, and as I perspired I felt like my stomach was beginning to rebel. It was what I would call low-grade nausea. The bus finally came, and by the time I got home I could do nothing but lie down on my bed. I awakened when the people arrived for the meeting and managed to attend that. When they left, I felt like I should eat something. Cup-a-soup sounded the best, and that went quite well—although Bernie, sitting opposite me, ate warmed-up chicken curry and that nearly got me.

Taking a just-in-case basin with me, I went to bed at 7:30 P.M. I slept well and this morning had only a bit of residual nausea. Our stove was out of gas, so my breakfast consisted of a slice of bread, a cracker and an orange. On arrival at camp, I was in pretty good shape and managed to get through the day by taking three naps.

You can judge my recovery by the fact I went to Fargo's and had deep-fried shrimp and French fries. No ice cream was available due to the electrical problem.

While I have been writing this, a lightning-and-thunder storm has descended on us, and now one of those tropical rains pounds on our roof. Aran has had problems with floods, but Ta Phraya does not. Houses on JVA [Joint Voluntary Agency] Lane have been flooded out. An enterprising Thai operates a rowboat ferry—5 baht per trip.

I have not written much about some of the people I work with whom you do not know. On my arrival, the nurse on Pediatrics was a young man by the name of Jeff. He is from Minneapolis, a good nurse and liked by all for his gentleness and kindness. His tour finished two weeks ago, and he was replaced by Jill, also from Minneapolis. She is also a good nurse and very interested in exploring new ways to help the Khmers.

More about the fellowship program: The Fellow is appointed for one year, and the goal is to help him to become a local expert in some field of medicine appropriate to the problems present. The farang agrees to spend one hour per day with the Fellow. Our first Fellow is Saly—married, two children, intelligent and pleasant, the first Khmer to demonstrate real interest in malnutrition. We spend our hour reviewing the charts of patients in the feeding center and reading a big book on nutrition that Fern left, discussing it as we go along. The only problem is the author is English and tends to use pompous language. For instance, how would you explain to a Khmer the phrase "by virtue of"? The nurse I work with tried, and it at first sounded like she was going to get involved in chastity.

11 October 1986

This is my day off. I went to the market looking for fish, but none looked fresh. Instead I bought a chunk—I can describe it in no other way—of pork, some potatoes, onions and pineapple. After dropping these off at the house, I went in to Aran to do a bit more shopping. At Kim Kim's, I had two pancakes followed by a scoop of chocolate ice cream. The other day, when I wrote about the packed bus, I forgot to mention that besides all the humanity there was a man carrying a large TV set. This time, besides the packed humanity, there were two chickens held by their tied-together legs. I could not blame them for cackling in protest.

13 October 1986

Things are in somewhat unstable condition in our house, with discussions of moving to another house here in Ta Phraya and of firing our maid. A musical band lives in the house next door there, and they practice at all hours of the night. There is a restaurant across the street, and loud Thai discussions go on late into the night. These things have not bothered me, but Arlys is finding them intolerable. Kunya, our maid, is not too smart, and we cannot seem to get her to do anything consistently except the washing and the dishes. I have given up having her mail my letters, and do it myself after finding them lying in the appointed place for one or two days. She also fails to buy and fix pineapple on a regular basis, and that is too much—minor matters perhaps, but irritating.

14 October 1986

This has been a long but nice day. I awakened at 4:30 and felt like getting an early start. I did some letter writing and studying, then fixed breakfast and lunch. At 6:15, I left for KID and was relieved and grateful to find the infant I had worried about overnight had arrived safely and was doing well with chest tube in place for his emphysema.

Our pediatric census continues low, and I am having a good time doing considerable teaching on rounds. My nurse colleague, Jill, is on vacation, and during her absence I must do the accounting for medicines used. This is a complicated procedure in which we seek to be sure all the medications used have gone to patients and not to the market. I insist on doing the counting in Khmer, so have become fairly good at Khmer numbers. I still hear the occasional laugh at my pronunciation, but I'm slowly learning.

I don't know what you hear about the military situation here. We have had a number of "Situation 1s"—Situation 0 indicates no military activity and Situation 1 is shelling in the distance. The Khmers are getting anxious.

16 October 1986

Safety in Thailand

During one of my previous tours, there was a physician who tried to promote the use of safety belts in our cars. To our shame, most of us paid no attention. Some even ridiculed this suggestion on the basis that there are so many other sources of danger here that the oftentimes frustrating process of putting on safety belts every time we got in our car or truck seemed not all that practical. Several months ago, a young woman farang suffered terrible injuries in a car accident. Whether it was that or just the gradual acceptance of the idea of making life as safe as possible, gradually the process of "buckle up" became acceptable, and today most of us try to follow it. Of course it isn't easy. The safety belt is often entangled beneath the seat. Often it is wet and muddy. In some vehicles the belt is either missing or inoperable. Nevertheless, today I am among those who try to use this simple device.

We are not alone in this emphasis on safety. To my surprise, an increasing percentage of motorcycle riders wear helmets. Of course there is a bit of the ironic in this, for it is not unusual to see a motorcycle roaring through the narrow street of our little town, chasing pedestrians to the side and wending its way between opposing traffic with only inches to spare. The driver's costume often consists of shorts and sandals, topped off with an expensive helmet complete with black plastic face shield. Of course, often enough he has wife and child or children riding behind without such protection.

Yesterday, I spoke at our weekly medic staff meeting. A woman's organization in Thailand is sponsoring a "one minute for peace" program, encouraging that at noon today everyone pause for one minute and pray or meditate on peace. I proposed at our ARC meeting that we discuss this in our various departments with our Khmer staff and try to join in this activity. The farang staff was fairly enthusiastic. When I discussed this with our Khmers in Pediatrics, I got a blank response. In a society and culture in which ethnic hatred runs deep, a society that has suffered and is suffering, it is hard to talk about peace. The article promoting this pointed out that before we can have peace between nations we must develop peace within our own hearts and lives.

Such is life on the border.

18 October 1986

We are still fortunate not to have had any deaths on Pediatrics. We have sent a few very sick ones to KID, and one of them, a child with aplastic anemia, did die after several days, but that was inevitable.

Arlys maintains a subscription to *Time* and to both the *Bangkok Post* and the *Nation*. While these are always a bit late, it does keep us aware.

19 October 1986

I'm sitting in House 1 as I start this letter and my journey to Phanat Nikhom.

Going to Phanat Nikhom is much more complicated than to Bangkok. One must go on the "Orange Crush" bus, which lived up to its nickname. Hot, blurry-eyed and squashed in, the four-hour trip seemed endless.

Finally, we reached the transfer point in the town of Chansansow. We debarked at a bus station, which consisted of a very large roof and beneath which was a myriad of small Thai restaurants. Each contributes to a continuous roar of Thai language, punctuated with scraping of chairs and clang of cooking pots. I sat down at the nearest table and ordered a cold *nam sodá*.

The next bus ride was for one hour and reasonably comfortable. I stopped for a Coke at the bus station in Phanat Nikhom. Sweet words came from the young man who ran the refreshment stand, for he spoke English. After total immersion in Thai, it was refreshing to hear those familiar words. He offered to find a taxi for me. The Thai driver had one of those little vehicles possibly unique to this area. It was a light truck with bench seats in back. The driver cruises the streets, stopping intermittently to pick up passengers and arranging his route according to the demands of his passengers. As a result, we went a very circuitous route. Gradually I became aware that the driver did not know where ARC House was. He asked a number of people and finally pulled in to a YWAM house. Two nice ladies there directed us, and finally we arrived, just a few blocks from the bus station.

I was welcomed to House 1 by the field director who, after seeing me settled, left on a previous engagement. I walked the busy streets of Phanat Nikhom and, wonder of wonders, found a little restaurant that had ice cream. I had a chocolate sundae and a cup of coffee.

I rode to the transit camp with the ARC team, and there followed a series of great reunions. I encountered Angie in the OPD, with whom I have worked on several previous tours and with whom Gwen and I shared a house during my second tour. LyRath and his brother, Yin Rit, met me at the restaurant as per plan. I had envisioned a large American-style breakfast, but my Khmer guests preferred the traditional noodle soup with bits of beef, and since the restaurant no longer serves bacon and eggs, it was just as well. I joined them in having soup for breakfast. It was such a happy time I could have eaten shredded wheat, a breakfast food I consider inedible.

I had urged LyRath to bring his whole family, but following Khmer custom his wife and children remained at home. We visited them after breakfast. They live in a small, concrete-wall-and-corrugated-roof structure with concrete floor, with only a grass mat to sleep on. They will probably be here for several months. On the way back to ARC OPD, we ran into Chop and family, another Khmer who has suffered much and now at last is en route to what we all hope will be a better life.

The Oreo cookies (six sent in a recent package) were just right. Just before I left Phanat, LyRath, his brother and I sat on a bench, and I explained the history and role of Oreos in our life. We each ate one, and I sent the remaining three home with him for his wife and two children.

ICM [Intergovernmental Committee for Migration] has a van that runs to Bangkok each morning at 10:00, and I was fortunate enough to get a seat on this. My seatmate was a young physician from Bangladesh. It was my first opportunity to talk with a person from that country.

23 October 1986

I am safely back in Ta Phraya. This has been a busy day. Peds has remained quiet and without deaths. However, several of our colleagues are either sick or on vacation, and as a result I also made rounds in Adult Medicine, where there are several very sick ones. In the afternoon, we had our weekly education class and my session with the Fellow in nutrition.

My eyes are much improved. They scarcely give me any discomfort. I am a little weary of the laughter of my Khmer friends, who of course sort of enjoy any evidence of fallibility in their farang friends. I had been using chloromycetin eyedrops. In Phanat, they told me that gentamycin or tabramycin has been the most effective, so I bought a bottle in Bangkok and have started that. There is a folklore tale here that mother's milk is most effective. Perhaps if I get desperate I'll ask one of the lactating mothers to squirt me in the eyes. (I'm not serious.)

29 October 1986

I wangled a ride with an early truck from here at House 1. (I had stayed in Aran because of a dinner date.) They routinely stop at Kilo Six. There I bought a package of Thai donuts (Dunkin' Donuts need not fear), coffee and a noodle-chicken mix for lunch. The day went rapidly. At the end of the afternoon, I again went through a complicated series of maneuvers, which allowed me to get to Ta Phraya, shower and shave and be picked up by the van headed for Aran.

At House 1, I claimed my little room again and spent some time reviewing *101 Famous Poems* with Mary Beth and her boyfriend, Bob. The good-bye dinner for Hal was at House 6. He and I have formed a nice friendship. Jill put on the dinner, and it was excellent vegetarian spaghetti, cucumber-tomato salad and Thai hamburger buns fixed like garlic bread. I provided flowers.

8 November 1986

We had our first death during the night of 6 November. The patient was a seven-year-old boy who was sent to Peds shortly after we left camp. His admitting diagnosis was pneumonia. About five hours after admission, he suddenly went into collapse, delirium and died. Questioning yesterday revealed that conceivably he may have been very anemic and possibly had congestive heart failure. Unfortunately, our Khmer staff had not recognized his potentially lethal condition. Had it been, it is possible the sudden end might have been avoided. At any rate, there are things to learn from this.

9 November 1986

Yesterday was a very busy day for me. With the usual half team present on Saturday, I had many responsibilities. Also there was the big soccer game. When it appeared that there would be not enough farangs to make up a team, I had offered to play, but as it turned out there were more than enough, and their level of play was far beyond my capacity. It was just as well, for after watching for a short time I was called back to Peds. One of our little charges was in respiratory distress. The ambulance had already left, so as usual we decided that we would provide our own transport—namely, me driving the van. The trip from Site 2 to KID is about 40 km. The route is generally west, and leaving at 5:00 provided me with a beautiful sunset scene. As I approached KID, a brilliant red sunset outlined the hump of KID Mountain. I wish I had had a camera.

10 November 1986

| Little Poa

Poa is a two-year-old boy, admitted to our Pediatrics ward 10 days ago. On admission, he had the history and physical findings of meningitis, and this seemed to be confirmed by spinal fluid examination.

Treatment here for this disease involves 10 days of intravenous and oral antibiotics. Meningitis is not as common in the U.S. and causes great concern to parents and physicians when it occurs. Here it is quite common, and while we have the occasional patient who fails to respond, in general most appear to recover without residual effects.

Poa failed to show good response during his treatment, and toward the end of the 10 days it was apparent that some other problem was present. On arrival at the ward yesterday, I found Saly with a weary and worried look instead of his usual upbeat expression.

He took me to Poa's bedside. During the wee hours of the night, Poa had spiked a high fever, developed a generalized convulsion and had periods of apnea (failure of respiration). In the steady tone of Khmer English, Saly described the treatment rendered. This included giving intravenous sodium bicarbonate, adrenaline, tracheal suction and mouth-to-mouth respiration. We farangs are not allowed in camp overnight, and one can only imagine the scene as Saly, the chief nurse and the health worker, the scene illuminated only by the always dim flashlight and small kerosene lantern, rendered this desperate and so-phisticated treatment.

As he finished his report, Saly, with tears appearing in his expressive eyes, said, "Please, you will excuse me if I do not work so well today. I am tired from making so many decisions in the care of this boy."

Little Poa lives, but his future remains in doubt. We will treat him for malaria even though his laboratory work-up for this disease is negative. We will also consult with the TB clinic.

There have been times in my past experience when it seemed to me that our Khmer health workers did well in the routine care of patients, but when grim signs of failure occurred they tended to accept this with philosophical resignation as if to say, "So be it." Little Poa remains very ill, his diagnosis not really known and his prognosis doubtful. However, this episode reveals the developed skill of our Khmer health workers and an example of care and compassion in the service of their people.

12 November 1986

Yit is a seven-year-old boy who was admitted to our Peds ward about two months ago. He had findings of neurological disease with progressive deterioration. Our efforts were to no avail, and with the aid of several consultations we concluded he had a brain tumor. One day, after he had been with us for about a month, we were making rounds and found his mother sitting with her back to us. This was real body language that said she no longer had hope or faith in us. At about this time the boy's grandmother took over his care, and she could be seen almost continually squatted on the bed, her wizened face revealing that she accepted the situation and awaited the end. A few days later, the mother asked if she could take the boy home, to be treated by the Krou Khmer, the native healer. We of course agreed.

Today, the maternal-child health worker, an English lady, told me she had visited this family at home, felt the boy would die soon, and asked if I would like to visit him. I would indeed, and promptly Bun-Sieth, the medic who had taken care of him, and I went to their hut.

The boy lay with unseeing eyes, only his respiration indicating life. His skin was dry and none too clean. The grandmother was in her position. The mother disregarded us. The father seemed to welcome our visit. There really was nothing to do for the boy. This evening I went to a little store here in Ta Phraya and bought a bar of toilet soap and some intensive care skin lotion for him. There are times of frustration and futility here.

15 November 1986

Our census on Peds rises to 37 with the influx primarily of children with pneumonia. We also have one child with severe malnutrition. The degree of malnutrition is based on a calculation of height/weight. Theoretically a normal child should be at 100 percent, but we accept 85 percent as satisfactory. Most of our children admitted for malnutrition measure in the low 80s. We have one boy at 74 percent, and he reminds me of Bang Phu days; I am concerned about his prognosis.

The boy who had meningitis and for a while failed to recover is now improving. Today, he took a few steps for the first time. You should see the smile on the mother's face; it encompasses gratitude, pride and love.

You asked recently about the volleyball net and ball. I did indeed complete Bill's deal—that was for the OPDs and the platform. After that, Saly said that the Peds staff would clear a level space for a volleyball court if I would buy the net and ball. Giving money to individual Khmers is emphatically illegal, but athletic equipment can be brought in legally with a pass, so I was happy to do it. As Reun, another medic put it, "When I am playing soccer or volleyball, I forget my problems for a short time." I have also supported some of their celebrations, such as the graduation ceremonies that occur tomorrow.

16 November 1986

Yesterday was Loy Kratong—they make small boats, put a candle in and float them. I had considered putting a candle on a plate and floating it on a mud puddle in front of our house. But then I thought the Thais might take offense, so I did not. I did persuade Arlys and Debbie to join the crowds walking by our house headed for the wat. Here there was a carnival atmosphere with many booths selling food and little boats, or *kratongs*. There were fireworks—rockets and indiscriminate firecrackers—being exploded. Not my kind of thing. Nearby there is a reservoir where the *kratongs* would be floated, but we found that would be at midnight and long past my bedtime. I did buy a *kratong,* which I will send to you. On our return trip, walking down the main street, I was the object of much friendly laughter. The Thais thought it was quite comical to see the farang bearing a *kratong* but headed in the wrong direction. I thought it was sort of typical of my life on Thailand streets.

18 November 1986

When I arrived at camp yesterday, I detected concern in the faces of our Khmer staff. Saly asked me if I had heard anything about Vu Thi. They had heard a rumor that Vu Thi had died during the night. Vu Thi was one of our medics when I first arrived. He told me early on that he intended to go to KID. Smart enough, he lacked the charm of many of our Khmer health workers, and I had found it hard to develop a relationship with him.

Saly asked me if I could go to KID and find out about their colleague. With some reluctance, I agreed to go. There I sought out Virac, chief of the Khmer clinic staff, and he assured me that Vu Thi had slept in the Peds ward that night and was healthy when he got up.

In a sense it was a wasted trip, but it pointed up the stressful life the illegal residents of KID live. They are most often caught by TF 80 at night. Some, like Vu Thi, find various places to sleep. Some have friends, legal residents who hide them, frequently in holes dug in the ground under their sleeping platforms. Recently, a snake bit one of the ladies when she climbed into her hole. Such are the problems of those who see no hope in their present situation and seek freedom.

Tomorrow I was to have off to go to a meeting in KID, but we are so busy that instead of a leisurely day it will be demanding. I will go to camp in the morning, make rounds and then drive to Aran for the meeting, returning to Ta Phraya in the evening.

21 November 1986

I am grateful to Amy for teaching me the radio call letters as I have become quite comfortable with managing radio traffic. Not so for everyone.

> SUZANNE (platform nurse, speaking on the radio to Sherry, OPD nurse): "I wish to report positive malaria smear to you. Patient's name is Phan—Papa, Hotel, Alpha, November. Do you read me?"
>
> SHERRY: "Please repeat."
>
> SUZANNE: "Papa Hotel Alpha November. Do you read me?"
>
> SHERRY (after long pause): "No."
>
> SUZANNE: "Papa Hotel Alpha November. Do you read me?"
>
> SHERRY: "No, I don't. I suppose you are speaking in some code I'm supposed to know."
>
> Great laughter.
>
> SUZANNE: "P-H-A-N."

I suppose Sherry may have thought Suzanne was telling her, "Papa is in the hotel with Alpha November."

23 November 1986

I started a letter to you earlier, but the lack of coffee or even a used teabag here in House 1 was too much for me. I found an unlocked bike downstairs and, without permission of its owner, went for a ride. I went over by the school, where there is a large pool, and was treated to a beautiful scene. Lit by the rising sun, the water, the green grass, the trees and the flowers were beyond description. To add action to the scene, a Thai man and two young boys approached the pool herding several water buffalo. These massive animals ordinarily seem eager to immerse themselves in mud or water, but perhaps it was too cold for them. The little Thai boys persistently pulled on their nose ropes or slapped their flanks and finally persuaded them to enter the water, where the boys washed them, swimming around and occasionally crawled on their backs. It was a delightful scene.

I came to Aran late yesterday afternoon. At 7:30, Mary Beth, Bob and I went to the Catholic Mass. There were about 20 people there, Volags from nine countries.

25 November 1986

After Mass, a large group of us went to the Bamboo Restaurant, where we ate one of those mixed meals, the menu decided by each person choosing one favorite dish. Everything tasted good to me, although some of it was quite hot.

I slept well at House 1. We went to Kim Kim's for breakfast, where a large group gathered for a last meal with Jill before she leaves for the States. One of the nice things about life here is the informality of such gatherings. One can start with two for breakfast and end up with a dozen—some close friends and others friends of friends, but soon part of one's own friendship collection.

My trip home was without spectacular incident. In Aran, I transferred to the Orange Crush bus to Ta Phraya. The only seat open was partially obstructed by a huge tractor tire, over which I crawled. The last passenger to get on brought two boxes and a huge duffel bag. With these piled on the tire, I was tightly compressed with just room to breathe.

29 November 1986

| *Thanksgiving in Thailand*

The ARC group here comprises about 30 people, mostly Americans, but including a few Europeans and Thais. It was decided early on to combine our Thanksgiving with IRC, which added about 12 people, and then at the last there were a number of visitors.

Thanksgiving Day we worked at camp until noon. Stopping at Ta Phraya en route, we proceeded to Aran. At House 1, the great peeling of potatoes commenced. The peelers I had bought worked well in the hands of Arlys, Debbie and the maid. I continued my search for a potato masher but remained unsuccessful. The girls managed to do that job with spoons. With butter, milk, salt and pepper, the potatoes, somewhat lumpy, turned out fine.

Mary had made arrangements for the bakery in Aran to bake the pies. She was to be there at 8:00 P.M., but what with the peeling difficulties they didn't arrive until 9:00. Mary had often stopped at this bakery and the baker was always nice. However, he must have had a bad day, for he, in a most un-Thai-like manner, berated her for being late. It seemed that he would refuse to bake the pies, and the verbal impasse went on and on. Mary understands Thai fairly well and, hearing this Thai man speaking so roughly to her, turned to Wichai, Mary Dunbar's Thai friend, for support. Thais do not like interracial confrontations, and Wichai sided with the baker. Finally, the baker agreed to bake the pies. In the turmoil, he must have misunderstood the directions, for he put the pies in the oven at 1:00 A.M. and took them out at 4:00 A.M. When Mary arrived, she found to her dismay they were like gingerbread. Actually, a downright miracle must have occurred, for at dinner they seemed quite good—although I must say different from yours. But then I don't think you ever had similar problems in preparing your famous pumpkin pies. The whole dinner was wonderful, with a nice mix of traditional American and suitable

Thai dishes. Of course I managed to put turkey gravy on my fried crab balls, but that was OK.

30 November 1986

| *We Break the Orange Together*

Working in pediatrics, it is rather common for me to serve as ambulance attendant accompanying a sick infant and concerned mother on the 40 km trip from Site 2 to KID hospital. I have always felt concern and compassion for these Khmers when they are locked into the steel tubing and aluminum walls of the ambulance, particularly when they or their child are sick nearly unto death.

The biblical phrase, "to break bread together," is familiar to those of us from the Anglo-Saxon world, but what relevance can it have in this land where bread is not part of the culture? One could hardly speak of breaking rice together; however, one could speak of breaking an orange together.

I try to carry an extra orange in my pack. The first 30 km of the ride to KID is over rough road, and I spend that time hanging on and checking the IV drip and the oxygen. When we reach the smooth road, I break out the orange, peel it and share it with the mother.

Today, my patient was a four-month-old girl. The mother seemed very distressed and much occupied with holding the oxygen mask over her child's face. Since both of her hands were busy, I fed the mother her half of the orange, placing slice by slice in her mouth. We arrived at KID in good shape, and I am sure that as I turned child and mother over to the KID staff, there was a look of understanding and gratitude in that mother's face.

9 December 1986

I now have an official Thai driver's license, so life should be simpler, but the process was complicated.

David is a small, thin and wiry man of about 40, from New Zealand. He is administrative assistant and takes care of details such as ordering supplies, arranging passes, getting driver's licenses, etc. He is well prepared for this, with two years' experience in Thailand in the Peace Corps, and speaks Thai fluently. He is married to a Thai lady and they have two boys, five months and 2½ years.

His job, like that of a mother, is never done, and he is frequently behind. Having three months' lead time on getting our licenses, one could well ask how come he didn't have this worked out a month ago and avoid this hassle? There are perhaps a number of answers to this, but in any case it is rhetorical. He has such a delightful personality, and his New Zealand accent is so delightful to my ears, that I cannot get mad at him, though I tried.

The drive yesterday to Pratchinburi was about 2½ hours. It was a clear but relatively cool day. Since we took our van, I put mattresses in the back and spent the time reading, sleeping and talking. Having left Aran later than scheduled, we arrived in Pratchinburi shortly after noon—not good timing, since the police department closes at noon. We had lunch at the local equivalent of Kim Kim's. I had noodle soup, which was wonderful except I put too much pepper in. That was all right because I had a good excuse to have a banana split to cool me off.

Back at the police department there were forms to fill out, small photos to take and questions to answer. Then there was a long wait for some higher official to affix his signature. It took two hours, and finally we were through with licenses in hand.

The trip home was uneventful. We arrived in Aran just before 7:00 P.M. and managed to clear the checkpoint for Ta Phraya just in time. I slept well despite presleep visions of a large snake (10 feet) we saw crossing the road and another smaller one who "passed under our wheels."

On arrival at camp this morning I immediately saw that the bamboo platform where our kwashiorkor baby had lain was empty. I sagged a bit when they told me the baby died yesterday morning. I was away getting my driver's license, and so was spared being present. The sad part was that on Sunday the child was doing very well, and the mother was heard to say that he now seemed to be the well child he was before his illness. Kwashiorkor is a complex metabolic failure in which proteins are involved and the child is swollen with subcutaneous fluid. We had found *E. histolytica* in the stool, and were treating the amoebic dysentery it causes.

At the end of that hopeful Sunday the child suddenly became febrile. Saly, the chief medic, was called from his home, and they discovered rales in the child's chest, probably from pneumonia. In the early-morning hours of Monday, the child vomited large amounts of blood. The few life support measures and medications were properly used to no avail, and the child died at 8:30 A.M. The medic reported that before leaving with her sad burden, the mother expressed her gratitude to the health staff for their efforts and kindness. This was a small victory in the face of a major defeat, for in Khmer culture it is rare when such a death occurs that the parents express gratitude. Indeed, it is not unusual for them, in the anguish of their loss, to speak angry and accusing words to the Khmer staff. And so we left that empty bamboo platform saddened, but perhaps having learned a little about medicine and a little about humanity.

12 December 1986

Today I rode in the ambulance with a man who had been badly beaten up. At a little village we were stopped by a Royal Thai Army unit. Soon an army truck pulled up and off-loaded a poor Thai village man. He had stepped on a mine and suffered the Nong Samet injury—one foot blown off and multiple soft tissue injuries. I started an IV and we loaded him in the ambulance. Because of the various regulations, we took him to the Ta Phraya hospital and then proceeded to KID with our original patient.

Tonight, we had invited COERR house for pizza and Trivial Pursuit. Only Mary, a young schoolteacher, and Father Andrew came, but it was fun nevertheless. The pizza prepared by a Thai restaurant was very good. Kunya made salad and I made dressing of mayonnaise, vinegar, soy sauce and pepper—quite good.

13 December 1986

Today on arrival in camp we found the surgery crew busy with a Khmer who had gunshot wounds; he was seen outside the fence by Thai guards. He was in bad shape but made it to KID. The rest of the day was satisfying. Due to a shift in schedule, I worked in Adult Medicine. That was good for a change.

On return to Ta Phraya, I took a long nap and got up at 7:30 P.M. to take a cold shower. Periodically we go across the street with our dinner plate to a small Thai restaurant. My current favorite is *potsiyou,* large flat noodles, bits of meat, mushrooms and pieces of green vegetables like broccoli stems, cooked in a wok.

14 and 15 December 1986

Sunday morning I arose early to help with the transfer of TB files from truck to truck. I caught the 7 o'clock bus, and we were well en route to Bangkok when I realized I had forgotten my credit card and checks to pay the dentist. Frustrated, I got off the bus at Kilo 6 and awaited the arrival of some of my colleagues. Vince and Mary Beth came along presently and I rode with then back to Ta Phraya. On the way, we heard Bob Maat, security, open the camp with Situation 1. This disturbed me and I considered going to camp instead of to Bangkok. We have had several Situation 1s recently, but they have always turned out to be transient local problems.

Now armed with proper paper and plastic finances, I again boarded the bus. I'm sure that local Thai farang watchers suffered from déjà vu as they watched "Papa" carrying his bags and boarding the bus the second time in one morning.

16 December 1986

Yesterday morning I got up early, wrote letters and had breakfast. I left the hotel at 9:00 feeling I had plenty of time to go to the post office and make it to the dentist by 10:00. However, that did not allow time for finding the post office and delays while there. The girl at the desk plainly wasn't interested and merely waved in a general direction to my query for directions. A man I asked on the street indicated, with French accent, that I should turn left on Sukhumvit, but neglected to say it was on the other side of the street. After several blocks, I encountered a Thai policeman who got me straightened around. Sukhumvit has changed since you were here. It is now one way, and it is impossible to cross that fast-moving traffic in the old-fashioned way. Fortunately, there is a traffic light at Soi 4, but I'm sure it is five minutes between changes.

Finally arriving at the post office, I promptly got into the wrong line—the people ahead of me all having complicated deals to consummate. Post offices in the States used to have a reputation for inefficient service, but their change for the better has not reached Thailand. The young man at our counter had to leave his post for stamps, change and who knows what for each customer, and each trip was delayed by conversation with his colleagues in the back of the room. Finally I reached the counter. Your letter required several stamps, and somehow I managed to affix the King's image upside down, and of course this would not do. Carefully the mail clerk made it right.

I hurried back to the traffic light crossing and again waited, meditating in the meanwhile on the fact that this is Thailand, the land of *mai pen rai*. That was appropriate since the dentist was one hour late in her appointments. The tooth cleaning went easily for me, and no cavities!

18 December 1986

Here I am back in my little room in Ta Phraya. I spent yesterday morning going to the Troc and shopping. All afternoon I spent in my comfortable hotel room, writing letters and working on a paper I am preparing. Last night, I had dinner with Fern and her friend, an Australian surgeon who speaks with an almost unintelligible accent. We ate in the hotel dining room and sat and talked for three hours.

I overslept this morning. Instead of catching the 8 o'clock bus, I found myself hurrying to catch one at 10:00. The taxi driver I dickered with assured me he understood and knew where the North bus station was. En route, I realized we were following a route I did not recognize, but he was still assuring me when we pulled in to the South bus station. We finally arrived at the North station at 10:10—bus gone.

20 December 1986

Saturday, and with half the crew working I was again the only MD, and thus it was busy. The Belgian ambassador came on his annual visit, so it was a big time for Bernie. He came at noontime, just when I thought I would be able to take a half-hour nap. After meeting him, I sneaked off to the empty medic classroom to stretch out on a bamboo bench.

Just before I fell asleep, I heard French conversation and approaching steps. These buildings are all bamboo, with much latticework, making privacy unavailable. It would not do for the Belgian ambassador to discover the American physician thus. I hurriedly found a hiding place behind a blackboard and was relieved to hear them pass by.

21 December 1986

There was Thai dancing at the last TF 80 party, and I came home determined to learn. None of my housemates responded affirmatively, and so I went to my Thai dictionary and found the words to ask Kunya if she would teach me. She almost fell to the floor laughing. Eventually she told me I would have to teach her, then more laughing. Not giving up, I went to the stereo store in Aran and asked for a tape of Thai dance music. Again laughter, but they found one tape. Arriving home, I put it in the tape recorder and started to play it for Kunya. Hilarious laughter. I gave up. A few days later, riding with Lek, my favorite Thai driver, in the van equipped with a tape deck, I asked him to stop at Ta Phraya. I ran into the house and got the tape, which he immediately put in the tape deck. Again, hilarious laughter. So much so he had to pull over to the side of the road. It seems that the lyrics to this Thai music are X-rated—something about a housewife who bids her husband good-bye, and while he is at work entertains a male visitor. I guess I give up on Thai dancing.

22 December 1986

I stayed in Aran last night. The Christmas party at YWAM was very nice. I was fortunate to sit between a good alto and soprano, and really enjoyed the carol singing, although I must confess to some homesickness at this time.

On Christmas Day, we are putting on a Nativity pageant on the stage at Site 2. Andrea (Jewish) will read the narration. I am to be Joseph. Too bad I have not grown a beard. More than that, I am playing the recorder in a trio composed of myself, John playing the harmonica, and Bob the guitar. John is a young man, teacher, who came to Bangkok looking for a job.

I happened to meet him at the ARC office and played a small part in getting a job for him with COERR. He plays the harmonica at about the same level that I play the recorder. Bob, Mary Beth's boyfriend, is a professional guitarist, and he carries us along. We are playing "Bring a Torch, Jeannette, Isabella," "O Tannenbaum" and "The Little Drummer Boy." We hope to have a Thai drummer for the last.

23 December 1986

I came into Aran in the ARC van and immediately headed for town. I had already searched Ta Phraya for razor blades, and it took several stops to find any here. Having succeeded in this, I proceeded to Ploen's for my favorite menu: deep-fried shrimp and French fries—decadent, but so good.

I proceeded to Kim Kim's for you know what. There I encountered Helen, an Irish nurse, married to a Thai man who works in Singapore. He manages to come to Bangkok once a month, and Helen says with her delightful Irish accent that life for her is a series of honeymoons. She is Lisa's coworker at KID. Helen and her friend left before I did, and she pulled one of my favorite tricks—paid for my coffee and ice cream.

We had a death in Peds last night. It was an infant brought in comatose at 5:30 P.M. Our medics and nurses strove mightily through the night, but the child died at 3:00 A.M. We are seeing an increase in that deadly combination of malnutrition and diarrhea. I hope it does not continue.

24 December 1986

In my time I have spent the Christmas season in some fairly exotic places—Vietnam, Japan, and now in this little village of Ta Phraya. The COERR group held a spaghetti dinner tonight to be followed by a Mass at 10:30. I did not attend and for reasons I know not. The past two or three days have been busy with preparations for the pageant tomorrow. Today, I was the only doctor in camp again and it was busy. This afternoon we received a six-year-old boy with a fractured femur. He was frightened and suffered great pain with each movement. With all the gentleness I could summon, I splinted his leg, and imaginary or not, felt sure I saw an expression of gratitude and understanding in his eyes as we placed his stretcher in the ambulance. What better Christmas present could there be?

When I arrived home I sacked out and, despite the entreaties of my housemates, decided to forgo the spaghetti. I got up about 8:00, showered and made my way to the restaurant we call ARC house. I had a very good plate of *potsiyou*. Next door is the YWAM house, and as I ate I could hear them singing Christmas carols. When I finished dinner, I entered their house and joined in the rest of the service. It ended with "Hark! The Herald Angels Sing." It has been a good Christmas Eve for me and I hope for you as well.

26 December 1986

The big pageant went off with all the characteristics of *mai pen rai*. It was produced on the stage overlooking the rice field, a stage that was a very good replica of a stable. At the last minute, we became aware that someone had forgotten about the baby to represent the baby Jesus. In a flurry, a Khmer baby was found, and so we started with Mary from COERR holding the baby and me sitting nearby. The baby behaved beautifully, sleeping peacefully until we were on stage. She, it was a girl, started then to wake up and obviously was hungry. Of course our Mary could not feed her. I told Mary to put the tip of her little finger in the baby's mouth. This worked wonderfully, but then Mary felt a spreading wetness and soon there was an odor that indicated more serious problems. Since Khmer babies do not wear diapers, as we know them, it was a bit of a problem, but we managed.

The narrator told the story of the Nativity. Shepherds, wise men and angels, played by various farangs and dressed in sarongs and *pakimas*, came to worship. Music in English and Khmer was provided by the Seventh-day Adventist Choir. While it was the most unprofessional of performances, and I'm not sure how much the thousands of Khmers attending understood, it was fun for us and somewhat of a spiritual experience.

By the end of the day I was tired and dehydrated. Having committed myself to going to the spaghetti dinner in Aran, with some reluctance I drove a truck into Aran. The dinner was very good, and it was 11:00 P.M. by the time I got to bed.

28 December 1986

It is Sunday afternoon here. On Sundays we have only half the crew at camp and only one person stays after 1:00 P.M. This is my turn. A quiet descends upon the hospital platform. I have little to do at the moment, so I scrounged up this piece of paper and perhaps will get my daily letter written. In Pediatrics we have a seven-month-old just coming out of a seizure. In OB there is a lady in the terminal stages of cancer of the uterus. I check on them every half hour or so, otherwise there is little to do.

29 December 1986

This has been a demanding day. It started with a flat tire on our van, which made us late. On arrival at camp I found Michelle, the nurse who works with me, dealing with a seven-year-old boy who had chicken pox and severe pneumonia. Michelle had recognized his tenuous hold on life. Over the radio we sought to make the ambulance driver feel the urgency of our call. It seemed a long time before he arrived. I arranged getting the boy in the ambulance and getting the oxygen started. Being the only doctor in camp, I could not accompany him. As I closed the ambulance doors on Michelle, the worried mother and the struggling boy, for the first time this trip there were tears in my eyes. My reaction was partly for the boy and his parents, partly the feeling that circumstances prevented me from sparing Michelle one of the tough experiences here. As it turned out, they made it to KID all right, and the boy's future is in other hands. Sometimes the rules we work under, such as no oxygen in border hospitals, are hard to accept even though they make some sense in the overall situation here.

30 December 1986

Michelle called me over to where she stood with a group of staff and Khmer family members, who surrounded the bed of a seven-month-old Khmer child. She told me that the father, an older Khmer, wished to speak to me. He was fluent in French but spoke no English. Translated, he said, "I ask that you help me save this little child." Then he described a scene on the Thai–Cambodian border where he had come upon this child and her parents. The father was leaving for military service, and the mother was about to abandon the child.

This Khmer gentleman, already responsible for his own family, decided to try to save this child, and he and his wife became adoptive parents. The child shows early signs of malnutrition, and it will be our privilege to participate in "saving this child."

31 December 1986

It is 7:15 P.M. as I start this letter. There is a big party in Aran, but none of us from Ta Phraya are going. The streets here are even noisier than usual, and I imagine that will continue on through the night. I am quite content to spend a quiet evening at home.

Yesterday, we had a practice evacuation of the camp. Even though it was just experience and practice, I did not like the feeling of leaving the Khmers on the Pediatric ward.

I have been studying one of those "easy Thai" books, which says all you have to do is learn the alphabet, which contains 44 characters having no relationship to the ABCs.

I must see about some dinner. I don't imagine that you will be doing much about New Year's—it never was much our thing anyway. Nevertheless, I send my best wishes and the hope that 1987 will be good year for us.

1 January 1987

This has been a busy day; our census is now in the 70s, and the degree of illness has increased. However, the degree of illness still does not approach that of Bang Phu days, and I think we are handling the sicker ones better. This is largely attributed to the excellent capabilities of the nurses and medics. The Khmer people, and we the farang staff, are indeed indebted to the education staff, which labored so hard in years past.

3 January 1987

| *IV*

The letters "IV," often used as an abbreviation in medicine, can stand for "in vitro," which means a reaction conducted by a technician in a glass or ceramic vessel of his laboratory, or "in vivo," the action of a drug observed in a living animal. The most frequent use of the abbreviation in medicine refers to the infusion of a liquid into a patient's vein.

Certainly the IV has had a marked effect upon the Khmer medical scene. While we try to control its use, the Khmers have great faith in it, and many are the little lectures we give encouraging more natural and simple measures, such as encouraging oral intake of fluids. The Khmer medics are in a bind over this, for parents and patients are frequently convinced of the magic power of the IV and they pressure the medics to start one.

Most of the beds in Pediatrics are actually bamboo platforms about two feet high and about the size of a king-size bed. It is not unusual for the platform to be occupied by three or more of our little patients, surrounded by any number of brothers, sisters, parents and friends. On rounds, when the medic starts to present the case, it is often difficult to tell who is the patient. If there is an IV hanging, one can follow the tube down and thus make the determination.

Trained by years of deprivation, the Khmers have become adept at improvisation and have found many uses for discarded IV tubing. Shaped with infinite care, they become caricatures of fish or birds. Woven, they become baskets. More pragmatically, they become cords to bind bundles.

In a more serious way, one must give credit to the IV. Admittedly sometimes used when unnecessary, nevertheless in this land of fevers, diarrhea and vomiting, the IV often is the saving procedure, and the Khmer health workers have become expert in its use.

4 January 1987

On Friday morning at camp, about 9 o'clock, I heard a small plane flying overhead. This is unusual, so I went outside as the small Thai observation plane flew over the hospital at fairly low altitude. A few moments later, I heard a burst of machine gun fire. I went over to the TB clinic to report this to Bob, UNBRO security. He left to investigate. A little later, there were a number of artillery blasts, followed by radio notice of Situation 1. Everything quieted down. Bob reported that the ground fire was from Vietnamese troops and the artillery from Thai units. We heard nothing further. I was amazed to read in the *Bangkok Post* about the sad denouement of this experience. The plane was hit by ground fire, had problems in landing, crashed. The pilot was killed and a second man badly injured.

Despite the above, all is quiet here.

5 January 1987

Our census has reached 80, and we are very busy. Fortunately, we have only a few very sick ones and have had no deaths recently. Most of the children have either pneumonia or diarrhea-dehydration and malnutrition. I am planning a little bacteriological study of the dust that fills our lives these dry days.

8 January 1987
Bangkok

Yesterday I spent alternating between sleeping, reading and shopping. As to the latter I had only one chore—to buy an intern's handbook for BunSieth, our chief medic. Not as simple as it sounds. Most bookstores here have medical sections, but none of them I went to had handbooks. I had heard of a bookstore at Chulalongkorn University. Using my trusty map, I went by bus and arrived there without difficulty. This university reminded me of the University of Washington—a large, tree-adorned campus. A student I queried spent 20 minutes drawing a map and giving me directions to the bookstore. It was a long walk and the day was hot. I didn't find exactly what I wanted but close enough.

I made my way back to a business district where there was a Pizza Hut, and I had a very good small dish of macaroni with tomato and cheese and super garlic bread.

8 January—later

I am sitting at the dining room table in Lois Visscher's house, Chanat Province, central Thailand. The bus trip here was delightful, much better than the Aran–Bangkok trip—better bus, nice service, better roads and interesting and different part of Thailand. There were vast fields of ripened rice on either side of the highway, and in most of them one could see conical hats and patches of color—farmers and families harvesting in their ancient fashion.

The bus let me off about a quarter mile from the hospital. In the distance I could see someone in a yellow dress approaching. She walked rapidly with vigor; at first I couldn't believe it, but it was indeed Lois. Of course the last time I saw her she was just recovering from surgery. I was very happy to see how well she appears.

Lunch was on the table—rice and several tasty accompanying dishes and pineapple for dessert. After lunch Lois had some surgery to do— repair of perforated peptic ulcer in an older Thai man.

9 January 1987

I am sitting at the desk in the little room assigned to me in the guesthouse. It is dark outside, but the roosters crow just like in Ta Phraya. When Lois came back, she took me on a tour of the Manorom Christian Hospital. In status and technology it appears to be about midway between our hospital at Site 2 and modern hospitals in the States. Of masonry construction, it has three floors and several wings and contains about 100 beds. Part of the effort here is in service to lepers. A surgeon, Dr. Grace Warren, makes her headquarters here. She does primarily reconstructive plastic surgery on lepers.

After the hospital tour, a quick shower and shave, we had dinner. This was cauliflower and a casserole of mashed potatoes, onions and pork, very good. Best of all was the homemade bread, which their maid prepares. For dessert there was chocolate pudding, excellent. We went to the weekly Thursday staff prayer meeting. They sang, unaccompanied, a number of hymns unfamiliar to me. The leader periodically listed various people to pray for, and then there would be several moments of volunteer prayer. The staff comprises about 20 people, the majority women appearing 35 years and up, two Thais and several Caucasian men. These people come from all over the world and serve for long periods of time. They are an impressive group.

I'm glad I came on this visit. Dr. Visscher is a few years older than we are. I certainly admire her surgical ability and her general knowledge of tropical medicine. She is a remarkable lady and an inspiration. Time to go to her house for breakfast.

Later, back in Bangkok

My bus trip from Manorom was without incident. Wonder of wonders, I managed to take a municipal bus from the North bus station to this hotel instead of a taxi. This evening I went to the Troc, and Cathy Glidden had arrived. I took her and Lori, another nurse, to dinner at La Paloma. It was a great evening. You and Peggy were with us in spirit; I wish you could have been here in person.

11 January 1987

Sunday evening and the end of one of those days when my heart is filled with gratitude for the opportunity to be here. We do indeed have some very sick children on the ward. Today, I gave digitalis to two of them for congestive heart failure. It is certainly possible that one or both of them may not survive, but the parents and all of us who have worked with them can certainly feel that they have had quality care. I am so impressed with the skill and dedication of the health workers. I hope I am communicating to them my admiration and sense of privilege to be working with them.

12 January 1987

A measure of my love for you is the conflicting pull between this blue sheet of paper and the white sheet of my bed. Today was a busy day. Our very sick babies are still with us, but their prognosis is questionable.

Actually, today I was to go to Site 8 to participate in a screening of children under three. This is a process to identify all those eligible for extra food. I begged off going, feeling that the demands of Peds were greater. Several of our team went. We heard over the radio that Site 8 had gone from Situation 0 to 1 to 2 to 3. Situation 3 means shells landing in camp, and requires evacuation. We haven't heard any details yet but assume our colleagues are OK.

13 January 1987

The Surgical Glove

This glove was probably manufactured in a factory in some eastern city in the United States. From its manufacture, through the various steps of packaging, sale, transportation and delivery, many people were involved. It is possible that one or more of those people gave thought to the lifesaving work for which it might be used.

This surgical glove ended up in the hospital at Site 2 on the Thai–Cambodian border. We do not know under what circumstances it fulfilled its intended purpose. Perhaps it shielded the hands of some Khmer medic as he sought to deal with some ailment of one of his countrymen.

We only know that somehow it came into the hands of a four-year-old Khmer girl. Responding to her need for toys and using the ingenuity of her people, she put it in her mouth to blow and make a balloon. Somehow she breathed in at the wrong time, and the rubber finger of the glove lodged in her throat, blocking all air passage.

I knew she was dead when I first saw her lying on the table. She was surrounded by Khmer health workers, who had rendered emergency treatment. I immediately sent one of the Khmers to summon Dr. Vincent, my young colleague. Reaching in her throat with my index finger, I could just feel the end of the rubber finger, but could not grasp it. Heimlich maneuver was to no avail. Dr. Vincent arrived and recommended tracheotomy. With him wielding the scalpel and some help from me, the tracheotomy was done, the offending rubber finger removed and cardiopulmonary resuscitation instituted.

It was to no avail, and after a suitable time we had to accept defeat. As we walked away from that table, we could hear the grieving cries of the mother and sister. We were further saddened to learn that this mother's

22-year-old son had been killed one week ago in battle. There are many happy and satisfying experiences here, but there is sadness too.

It's probably therapy for me to write the above. I am indeed sad about that episode, but confident we did our best in a hopeless case.

BunSieth is 25 years old. He is short, perhaps five feet in height, and weighs no more than 100 pounds. He is married and has two children. He is currently Khmer chief of the Pediatric ward, and we are close friends.

He dresses neatly, usually a Western-style shirt, pants of thin cloth and thongs. This is in contrast to his colleagues, who often wear fancier shirts, jeans and tennis or running-type shoes. Simple garb in the Khmers usually indicates that they either do not have a generous Western support person, or what goodies come their way are used to support their families.

BunSieth was 13 years old in March of 1975 when his father came to their home in Battambang, having left the Lon Nol army to try to help his family through the Pol Pot time. The family consisted of father, mother and four children, ages five to 20.

Their first requirement was to move from their neighborhood, for the father's life depended on hiding his military service. They moved to a farming area several kilometers away, where they were encompassed by the Pol Pot army. Following its usual procedure, the new state separated the family, sending each of them to rice farms about 5–10 km apart. In their new locations the family worked in the fields, and survived on minimal rations of rice and soup. The oldest daughter died of disease and malnutrition. In 1979, with the withdrawal of the Pol Pot forces, the family reunited, and for six months tried to make a living in the rice fields.

They heard of a better life in the border camps and made their way to Nong Samet in 1980. The father joined the local army unit and was recently wounded in battle. The children have married. BunSieth studied in the health worker classes and has progressed to his present position. As the years pass they ponder the future—to a third country or back to Cambodia or continued life in a refugee camp.

BunSieth's story of Pol Pot days is not nearly as dramatic as many.

For us who have been blessed by the good fortune of living in America, the picture of a 13-year-old boy working long hours in the fields during the day, subject to hours of political educational harangue every evening, and separated from his family is a humbling one. BunSieth is a survivor, but one who has not let the hard experiences of the past defeat him. It is a privilege to know him and to work with him.

14 January 1987

Tonight was staff meeting in Aran. Due to arrival of new folks and Bob Medrala and Supot being in town, there was a shortage of beds available. Rather than suffer through the complexities of it all, I just went to the Inter Hotel. And so here I sit in a nice little hotel room, neat and clean with air-conditioning and hot water. It was a nice short meeting, and as soon as I finish this I will climb into bed by 9:30 and read several letters brought up from Bangkok.

16 January 1987

This was a very nice day. Cathy made rounds with us; it was very good for the Khmers and for me. It was a mutual learning experience. She is spending the night at Ta Phraya house. I made an omelet with fried boiled potatoes and onions for dinner, and Cathy and Bonnie made a tomato and cucumber salad.

I sometimes feel like my mother is here, for several people, including Cathy, have said, "You look very tired." I don't know what they are referring to, for except for getting weary by evening like everyone else, I have felt very well and have plenty of energy.

18 January 1987

Today, Sunday, is my day off. Bonnie, nurse practitioner in Surgery, leaves tomorrow, and partly in observance of that I will spend today cooking. Going to the market this morning, I bought 1.5 kilos of beef, fruit, potatoes, onions, and tomatoes, and now have a pot roast simmering. Since this is also Kunya's day off, my first job was to wash dishes, which I did in Western fashion, rinsing them with boiling water. This is a step that Kunya avoids.

The balance of the day I will spend intermittently sleeping, reading, writing, and preparing dinner in steps.

21 January 1987

TF 80 has a party tonight celebrating the opening of their new offices. All Volags are "invited" to stock booths with goodies to eat. We are providing fruit salad, and Ta Phraya House provided the papaya. Kunya did most of the work of peeling and slicing.

23 January 1987

Yesterday a Dr. Van showed up at Site 2. He is a child psychologist and was quite willing to make rounds with us. I am always happy to show off the skills of our Khmer staff. In the afternoon, we had an education session with our Khmer staff and that went off very well.

24 January 1987

This morning I went to the market to buy some Thai-style donuts—*Fa Ta Ko*. These are X-shaped and made of dough similar to raised donuts and are fried in hot oil. They are very greasy, but the closest thing to Dunkin' Donuts available in Ta Phraya. Inside, there are large air spaces so one can break them open and pour in some sugar, thus making a thoroughly decadent Thai–American treat.

25 January 1987

Today was my Sunday to work, and as usual I volunteered to "stay late." Patty Anderson and Bob also stayed late, and it was 5:30 by the time we were ready to leave. Just as I was getting into the car, one of my medics came running. A 20-month-old child had arrived, his father reporting that the child had eaten 20 of his mother's iron pills. We put a nasogastric tube down but did not retrieve any. A trip to KID was in order for administration of deferoxamine. And so I took a late ride in the ambulance and got home at 7:30.

Supold, who works in our staff office and speaks excellent French, told me of a "Voice of America" broadcast he heard recently in which they listed Patty, Suzanne, Bernie and myself as part of the ARC staff. They gave a short biography of each of us, stating I had recently retired from practice in the U.S. and now am taking care of Khmer children. I don't know how all of that came about—it must have originated with one of the journalists who came through.

Today was a good day in Peds, although it started out sad with the report of the death of one of our neonates who had sepsis. Bernie has a baby in obstetrics with a strange skull deformity. By radio, I invited a new pediatrician at Nong Chan Hospital to see the baby. The doctor's name is Paul. He stayed the whole morning with us; he said he really enjoyed it and gave us some good tips.

26 January 1987

Here I sit in a little room in House 1, by now so familiar to me. You may well ask, "Why are you in Aran again?" Well, let me tell you about Grandma running down the road.

Today started very well. On arrival at camp, I found the babies and children all doing quite well. About 9 o'clock, the cars from Aran arrived bringing Dr. Nancy Thompson. It was another of those wonderful reunions that are part of the spice of life here. I looked forward to her visit, both on the basis of our friendship, and the opportunity to show her our Pediatrics ward and to learn from her observations.

Rounds went very well, with the Khmer health workers presenting their cases in good style and Nancy in her gentle and kind manner asking questions and offering suggestions. I was vaguely aware of the noise of artillery shelling in the background and not really surprised when Suzanne came by to announce Situation 1. Rounds continued, and gradually the rumbling became louder and more frequent. Almost as if a cosmic switch had been thrown, I sensed an aura of heavy tension. A few minutes later Suzanne ran into the ward and yelled, "Situation 2."

A month ago we had a practice Situation 2. Even though it was simulated, I felt at that time that if a real Situation 2 occurred I would not be able to leave my little Khmer patients, their families and my Khmer health worker colleagues.

Realizing that refusing to leave would cause great concern to ARC and expose some of them to danger, I had determined that if a real alarm occurred I would make myself leave immediately without looking at my Khmer friends. My plan worked well. At Suzanne's shout, I grabbed Nancy's arm and told her to follow me immediately. We ran out of the ward and to the pharmacy, my place of duty. There the pharmacy workers were madly jamming medications and solutions in boxes, and Nancy and I carried these to the truck.

With this completed, we were told to board a waiting truck. It was then I looked at the nearby road. It was crowded with Khmers. It was then that I saw the grandmother running. Where she was headed I know not, but her expression and stride said to me that she had been through this before. My spirit convulsed with grief for these poor people. I thought of the families in the Pediatrics ward who were leaving to gather together at their bamboo huts. I thought of my Khmer medics and nurses, who no doubt were running to see to the welfare of their wives and children.

My vision blurred with tears, I made my way to the waiting truck. Soon we were at the rendezvous point outside of camp. In beautiful sunshine, far enough away not to hear the shelling, we awaited orders. Soon they came and we continued the evacuation to Ta Phraya. There we gathered at Ta Phraya house, a strangely quiet crowd, divided in small groups huddled about the radios. Each of us had a story to tell, and we each sensed that our listener understood and sympathized.

I was impressed that, in myself and as near as I could tell in all of my colleagues, there had been no real fear for personal safety. There had been an overwhelming desire to perform our duty, and at moments this feeling of sadness and compassion for the Khmers.

By radio we learned that Situation 3 had been called, meaning shells landing in camp. Later we learned of nine casualties, five serious, but no deaths reported.

Tomorrow a limited-access team will go into camp. In rotation, I will go in on the next day. It is expected that limited access will go on for about 10 days. There are many times when I wish I had a camera. But I do not need a photo to remind me of this day, for I will always remember Grandma running down the road.

27 January 1987

I hope this letter does not disturb you unduly. The regulations set up for our safety are very conservative, and I am determined to follow the rules. Except for the concern for the Khmers, I am in good shape physically and in spirit.

27 January—later

It was good to talk with you this morning, although it leaves me with very little to write about. Leaving the phone store, I went to the PO and then did some shopping. I bought a K4 Kodak 35mm camera. It is one of those automatic focus and shutter speed cameras, but instead of a motor-driven film advance one must wind it by hand. I think I can tolerate that. I will hurriedly take up the 20-exposure film they gave me for free, and get them developed rapidly so I can get some idea how well it works.

Word from camp is that all is quiet—Situation 0.

28 January 1987

Today I was part of the limited-access medical (LAM) team. All was quiet at camp yesterday and again today. On LAM we are allowed to stay only until 1 P.M. Since only one doctor is allowed, I was very busy for the first few hours, checking with the medic chiefs of the various wards. Actually, the medics did most of the work. Only about half of the patients returned, and no new patients showed up on Peds; in fact, it was relatively quiet. The Khmers were all in good spirits, revealing no particular anxiety, except many packed up their books and precious papers and possessions to send home with us. Tomorrow the authorities will relax restrictions a bit, allowing most of the team, except education, to return.

It is 3 P.M. as I write; we must go into Aran again at 4:30 for a town meeting. I really admire the way Patty, Suzanne and Bob have led the team through this episode. I suppose it is to be expected that such experiences tend to unite a group. That effect is certainly visible here.

29 January 1987

In the 2 February *Time* magazine (Asian edition), there is a picture of me, Saly and BunSieth. The picture primarily features my bald pate and identifies me as a Minnesota pediatrician, but nevertheless it is I. [The 9 February 1987 U.S. issue carried the same story and picture.]

1 February 1987

The recent Chinese New Year, January 29, has had a negative effect on us. It seems that all or nearly all the bakers are Chinese, and they closed up for several days. As a result, there hasn't been a loaf of bread available in either Ta Phraya or Aran. And you know how I like bread. Early this morning, I took the bike and went searching—no luck. I ended up eating in a Thai restaurant—fried eggs and rice. Afterward, I went to the market and bought fixings for dinner—potatoes, onions, papaya, banana, pineapple, cauliflower.

Kunya does not work on Sundays, so as preparation I had to do a big pile of dishes. I just about have everything ready. The balance of the day I spent cleaning up my room, changing the bed and doing some preliminary packing for the big move at the end of this month.

2 February 1987

The following is copied from the book *The Big War,* by Anton Myrer. The book rates about an "8" on my scale. It relates at least part of the reason I am here:

"All of it—in this one dirty, wasted, fearful, ecstatic face of a half naked child. He does not know me, nor I him, we cannot speak the same tongue, he has lived his short life ten thousand miles from mine; but he is a part of us all the same. One momentous, indissoluble entity we are, and he needs my succor. And it is just as much my need to succor him. This is the vindication of our destiny—not the high heaped verbiage of ideologies and waspish reasonings, the chill mash of thoughts, but simply in the comforting of man where he is in misery. There is no security in this world—none at all in heaps of weapons and war gear or splendid isolation or boundless wealth or knowledge—no security except what is in love and selfless suc-cor and generosity of spirit. That is the only rock immutable and anything else is a dance of shadows painted on a gaudy screen."

4 February 1987

Here in the city of Chasansow, I am sitting in a bus that I hope will soon depart for Phanat Nikhom. I say "hope" because I sat in another bus for 15 minutes before another passenger arrived and assured me that the bus we were on went to some other town. Fortunately, we had not left the bus station yet.

The bus trip from Aran to this city was much as I recall it from my previous trip—long and crowded. Thai buses are scientifically designed so that the space between seats is 1 cm less than the distance from my patellae to my sacrum. Added to this, when you crowd three people into a seat for two, it makes for an uncomfortable ride.

4 February—later

The balance of my trip to Phanat Nikhom went very well. On arrival, I expected the bus to go to the bus station like the last time, but before I knew it we had gone through the center of town and into the suburbs. I had a bit of a walk as a result, but never mind, for en route I passed an ice cream store, and of course had my one scoop of chocolate ice cream.

As expected, all of the House 1 people were still at work when I ar-rived, and the doors were all locked. I put my *pakima* and towel down on the concrete floor of the porch, and with my zipper bag as a pillow, I lay down and to my surprise had a good nap.

When the people arrived home they welcomed me. For dinner, we went to a sidewalk food stand and bought a variety of barbecued dishes and cucumber salad. We took this home and had a nice dinner. I walked the streets of Phanat Nikhom for a short time after dinner, and here I am ready for bed.

It is interesting to talk with these people. They deal with a different group of Khmers and Vietnamese. Rather than the melancholy we deal with, they have anxiety tension states to deal with.

Well, tomorrow I hope to see LyRath and then off to Bangkok.

6 February 1987

| *A Morning in Bangkok*

Living in the little village of Ta Phraya, I periodically build up a list of errands or purchases I need to do in Bangkok. Accordingly, I left my comfortable little hotel room early this morning and embarked on the streets of Bangkok.

Readers of this journal will perhaps have grown weary of descriptions of Bangkok traffic. Motorcyclists on Sukhumvit who wish to turn at the corner use the curb driveway, drive around the corner on the sidewalk, and then leave the sidewalk on the second curb driveway. They scarcely slow their speed from the street. Pedestrians, I among them, flee the peril of these monsters.

Later on, I encountered a real monster on the sidewalk—an elephant. It was a moneymaking scheme. There was a mahout perched on the beast's shoulders and an attendant on the ground. For a coin, a passerby could place a morsel of fruit or vegetable in the snout of the elephant's questing trunk. If instead of a coin a person placed a 10-baht paper bill in the snout, the elephant sensed the difference and raised his trunk to the mahout above, who pocketed the bill. It was an interesting scene, made all the more piquant by the cars maneuvering around this giant beast. Mini cars indeed seemed mini. For those who wonder how fast an elephant walks, he walks slower than the average person walks on the city sidewalk. I know, for I paced him.

Mai Pen Rai?

My major purpose for this trip was to see my friend, LyRath and family. I first met LyRath in 1981, and since then we have been good friends. I have helped him somewhat in his migration from Nong Samet to KID, given him some support during his two years in KID. Two weeks ago I received a letter from him indicating he would be leaving Phanat Nikhom, the transit camp, for Canada in February or March and asking if I could visit before he left. By two different routes, I sent letters advising him I would visit on 5 February and asking him to get word to me if he was to depart before that date.

Yesterday, arriving at Phanat Nikhom camp, I found LyRath's former hut occupied by a new family, who advised me that LyRath and family had left for Canada on 26 January. My time, expense and a hard bus trip were for naught.

Mai pen rai is Thai for "never mind," but it represents a much deeper philosophical mind-set encompassing karma, "don't sweat the small stuff," "so be it" and so on. Westerners who come to Southeast Asia are blessed by exposure to this philosophy. Some embrace it too wholeheartedly. In moderation, it is a great antidote for the anxieties and tensions of life in that other world.

And so I accepted LyRath's precipitous departure with the spirit of *mai pen rai,* and instead of fretting and feeling disappointed, gave my mind over to good thoughts of hope for happiness for this family as they start a new life in Canada. May they take just the right amount of *mai pen rai* with them.

7 February 1987

I will start this letter while sitting in the bus awaiting departure to Aran. I had a super sleep last night: asleep by 8:30 P.M., barely awake when my watch alarm went off at 6:00 A.M., and finally getting up at 7:00. My cold is much better. Over this trip I completed a book, *City of Joy,* by Lapierre—a long tome about life in the slums of Calcutta. I found it depressing and not really good reading while over here, except it does make one realize that there are people worse off than the Khmers. While not encircled by barbed wire, these people are as surely imprisoned by poverty. Now I am reading *The White Nile,* by Moorehead. This is a history of the exploration of central Africa and includes a considerable amount of the history of the Sudan.

I did some shopping in Aran and ate at Kim Kim's. Cathy came by and brought me up-to-date on doings at camp. All is well. There being a number of people leaving in the next few weeks, there's a good-bye dinner in Aran for several at one time.

The bus trip from Aran to Ta Phraya was draining. It was hot, the bus packed, and they had rock-and-roll music blasting out. I was happy to get home. A French OHI man came to talk with me. He wanted to know if I thought it was foolish for him at age 35 to consider going to medical school. We had a nice talk, with me gently on the positive side.

10 February 1987

Here I am back in my little room at House 1. It is 10:30, late for me, but I will write anyway. Today several men from the U.S. Embassy brought a delegation of two Vietnamese and two Cambodians to visit Site 2. These Asians are former refugees, now established in the U.S. and representatives of coalitions of SE Asian refugees. They are seeking information to present to the U.S. Congress in March—seeking some alternative to closing KID and some redress regarding the de facto status of the refugees. One of the embassy men, Soo, I have known from several tours. He invited me to dinner with them. I had a good dinner courtesy of the U.S. government. I sat next to a Cambodian—a former social science teacher in Phnom Penh. It was very interesting to talk with him.

15 February 1987

One of very few positive developments of the U.S.-Vietnam war has been the manufacture of Ho Chi Minh sandals. The sole is made of discarded auto tires, and the binding of strips of inner tube.

At our camp there are several older men whose job is keeping the grounds clean. The nature of their job and the fact that they do not work closely with the farang staff makes them somewhat loners. Because of this, I try to be friendly with them and often give them a banana or orange.

Yesterday, one of these men drew my attention to his worn-out sandals, and I perceived he was asking me to get him a new pair. Feeling that I was demonstrating clever Western technology, I took his worn sandal, placed it on a piece of paper and outlined it—this to ensure I got the proper size. He was not to be outdone, for he asked for my pen and wrote the figures "10½" for the size.

16 February 1987

Paul is a pediatrician who was good enough to spend a morning doing rounds with me. He told me he played chess, and as a result he and his girlfriend, Geraldine, are spending the night with us in Ta Phraya. My dinner of yesterday was calculated to yield leftovers for dinner tonight, and as sometimes happens they turned out to be even better than yesterday. We played three games and I won them all, so it was a nice evening for me.

As my days here decrease in number, my list of things to do increases. BunSieth and Sam Ol, recently sick, were back at work today. I managed to take them to the Khmer restaurant. They have a special drink there of sweet milk and a raw egg, which the Khmers believe has restorative power. I bought them each one but for myself had café au lait. Tomorrow for lunch I will have a roast beef sandwich. I can hardly wait.

18 February 1987

This is the magic hour of the day. Our house is quiet, my housemates still asleep. Outside light steals silently to the scene. Only noises herald the dawn. A hundred roosters vie for attention with their crowing. There is one in particular whose greeting I recognize. I think I should search him out and make his acquaintance. The garbage truck grinds its way down the street, a mark of the progress of civilization in this village. Birds are chirping their part of this symphony. Periodic roars of a motorcycle accent the human part of starting life in Ta Phraya for another day.

18 February—later

I will have tomorrow off; today I worked. A family by the name of Cohen visited us: the father is a psychiatrist, the mother is a psych clinician, the son works in Surin, and a daughter is college age. Patty asked if I would give them a tour of the camp. It was a pleasant time for all of us, for they were very interested and asked very good questions. They came without cameras, feeling that perhaps the Khmers would not appreciate their photos being taken. I must say they were unusually sensitive to the feelings of the Khmers.

Things go well on the Peds ward. Our very sick ones are responding. It appears I will end this tour with a death rate of less than two per month. I don't know how this compares with the past year or so, nor do I claim any credit for this. It is no doubt primarily the result of educators of the past, the dedicated work of the Khmer health workers, and the improved health of the population.

21 February 1987

At his invitation, I had dinner last night with Gilles, a young and very handsome French doctor who is medical coordinator for MSF. It was a nice time for me. I regret that neither of us found time to develop our friendship earlier.

As often happens at the end of a tour, I am prepared to take pictures during my next few days at camp. I am also making some tape recordings of some of the sounds of life here. I just captured the roosters crowing and I'm half listening for one of those motorcycles to roar past.

24 February 1987

I rode from Bangkok to Aran with Bob and Neal Ball. Neal is an interesting man—a combination of real commitment to helping refugees and real American-type business capabilities. There was a very nice dinner for him last night at House 5. It was late to bed and early up this morning. Today was busy with orienting Dr. Bill Heegaard. He is 60 years old and a family practitioner from Alexandria. He did a three-month tour in 1980. Bill has many characteristics that indicate he will do well here.

Of Time, Place and Person

There are several stamp collectors amongst my friends here. This caused me to hang a plastic bag on the wall of my room and to save in it all the envelopes from letters I have received during my time here. Yesterday, I dumped these on my bed and proceeded to cut the stamps from them in preparation for giving them to the collectors.

I noted the dates of the postmarks, some from the beginning of my tour and some heralding the end. This reminded me not only of the passing of time but also of the hours spent by my family and friends in writing. I consider each letter a compliment and together a mighty support and reassurance.

Like a slide show, as I noted the various postmarks and return addresses, I mentally pictured the people who had written and remembered fragments of their messages. There were more than 100 letters from you, who with your characteristic concern and caring had made a special effort to use various stamps to the benefit of local stamp collectors. There were letters from all over the United States, from Europe, from Africa and from Asia.

In Thailand, one is often greeted with the question "Benai?" "Where are you going?" In America, a common expression is, "Where are you coming from?" Many of my friends here ask me, "Where will you go next?" People I correspond with are interested in where I am.

My friends are busy people, occupied in the demands of their work, their family and their contribution to the world. And so, as I noted the return addresses on all those letters, I pictured the writers and gave thanks that I could list them as friends, for friends help establish who a person is.

In interviewing a patient to establish his or her mental awareness, we seek to determine orientation to time, place and person. My little job of cutting out the stamps led me to thoughts about myself in regard to time, place and person. In the next chapter of my life, I want to take time to be a friend to those who have written. I want to be where I can best promote friendship. I want to be a person who does a little to promote love and peace in the lives of family and friends, in the society in which we live and in the world about us.

Good-bye

Good-byes are not my forte. Indeed, I have been known to skip them entirely. Recently in one of your letters you lectured me about this, pointing out that I frequently talk about moderation as a worthy quality of one's life philosophy, and that I was really not moderate in this aversion. As often happens within long marriages, I had been thinking along the same lines and had decided that this tour I would end with a proper good-bye.

Shortly before the end of my tour, I came upon a group of our health workers sitting on the bench outside the Pediatrics ward. They were discussing the arrival of a supply of English–Khmer dictionaries, and how they would each raise the 55 baht to purchase one. I proposed to them, in observance of the end of my tour, that I would offer them a choice. I would buy them each a dictionary; or I would put on a party with food and goodies; or I would purchase a basket of food for each of them. There were at least a dozen of our Khmer workers there—nurses, health workers and medics. They voted unanimously for the dictionaries, in itself a manifestation of their hunger for knowledge.

As the last day of my tour approached, I decided that—even though I had given them the dictionaries—we would have a small party with soda pop, cookies and fruit. We gathered in the afternoon of my last day around a long table. In true Khmer fashion BunSieth, chief medic, gave a speech and presented a gift [a carved wooden vase and piece of Thai silk].

| BunSieth's Speech

Welcome to ladies and gentlemen. This party is holding as a small meeting for all of us to say good-bye to Papa Louis and appreciate his help.

Papa Louis has been worked in Pediatrics ward as a doctor for six months. On that time we were enjoy to work with him very much. Papa always stayed in the good manner and was very kind to all of us. Papa has tried to work very hard even he is in the old stage. On the other hand Papa has built up our spirit for being self-confident and to be the good workers that would help our people on ourselves. And once a week Papa has spent several hours to teach an extra class to the medics to make them more stronger. All what Papa has been done are the unforgettable memories that would be stuck in our heart forever. How wonderful and how nice to work with Papa Louis. Unfortunately, the time is coming he has to go back home and we have to cry out with pain to say good-bye to him. At last we would like to say and we mean we were very much pleased with his work and thank him very, very, very much. We all wish Papa Louis in the good health. Be happy.

BunSieth and All Khmer staff in Pediatrics Ward

The publication of this speech has aspects of self-aggrandizement, but I do so in all humility. The speech is an example of Khmer English language skill, their sensitivity and insight.

Previous good-byes to the Khmers for me have been moist eye occasions. This time, my overwhelming reaction was not sadness but gratitude—gratitude for having had this opportunity, gratitude to these Khmers who have given so much to me, and gratitude to my Western colleagues present and past who have made all of this possible.

21 March 1987—home

Vietnamese troops have penetrated two miles into Thailand to occupy two strategic hills, and Thai troops are preparing a counteroffensive. This is the news per radio this morning.

I have been home for one week. I was warmly welcomed by family and friends. I have indulged myself in a few hedonistic pleasures such as French dip sandwiches and Dunkin' Donuts. I have enjoyed some of the qualities of life we often take for granted, such as pure water, plumbing facilities that work, bounteous electric power, and good roads. These may seem like trivial matters, but they are a part of life here.

Jet lag overcome, I am now ready to get to work with shovel, ax and saw. I shall try to be a good family member, a good friend, but part of my mind and part of my heart remain with the Khmers, and no doubt I will try to keep other Americans aware of their plight and their needs.

Move As the Spirit Leads

8 January 1988

Fear, apprehension, regret, melancholy, anticipation, gratitude, conviction; all of these characterize my mental state as I sit in the plane awaiting takeoff. Fear: who can fly today without some awareness of recent tragedies? Apprehension: do I have what it will take to meet the challenges that face me, to respond to the needs of the Khmers? Regret: I just said good-bye to Gwen. She is strong, but there will be times of loneliness. Melancholy: for the realization that a happy chapter in our lives has closed and a new one starts. With these negative thoughts, some who read these words may ask, "If you feel that way, why go?" Anticipation: of the thrills of travel, the reuniting with old friends, refugees, and refugee workers. Gratitude: for having arrived at this point in my life capable of undertaking such a journey, gratitude to friends, family, American Refugee Committee personnel, and Gwen, in particular Gwen, without whose understanding, this tour would not be possible. Conviction: that in the course of the next few months I will be in a position to render some service, to speak some word of compassion, to provide some word of encouragement that will make it all worthwhile.

10 January 1988

The Los Angeles airport is a big, busy, hot place with more than its share of nonoperative telephones—up escalators located long distances from down. I had a number of details to attend to. I was through with these and standing at the end of a ticketing line when I reached for my wallet and found my pocket empty. What a sickening feeling that was. Carrying my bags, I retraced my steps and then concluded that in the crush of crowds someone had filched my wallet. Perspiring, angry and frustrated, tired of carrying those bags around, I realized this was the classic situation for an airport coronary. I found a secluded corner and summoned those philosophies: "What is important in life?" "Don't sweat the small stuff." "Let 'er go how she looks." And I felt an acceptance of what happened. My plans for visiting refugees in the Los Angeles area erased, I proceeded with the necessary details of phone calls related to the loss.

I had decided to take an overnight bus from Los Angeles to San Francisco. The ride was great; I slept most of the way.

In San Francisco, I attended Glide Memorial Church on Sunday morning in preparation for the long Pacific flight. This Methodist mission, devoted to street people, is world famous. The major song featured was "Blowin' in the Wind," a song I have dearly loved. Just before leaving, Gwen had bought me some tapes to play on my cassette player, and one of them was Peter, Paul and Mary singing "Blowin' in the Wind." I listened to that for many miles across the Pacific.

Some American airlines are emphasizing the rule of one carry-on per passenger. Not so China Airlines. Our flight, largely filled with Taiwanese, was packed by bodies and all kinds of packages. My seatmate was a young Taiwanese computer engineer. He travels for business a great deal and was in a spirit of elation, for on return to Taiwan he was to be married.

13 January 1988

The Bangkok airport has been vastly improved, and immigration procedure for me consisted of passport inspection and a wave through customs. I was met by Bob Medrala, an honor, and Jean Jachman, a delight.

Arriving at the Trocadero, we had a quick cup of coffee and then I was off to bed. I slept restlessly for one to two hours, awoke, got up and read, and then went back to bed for six hours of real deep sleep. I walked to a restaurant I knew had American breakfasts, and then shopped for pocketbook and *pakima*—no success with either. This evening I went to dinner with Jean, followed by a Scrabble game—close, but she won. And now I'm up to date. You may thank the mosquitoes for this letter. I really don't care for the air-conditioning and prefer the windows open, since it's not too hot. Unfortunately, the mosquitoes found me.

14 January 1988

There are some advantages to being an old-timer here: they sent me by taxi to Aran, a four-hour ride spent partly in sleeping and partly admiring the beautiful green fields. We arrived at House 1 just about the time the workers came back. Most of them are new to me.

I stayed at House 1 last night, crashing at 9:00. En route to camp, Nancy Thompson dropped me off at Ta Phraya. Being hungry and looking for a cup of coffee, I deposited my bags and went to ARC House, a Thai restaurant ARC folks routinely stop at for breakfast. They were sitting around a table and in one corner was BunSieth. When emergency cases are transferred at night, Khmer medics are now allowed to accompany.

Returning to Ta Phraya house, I looked the house over. There is a new building immediately next door, housing a noisy motorcycle repair shop. Unpacking your neat packing gave me pangs of loneliness. I'm pretty well established now, except I have the bed to make. At noon, I went to the market—chicken-on-a-stick, cooked rice, pineapple and bananas. There is no source for bread in Ta Phraya, and you know how I like bread. Bread is to a Frenchman what pasta is to an Italian. I found *pakimas* in a shop and bought one.

15 and 16 January 1988

This was my first day in camp, a day of great reunions. They have built a new hospital since my last tour. It is still bamboo with dirt floors but much larger and airy. My Khmer coworkers all look healthy, although some of them are thinner than ever. David, an Australian who is doing adult medicine, is on vacation, so I spent most of my time on medicine. They had four interesting and challenging cases: a man with appendicitis, an overdose of aminophyllin, a gastric hemorrhage, and a man with hemorrhagic purpura. Not a bad reintroduction to the challenge of Third World medicine. Peds is currently slow (25 patients).

By noontime we had two cases ready for transfer to KID and I offered to be the ambulance attendant as I wanted to see old friends there. The poor mother with her sick child did not tolerate the trip well. Fortunately, I had a plastic bag which she nearly filled.

At KID, I visited Kariv, a good medic and my own personal nomination for the Nobel Peace Prize. Kariv and I have been friends since my early days on the border. I took care of him when he had a renal stone, and later cared for his son when he had meningitis. His wife is an equally lovely person. There is now a second child.

About two years ago, Kariv and his family made the perilous trek from Bang Phu border camp to Khao-I-Dang Holding Center. They took this trip at risk of life and limb from snakes, predatory bandits, wandering military, and antipersonnel mines. At KID, they entered the life of illegals, hiding from authorities and scrounging for sustenance. It was a high price to pay in search of freedom and a better life.

Their time of terror lasted for about one year, and then—in one of those unexpected turns of events that occur here—the authorities granted limited legality to those who had been in hiding. For Kariv and his family it meant a home of their own, a rice card and, most important, an opportunity to work. Kariv found a job in Admissions, made steady progress and soon became chief. He did not forget their difficult time and quickly became the unofficial receptionist for fellow Khmers who followed the path he had trod. On arrival at KID, those new illegals found a trusted friend who directed them to safe houses and hiding places and who taught them survival in a new set of dangers and deprivations. He had nothing to give except advice and encouragement—and always a beautiful smile.

The bus ride from KID to Ta Phraya was fine. It was hot during the afternoon, but nevertheless I did my first exercise session—stretching exercises, sit-ups, push-ups, etc. After dinner, I went to my room and fell asleep and only now awakened, somewhat chilled by the fan I had left going. I remain in good health, although the Khmers say I am fat—very good, they say.

17 January 1988

Sunday, and my day to work. The big deal today was the visit of Senator Rudy Boschwitz from Minnesota. There are a number of people here from Minnesota, and they were to meet him. Two of the men in his party were old friends of mine. When they spied me on the periphery of the crowd, they made a big to-do. The result was, I was ushered up and spent several minutes with the senator and many pictures were taken. Who knows, you may see them.

18 January 1988

| *Two Khmer Ladies*

They sat at a bamboo table in the classroom, these sisters, one 38 and the other 52. Across from them sat Glenda Potter, an American attorney, devoting her life's energies to aiding the expatriation of Khmers at an income probably one-tenth of the average of U.S. attorneys. I had been asked to see these ladies to make a medical statement about their condition. In most situations the desire is to make sure of their physical fitness, but in this case it was to determine if they had any physical condition that would be benefited by expatriation to the United States. Rasy works in an office and Pam manages their house—no mean task here where water must be carried and food is acquired by scrounging and long standing in line.

At first I couldn't come up with anything, and then Glenda suggested that possibly there might be some psychological condition that might warrant treatment or counseling. I had detected the sound of French in their speech, and so in the best French I could muster I asked them if they would prefer to use that language. That opened the dam, and they began to speak of the Pol Pot years.

They spoke of starvation, of working in the fields and being beaten when their work did not satisfy their masters. The younger one told of being suspected of being a CIA agent and of a pretend beheading that was carried out to force a confession. Acute fear attacks, depression, weakness, insomnia and headaches were very believable residual symptoms from those grim years.

We have read and heard many accounts of similar experiences by these poor people. We often hear the descriptive term "these are survivors," and we know that in order to survive and reach safety and freedom these people are capable of fabrication and exaggeration. There was something about their speech, the eyeball-to-eyeball contact, that made me feel this was genuine. I had no trouble in writing a statement recommending psychological treatment such as is available for victims at the Center for Treatment of Torture Victims.

24 January 1988

It's Sunday, my day off, but also the day of the hospital dedication, and feeling some compulsion, I went. Edie has a car, so I went with her. I got home about 1:30 P.M. and sacked out. It is really getting hot here, and I awakened to the tickling sensation of rivulets of sweat.

25 January 1988

The general status of our Khmer health workers is improved. Their technical skill is amazing. In general the health of the population is better, although we still see the occasional child with malnutrition. Our biggest concern is the fact of a population growing up in a penal colony: a whole generation of children who do not know how to grow rice, to fish, to ride a buffalo.

26 January 1988

My friend Jean Jachman is "Alpha III"—also known as platform coordinator, the central radio link for Site 2 South. By custom, Alpha III should be first in camp and last out. It is a tough job and occasionally I spell her at it. And so here I sit at the end of a long day waiting for the magic 5:00 P.M. hour. Then I can jump into our aging Toyota van and head for Ta Phraya. I had a good day, particularly this afternoon, which I spent with Kosol, the Pediatrics chief. We went to the Site 2 South library, where I reviewed with Kosol the use of the few reference books they have there.

29 January 1988

Yesterday I awoke with a sore throat and it bloomed into one of my super colds. I managed to work but left camp a little early. On arrival home I collapsed on the bed for two hours. I then went to Fargo's for a decadent American meal—ham sandwich, French fries, chocolate ice cream and coffee. On return home I took three aspirin and went to bed.

It was a long night. This morning it was clear that I could not go to work. I have spent the day up and down, doing some writing. I feel much better now and will go to work tomorrow.

31 January 1988

Yesterday was a great day. The only good thing about being sick is the wonderful feeling of appreciation and gratitude when one feels well again. I still have the dregs of my cold, but my strength and energy are back. The bright spot of the day was a nice letter from Peggy. Scarcely a day goes by but that someone asks about her. What a lovely young lady you bore and raised.

2 February 1988—morning

Last night the MSF put on a dinner in Aran for the platform people of Site 2 South. It was a get-acquainted meeting for all and very pleasant. I stayed at Cathy's House 5. This morning Cathy and I had a nice breakfast at Kim Kim's, and then she drove me to Ta Phraya. I am now awaiting the van to Site 2. I had planned to take today off, but we had a death on Peds yesterday. It was an infant under the care of Sok Saly in Feeding Center. The child appeared in extremis and died within one hour. Sok Saly was very upset about this, and I feel I should go today and provide him some support.

2 February—evening

Two letters in one day—not bad. I have just enough energy to write one letter tonight, and even though I've fallen behind on writing to other folks, I'd rather write to you. This morning when I wrote I was facing a demanding day. But all went well, and I had plenty of energy.

Last night I spent at Cathy's, House 5. That is the fanciest house in the ARC group, in absolute contrast to our house here in Ta Phraya. Only the hard-core refugee workers and this strange old man are willing to live here. The constant roar of traffic and the dust it raises are too much for most. Of course, the fact we are not housekeepers is a big part of the problem.

6 February 1988

With today off, I went to bed pondering a lazy day or a trip to KID to see Kariv, to Aran for potatoes and preparation of a big dinner. I awakened at my usual time and took an early bus to Aran, where I had an excellent breakfast at Kim Kim's, and on to the market. *Man fa rang,* Thai for "potato," isn't hard to say, it's just hard for Thai people to understand it. I finally succeeded and bought three kilos of potatoes and one kilo of carrots.

Standing at the bus stop, I was really fortunate to flag down a car driven by Ranee. She was going to stop at KID and then was going to Site 2 by way of Ta Phraya. I was able to see Kariv. He is in the process of preparing his biography and will send me a copy. Next week in Bangkok, I will plan to go to the embassy and put in a word for him.

As a result of my good fortune re transportation, I was home at 11:00 A.M. A ham-and-cheese sandwich for lunch and here I am writing.

8 February 1988

Every morning at about 7:00 a group of monks parades down the main street. Each holds a bowl and periodically stops in front of a home or business. A man or woman comes out and with great respect puts food in the monk's bowl, and then kneels while the monk utters a blessing. At the same time, I come out of our house bearing a bowl. I kneel as well, but I am on the floorboards of our van and my bowl contains water for the radiator.

Sok Thim is the Khmer chief of the TB treatment center. Under the guidance of Bob Maat, he has become a real expert in the diagnosis and treatment of TB. He is totally dedicated and has his own discipline of applied Western science. The average patient is under his care for one year. At the end of that time, the chart of this recovered patient must be completed and summarized. It is wonderful that this Khmer man, so dedicated to science, ends his report with, "May this patient have a long and happy life."

10 February 1988

Today was a sort of routine day until the last two hours. Jean suddenly had to leave early in order to spend the night in Aran, in preparation to go for her driver's license tomorrow. I took over as Alpha III, and they had no sooner left than we had a transfer to arrange: a four-month-old with congenital heart disease, congestive heart failure and pneumonia. I had great trouble with the radio, possibly related to the lightning strikes on our antenna two days ago. I finally got that arranged. I then walked over to the TB center to pick up the van. I heard a single shell report fairly loud—closer than any I have heard before on this tour. The radio immediately came alive; not surprising, soon came the announcement of Situation 1, a rather familiar condition for us. Alpha III's responsibility is to alert all team members of Situation 1, so I immediately went to the van, stared into the mirror and waved my index finger. You understand I was the only team member still at camp. What else could I do? Don't worry about the above—things are really relatively quiet.

13 February 1988

I am sitting in the pleasant living room of House 5. Jean is across the table from me, eating soup and listening to tapes—including the one of her appearance on the Jim French show, and including a nice commentary by you. It was good to hear your voice. The ants have arrived here too. For the first week or two I was in Thailand, I was happy to miss the little buggers, but they are back in full flood now.

I came to Aran primarily to go to Father Pierre's Saturday evening Mass. Fr. Pierre's Mass was dedicated to the Thai water truck driver who died as a result of a land mine on the road. (Water trucks take a different road than we do.) This was the first death of a UN employee.

The past 36 hours have been disturbing. Yesterday, Mary Dunbar and her Thai driver were menaced by a rifle-pointing TF 80 trooper. We have been at Situation 1 most of the time. Mary was not injured and is fine, and the TF trooper is in jail. It is depressing, since it is an example of the terror under which the Khmers live and have lived for years. I hope you will not worry unnecessarily. Every effort is made to guarantee our safety, and I remain convinced that Interstate 5 back home is more dangerous.

15 February 1988

Today was a good and busy day. I returned home and had enough energy to do my push-ups and sit-ups. Then I went down to the bathroom for shave, dental care and shower. I have been very diligent about flossing since I miss the Waterpik. It is not unusual for the floss to stick, and usually with a little extra pull it comes out. Only this time I heard something hit the floor. I bent over to find it but with no success. It was then I realized that the exposed section of my right upper lateral incisor was missing. With renewed diligence, I searched the floor, and there it was—a chunk of dental ceramic complete with extended silver post. This is the tooth that Dr. Arakasaka worked on, followed by two attempts by my dentist in Renton. Both had warned me it might not last. I washed off the fragment and with care reinserted it. How ironic that this occurred the night before I go to Bangkok. I hope I can keep this in position through tomorrow, for my Khmer crew would roll on the floor in laughter if they spied the gaping space in my upper teeth.

Tomorrow is the first day of my vacation. A clinical-pathological conference involving all the doctors of Site 2 North and South is scheduled at noon, and I feel constrained to go, since I sort of promoted this. I will proceed to Bangkok in the afternoon, and hopefully on Wednesday will see my friend Dr. Arakasaka.

I don't know if you will laugh or cry over this episode, but after my first exasperation "let 'er go how she looks" took over.

17 February 1988

I am sitting in a comfortable room in the Quality Inn on Sukhumvit. Yesterday was tough. My basic mistake was failing to realize that 16 February is Chinese New Year. I got up at the usual time and went to camp. I was Alpha III again, and my schedule was made more hectic by the visit of a couple who were sent by UNBRO. Early on, a six-year-old girl was brought in—her condition was near terminal. Our medics had a hard time getting an IV in, and by the time they did, CPR was required but no response.

It turned out that the meeting for which I came to camp was scheduled for 2:00 P.M., and I realized I would not be able to get off to Bangkok until late. I decided to forgo the meeting and managed to get a ride to Ta Phraya at noon. I had already packed, but during the short time I was at Ta Phraya house a Chinese New Year's parade passed by.

I took the bus to Aran and got on the 1:00 P.M. bus to Bangkok. By 7:00 P.M., we were approaching the Bangkok bus station. When I finally got off the bus, I went directly to a sidewalk stand and while eating my noodle soup considered the most fantastic crowd of intermingled people, buses and taxis I have ever seen. I tried to take a bus into town, but short of risking life and limb it was impossible. I ended up taking a taxi. At the Ambassador, it was no surprise to be told "no room." And so here I am at the Quality Inn. My greatest amazement is that I took all of this without an iota of anger or frustration. A great hot shower and a good sleep and now to my errands.

18 February 1988

This trip to Bangkok has worked out all right. I would rate this hotel about midway between the Trocadero and the Ambassador. It does have a nice little desk and chair, and is just right for studying and writing.

You have probably read about the new wave of Vietnamese fleeing to Thailand and the push-off policy Thailand is following. A number of people have landed on Trat, an offshore island. IRC is attempting to provide medical care and has asked ARC for backup.

Today I went to JVA [Joint Voluntary Agency], the organization that Liz Anderson works for. I met with Mr. John Crowley, a fine man and a credit to our State Department. Residents of the border camps are considered illegal immigrants, and barring unusual circumstances are not eligible for interview or consideration as refugees. Residents of KID are considered refugees, and if they can prove connection with the U.S. during the war or real danger in returning to Cambodia, they are eligible for interview. A positive result of interview is more likely if they have supporting testimony about their work in the camps. It was for that reason I made the appointment with Mr. Crowley. As a refugee, Kariv would be eligible for federal and state public assistance programs.

I realize I haven't mentioned my dental story. I saw Dr. Arakasaka at 9:00 A.M. yesterday. She grinned when she saw me and was, I think, somewhat pleased to be in a position to work on a tooth and a patient that an American dentist had previously tried. This tooth, having had the benefit of previous root canal surgery, needed no anesthetic—although it was hard for me to believe when she had that drill going. She temporarily replaced the fractured piece, and I will need to return on my next days off. She will insert a pin, three days later make a mold and then on a third visit at my convenience, put in the crown. It is hard to believe and accept so many dental problems, but perhaps it's the price one pays to be 65 and still have one's own teeth.

I was going to return to Aran tomorrow, but instead I will meet Arlys at the airport and ride in a taxi to Aran with her on Saturday.

21 February 1988

It turned out Arlys arrived at a different time than I thought, and I missed her at the airport. Yesterday morning I made my way by bus and foot, carrying my loaded backpack from Quality Inn to the Troc, where I met Arlys. Our trip in the taxi went fine, except we decided to ask the driver to take us directly to Ta Phraya. He tried a short cut from Wattana to Ta Phraya and got lost. As a result, we had a very pleasant ride through many small Thai villages, and even came across a working elephant.

22 February 1988

Yesterday I went to the wedding of BunSieth's wife's sister. It was a big wedding. Actually we were invited to the reception. On arrival, we walked down an aisle formed by the wedding party with the ladies on one side and the men on the other, all dressed in their resplendent best. It appeared to me there were more than 100 guests. We were seated at what I'm sure is considered a table of honor, directly in front of the band, which consisted of electronic string instruments and drums. We could only converse for the few moments between pieces. Shortly, there began a parade of plates laden with Khmer food. Some were beyond my diagnostic ability. The most outstanding was roast duck. At a Khmer wedding, instead of gifts of dinnerware, electrical appliances, etc., each guest is given an envelope and places money inside; quite reasonable I think.

At this point, I went back to the platform and Jean took my place—one of us had to be on duty.

24 February 1988

Sothara is a beautiful, graceful lady. She is a medic for ARC and has been in this border camp for as long as I can remember. She tells an interesting tale about her family. Her father is a well-educated man, who speaks beautiful French. Sothara remembers life before Pol Pot. Every night after dinner, her father would take down from his bookshelves a book and read to his family. For a time during the Pol Pot chaos, part of this family managed to be together, but now there were no books, and instead the father told stories. Some of the family survived, and several of the sons were able to go to the U.S. to build a new life. Sothara and her father remained in the camp. Then, through one of those miracles that occur here, it seemed that father and possibly Sothara could be expatriated. Feeling that her father's chances would be improved, Sothara withdrew her application, and the old man's application was granted. My route this morning led me by those buses, beside which stood a group of Khmers. The gray-headed gentleman stood out. I don't doubt there were tears in his eyes; mine were a bit moist.

26 February 1988

As I ate breakfast this morning, I read a report of a speech by Senator Hatfield that was highly critical of the U.S. policy in regard to the situation here. I will use my last aerogram to send him a letter. While I don't agree with him completely, he does seem to be one of a few voices trying to get us to use communication instead of armaments as a way to straighten things out here.

To obtain humanitarian release from these border camps, a Khmer must prove previous connections with U.S. forces or unusual physical disability for which treatment is not available here. Recently, I have been asked to do histories and physicals on several of these seekers. The man I examined yesterday was unique and interesting. At age 59, he moved and walked like a very old man. Nevertheless, his bright eyes and expressive smile indicated he was very much with it. In pre–Pol Pot time, he was a rich man, owning 10 taxis that ran between Phnom Penh and Battambang. He is the only Khmer who, to my question, "How were things for you during Pol Pot time?" answered, "Oh, not so bad; you see, I was rich." Unfortunately for him, I was unable to find any condition present that would strongly support his appeal for humanitarian parole.

27 February 1988

Our team on Pediatrics is made up of medics, nurses and health workers. I see my position as almost solely adviser and educator. I am most closely associated with the medics. Three of them are well experienced and reliable. Three are relatively new medics. The latter group's performance seems to vary considerably, so that one day they do excellent work and the next day not so well. On not-so-good days, it is important that they be corrected and encouraged in such a way that they not lose face. I usually try to get the senior medics to do this.

One of the things I am working on is the concept of teamwork. On our totem pole, the medics are at the top, the nurses at the middle, and then the health workers. Following the advice of Debbie, the nursing teacher, we are trying to make rounds a team function. Most of the nurses and health workers see their present position as a step on the way to becoming a medic, so in general they are eager to participate—although often shy.

29 February 1988

I spent yesterday reading, writing and sleeping. I finally loaded my camera and took 24 slides of Ta Phraya life. Now I have it loaded with print film. It is very difficult to get a camera pass. Peds has a camera, which stays in BunSieth's care. I will bring a load of film out and ask him to take some pictures of Peds in action.

2 March 1988

Another socially busy 24 hours. I had breakfast this morning at the market restaurant with John Henderson. I first met John 1½ years ago when he wandered into the ARC office at a time when Bob Medrala was away. We spent more than an hour talking about life and opportunities. He was 26 years old at the time, somewhat disillusioned with teaching high school in the States and looking for a job. While we are far apart in age and life situation, we have much in common in life philosophy and values.

I will go to dinner tonight with Corinne, a French nurse who works with Edie. Unlike some of the French, she is willing to put up with my fumbling attempts at her language.

Today at camp was good. Rounds went well. Kosol and I went to the MSF hospital this afternoon to see a number of patients suspected to have typhoid fever.

3 March 1988

Each unit in Site 2 South has a radio call sign. The ambulance call sign has been changed recently to Omega. Our call sign is still Alpha. So I asked Bob—if I go in the ambulance carrying one of our radios—whether he would put in a call for the Alpha and Omega. Karen Johnson Elshazly from ARC arrives for a visit tomorrow. I explained her position to our Khmer staff today, and Sam asked if she is single or plural.

5 March 1988

Karen visited camp. I was taking a short nap at noontime when Jeff came running in to announce Situation 2. I cannot describe the sick feeling engendered by the act of getting in our cars and leaving our Khmer friends to face whatever is coming. Situation 2 requires us to pack up and move out. (Situation 3: leave without packing; Situation 4: hit the dirt.) We drove to the Situation 2 rendezvous and sat in the cars in the hot sun for more than an hour. In bits and pieces, we learned that there had been a firefight in a nearby village, presumably between black marketers and legal marketers. We returned to camp by late afternoon. We went to Aran last night for a dinner meeting with Karen, and it was 11:30 when we got home. They brought mail—a bonanza for me, with letters from friends and nine from you. Though I was tired and sleepy, I could not resist reading at least one of yours, and the inevitable transpired: I read them all and got to bed at 1:00 A.M. Is it really busier this tour, or is it my age?

8 March 1988

We went to Aran last night for a meeting, aimed at collecting farang opinion about the choice of Khmers for the new medic class. This is a complex matter, taken very seriously by the Education department and by the Khmer, for it is a giant step in Khmer society to become a medic. The Khmers take a test on general knowledge, including math, ability to translate and basic knowledge about health and illness. A group of senior medics and leaders then write an evaluation of each Khmer who has passed the test. When their choice for candidates is complete, the farang staff reviews the papers. Finally, the conclusions are turned over to the Khmer seniors, and they make the final decision. It sounds complex, but this system has worked well, since it turned out such wonderful medics as BunSieth, Saly and Kosol. It is also a significant educational experience, since the deciding factors, if done strictly in Khmer fashion, would be social position, wealth and family status.

11 March 1988

Tim Mastro came to camp today. On an earlier tour he did adult medicine for ARC. He is currently here for a three-month tour, preparing a report for UNBRO. I was glad to see him, for he is an old friend. Tim starts a fellowship at CDC in Atlanta, Georgia, in October in epidemic intelligence.

I just learned that the Khmer word for money is "Louie," and unbeknownst to me they have a good time making jokes about that. No wonder I get hit up for donations periodically.

12 March 1988

After a week or so of pleasant, almost cool weather we are back in the hot season. Already I can feel the sweat gathering. Today is Saturday and my last day of work for one week. I plan a leisurely pack-up this evening, and leave tomorrow for Bangkok. I should get there soon, for this morning, chewing on a piece of hard Khmer bread, I broke off a piece of tooth, the one that had the $1,000 root canal and crown. I wonder what percent of my letters have to do with dental problems?

16 March 1988

I thought I would get lots of writing done here at Ko Samet, but this is my first effort. I am sitting at a restaurant on the beach having just consumed an excellent bowl of noodle soup. I have a little hut about the size of our bedroom and furnished with a mattress and a small blanket, period.

The trip from Bangkok starts with a 3½-hour bus ride from the East bus station. I left from the dentist's office about 11:30, and thought I would be able to eat at the bus station, but the bus was ready. By the time I reached the little town that is the take-off point for Ko Samet, I was really hungry and paused for noodle soup.

By the time we arrived at the dock on Ko Samet, I was weary of public transportation, so I adjusted the straps of my Dolt pack and hiked down the road to the resort area. I walked along the whole beach, enjoying the meandering road and the beautiful scenery. Ko Samet is quite crowded at this time, and I had to reverse my course and go back to the first part of the beach to find an open hut. By this time, I was tired and sweated and ready for my first swim. The water was just as perfect as I remembered it.

It is the end of the afternoon as I write this now. My trip to the dentist went well. She repaired the filling on my molar and cleaned my teeth. Perhaps that's the end of dental work for this tour.

I am now writing from a hotel room enjoying the air-conditioning. I slept very well last night. At 6:30 this morning I could not resist an early swim; it was wonderful. Following that, I showered, shaved and packed up. I rode one of the trucks to the boat dock. I had hoped to buy breakfast at the dock, but the boat was ready and waiting for me, the last passenger.

Arriving on the mainland, there was a Bangkok bus waiting, so once again there was no time for breakfast. Three and a half hours later, arriving at the bus station, I was really hungry, but deferred lunch until a taxi deposited me at the Victory Hotel.

I checked my bag, had lunch and then checked in at the ARC office. Nothing especially new there. Letters 50 and 51 awaited me. A Thai man who also sought a room at the Victory told me of a hotel on Sukhumvit for 300 baht. So here I am, quite comfortable.

18 March 1988

Arriving at Aran, I was most grateful for a safe trip, but also fairly well worn and water depleted. I had lunch and made my way to the place where I usually catch the bus. I went to the appropriate spot, and there were some Thai women and children who looked familiar. An hour and a half later, there were many more waiting. Picturing how crowded the bus would be, I decided to stay in Aran. Adjusting my bag for backpacking, I walked to House 1.

Here I found all the rooms locked, but eventually found one of the Thai men who works here. He gave me a set of keys, and I spent a half-hour trying them in various doors with no success. He then told me all the rooms were occupied.

I am now awaiting the return of the ARC workers, and hope there is a bed available someplace.

It is now Saturday, 19 March, and I am at Ta Phraya house, alone and sitting at the table downstairs in the living area, the coolest place in the house. Nevertheless, I am drenched with sweat. I have just completed reading several letters from you and four letters from other people. I have lots to catch up on. First, I will bring you up to date and then answer your letters.

The cars began arriving at House 1 about 6:00 P.M. Bob Maat had taken everyone on a mountain route that would be used as an evacuation route should it be necessary. I stayed at House 5. Most of the team ate dinner at "Seafood Place" next to Ploen's. The food was excellent, particularly the fried squid and the crab rolls. It was nice to eat with this Aran group, whom I don't get to see often. I slept well and this morning rode to Ta Phraya with the people who work today.

21 March 1988

Yesterday was a busy day. There has been a considerable amount of violence in the past two or three days, but all at a distance from us. Five Khmers getting firewood outside of KID were shot, none killed. Two Khmer soldiers in Site 2 North had a firefight, ending with one throwing a grenade in a house. Several were wounded. Three Thai COERR employees going to a meeting in Pataya were in a car accident—one dead, two injured.

As a result of the car accident, I am going to promote an ARC emphasis on driving safely. Our Thai drivers and some of the farangs drive too fast.

24 March 1988

Today I have the pass making it legal for me to bring into camp the clothes Fern sent. I know it seems like this has been long delayed, but there seemed no way to hurry the process of getting a pass short of getting angry. At long last, I will have completed the list of errands I brought with me. There is a meeting here tonight. I will call you sometime today. Furthermore, both Chris and David are on vacation this week, so I am the only ARC physician present. Besides Peds, Adult Medicine has been quite busy.

30 March 1988

Khmer Weddings

Despite the atmosphere of hopelessness, the restricted life situation, and the almost total lack of privacy that characterize Khmer life in Site 2, love does occur and marriages result. The formal marriage occurs in the Buddhist temple, and this is a family affair. The public celebration is held later in the day and follows a fairly regimented pattern.

The wedding reception is held at the home of a relative. Those famous blue plastic tarps, so much a part of refugee life, are stretched and supported to form a roof. Tables and chairs are borrowed from neighbors and friends. A band is hired and neighbors and friends become cooks and servers.

At noon, the bride and attendants, beautifully dressed and coifed, form a line at the entrance. The groom, dressed in Western style and often bolstered with cosmetics, and his attendants form a line opposite from the ladies, constructing a line through which guests will pass. Usually promptly at noon, the band starts to play and guests arrive. Passing through the aisle, the guests are greeted with *wais,* that beautiful Asian expression of welcome and respect, made by clasping palms together and raising hands to a slightly bowed head. The bride pins a small artificial flower on each guest, who is then led to a table.

The guests are mostly Khmers, with a sprinkling of farangs, who are frequently placed directly in front of the band, which plays loudly, often enhanced by electronic audio equipment. Food is served in courses, typically consisting of a pickled vegetable salad, a variety of cut-up meat and rice. Soft drinks, Mekong (Thai whiskey) and ice are provided in profusion. Whether it is traditional custom or commonsense adaptation, each guest brings an envelope containing a monetary gift for bride and groom.

The food is always good, the general atmosphere is happy, and it is always a time of greeting friends. For this foreigner, it is also a time when the bittersweet quality of life over here is very much present. One cannot look at the honored couple without pondering the perils of marriage under the best of circumstances, and of this present marriage so surrounded by danger, deprivation and the ache of unfulfilled hopes for freedom and fullness of life.

31 March 1988

Yesterday, we admitted a nine-year-old girl with a skin disease marked by large blisters all over her body. The diagnosis is bullous impetigo with pemphigus and Stevens-Johnson syndrome as possibilities. Involving so much of her body, this could be a lethal disease and constitutes a real challenge for our nursing staff.

When I first saw her, she was lying on banana leaves over the rough matting on the bamboo bed. It was apparent to all of us that she needs frequent bathing and clean sheets to protect her from the always-present dust. I drove to our Ta Phraya house and picked up two white sheets and my last bar of Basis soap. Shortly after I returned, the nursing staff had her cleaned and protected by the white sheets. To these Western eyes we had done a good job, but my pride and confidence were shaken when the medic told me that Khmer custom dictates use of white sheets only for the dead. The mother, however, had insisted on a layer of banana leaves, so perhaps that will protect her.

1 April 1988

Today started out as routine. I was in the middle of rounds when Jean came hurrying in with the words "Situation 2." We were the only group in Site 2 South at this time, so our departure went quickly but not without a feeling of shame that was induced by our flight—leaving the Khmers behind. At the Site 2 rendezvous point, we learned that bandits had attacked UNBRO vehicles as they passed through one of the villages that we had traveled through only a few moments before.

Gradually more information reached us. Our ARC van had not escaped unscathed. A bandit had stopped the van and approached, aiming his rifle. Our Thai driver, sensing a moment of distraction in the bandit's approach, let out the clutch and roared away. The bandit fired once, the bullet struck the right front door, penetrating the outer metal and fracturing the glass but not making it into the cab. The sole passenger was Denise, our newest colleague. Following our van was a YWAM van, with Thai driver and a young woman volunteer. One bandit got in that van and forced them to drive down a nearby road. A military unit happened to be there. The bandit and his captives fled the van and a firefight followed. The two captives dropped to the ground, but the bandit was killed, a Thai soldier was killed and two were wounded. We are filled with gratitude that none of our people were injured.

After a long wait at the rendezvous point, it was decided that a bare minimum medical crew would return to camp, and remaining personnel would be escorted by military convoy to Ta Phraya. Jean and I returned to the hospital, where the Khmers had carried on in good fashion.

We were escorted out by the military in midafternoon. Later, we had a meeting at House 1 in Aran, where it was decided that we would probably return to camp tomorrow. After that, the four of us went to ICRC, where we had a very nice dinner.

2 April 1988

A Buddhist Wake

The recent incident involving bandits, Volag vehicles and personnel, provincial militia and Royal Thai army, resulted in the death of one bandit, two Thai soldiers and several wounded. The emotional trauma to our Thai drivers and two Volag ladies is not measurable, but they seem to have weathered this trauma well. I should also note that the ARC team has dealt with the dangers of life here with calm acceptance.

There are a number of Buddhist rites that are followed when death occurs. On the day of death, the body is ceremonially washed. Ceremonies somewhat akin to Irish wakes and Catholic rosaries occur during the following day or two. There are special ceremonies 100 days after the death and again at one year. Cremation is the common procedure, and seems to be done at some propitious time during the following year.

One of the Thai soldiers who died was from a nearby village, and since his death occurred in connection with Volag activities, it was considered proper that some of us should attend the service last night. It was held in a little village about 10km from Ta Phraya.

The building was large, its single floor supported by wooden pillars, the roof and partial walls of corrugated steel. Seated in a line along the center of the back wall were five saffron-robed monks, chanting. Directly in front of the monks were several chairs, mostly occupied by military. The rest of the audience sat on the floor, all holding their hands in prayerful *wai* and careful not to have their feet pointed at the monks, for this is considered grossly disrespectful.

There was only one other Caucasian there. We were ushered to chairs, except for Elsie. Our chairs raised us even with or higher than the monks, and women are not allowed to be in that position. The chanting went on and on with only short breaks. After getting settled, I looked over the audience. Those near the monks maintained a worshipful pose, but those farther away seemed to talk and laugh. At one point, an elderly monk, assisted by a water bearer, passed among the audience and sprinkled us with water, using a sort of whiskbroom, which he dipped in the water jug carried by his helper. I had the definite feeling that the aura of this service was of happiness and celebration.

The chanting stopped abruptly and the service was over. Thai men rarely have insurance, and the death of a young father usually leaves widows and children to struggle. As the audience left, many approached a young woman seated on the floor, dressed in black. Her eyes were dry, but her facial expression was of grief and stress. Those who approached left white envelopes containing a monetary gift. In the Thai fashion, it was both practical and beautiful.

5 April 1988

I have reached that state of tour when the ARC office and many others are asking me when I will return after I complete this tour. My forthright answer is, "I do not know." More than ever my mental set is "move as the spirit leads." For now, I look forward to reuniting with you, family and friends, and we shall see what the future holds.

8 April 1988

David and Jip have moved into the new home, and we are scheduled to move on Sunday. Our house stores the TB drugs and a number of files filled with records that I doubt anyone will look at. Obviously, the files should be reviewed and much thrown out. This would take time, energy and—most important—the necessity of making decisions. We will no doubt take the easy way and move it all. Sound familiar? Much like I would do at home.

Arlys and I went to the Cambodian Lady's Restaurant for dinner this evening. Along the border here there are a number of people living who are at least part Khmer. Indeed, Khmer is the second language here, and when one gets mixed up on numbers when dealing at a store one can almost always shift from Thai to Khmer and be understood.

10 April 1988

Today was moving day, and we worked hard from 7:00 A.M. to 7:00 P.M. I worked hard, but must confess that the ladies worked even harder. We had expected help from Aran, but nobody showed up until about noon, when Brian arrived. He speaks Thai very well and hired three Thai men. With them working, our job that had seemed insuperable became manageable. Moving my own stuff was not so difficult, but the long-term ladies have accumulated a lot. Besides that, ARC House Ta Phraya is the storehouse for TB, X-ray and Education. It was a big day, with many trips up and down stairs and numberless loadings and unloadings of our truck.

Our house has five inside bedrooms, a storage room and a little one-room house in back. Since I have such a short time here, I told the others to make their choices and I would take what was left. I hoped no one would want the little separate house and I was lucky. I call it the "outhouse." The room is small, but I think I will like it.

12 April 1988

Our maid is having a hard time with this move. The house is much bigger, and with the addition of Jip and David we are now six instead of four. Even worse, Rancy thinks the house has ghosts. It seemed like she was going to quit, but yesterday she showed up with a helper to face a huge mountain of washing and the general chaos.

13 April 1988

With David living here I have a new companion. We generally go out to eat together. David is a really nice young man, and we exchange descriptions of various aspects of life at home. He grew up in a little town about 400 miles from Sydney.

You will recall that pouring water on people is a part of the celebration of New Year's. In addition, spreading white powder on the face has been a part of it, but even more so this year. This is done in such a friendly fashion, it is sort of like a blessing.

At camp, we have few patients, since all the families wish to be at home. I understand the celebration goes on until Friday. While it is a happy time, I will be glad to get back to our regular schedule.

15 April 1988

Communication in Thailand

David, young Australian physician, has become my frequent companion. He recently moved to our house here in Ta Phraya and is getting acquainted with the town. On a recent day off, he awakened late with a great hunger for a pancake breakfast. He made his way to Fargo's, which features a Thai–Dutch and somewhat American menu. David speaks considerable Thai, and with great confidence gave his order for pancakes to the Thai waitress. What he received was scrambled eggs and a small pitcher of syrup. It is most probable that if he had ordered scrambled eggs he would have received pancakes with an accompanying bottle of fish sauce.

Communication on ward rounds is largely by way of written records—the patient's chart. These remain with the patient. Many of these folk roll their own cigarettes, using a coarse tobacco and whatever paper they can find. When nothing else is available, they will often tear off a bit of their chart. The result is that their record, instead of getting longer as the days go by, gets shorter.

One of the problems in communication here is that we live in Thai society and work in Khmer society. In dealing with the Khmers, there is the additional problem that their past experience of survival and their present circumstances of deprivation leads them to understand and hear only what they want to understand and hear.

The New Year's celebration is very important in Khmer society, and much subtle pressure is put on farangs to underwrite New Year's parties. Like most of us, David succumbed to this pressure with some reluctance and informed Ry, his chief medic, that he would provide 100 baht for a

New Year's party. Ry said he would make a budget and did so promptly. His budget called for 1,500 baht. David sternly and forthrightly told Ry that the buying list must be reduced. Ry gave him that charming Khmer smile, promised to cut the list, and suggested that since some foods are expensive in camp perhaps David could buy them in Ta Phraya. The result was David bought fruit and cookies in Ta Phraya for nearly 500 baht. We all enjoyed a very nice 1,500 baht party meal, and David had learned another lesson in communication.

Jip is much more facile in speaking Khmer than the rest of us, but even she has her problems. Yesterday, she and a group of Khmers were considering a patient with a urinary tract infection. In Thai, water is *nam,* in Khmer, *nom* is urine, and so it was a simple mistake to say to the patient, "You must drink lots of *nom.*" When Jip saw the look of lack of understanding on the faces of the Khmer, she repeated it several times, bringing on great laughter until they could tell her of the mistake.

18 April 1988

Yesterday was my Sunday to work. During the New Year's celebration days, we had few patients and thus had time to play Scrabble with some of the Khmers more literate in English. They really don't have much chance to win, but it is humbling for us since we could not even start in Khmer.

19 April 1988

It is relatively quiet here this early in the morning. A rooster crows, there are distant muted sounds of other early risers and the occasional croak of a *tokay* (lizard). Living in this new house is different and much more pleasant. The house was clean when we moved in and quite suited to our mutual agreement of no shoes in the house—a marked contrast to our previous house. We have increased the maid's pay, and she is doing a better job.

20 April 1988

| *Rabies*

Louis Pasteur did the first scientific work on rabies, and I read about it as a student. Until two days ago, I had never seen a case, but now the scene will forever be imprinted in my mind.

Word reached us that they had a case of rabies in the COERR hospital in Site 2 North. Call it morbid or scientific interest, but several of us from our hospital went to view this case.

Rabies is a viral disease usually transmitted by animal bite, in this case a cat bite. The virus attacks the neuromuscular system, and as a result causes convulsions at the slightest stimulation of sight, sound or touch. The frightful thing about this disease is the victim remains very alert.

The patient was a seven-year-old boy. Partially screened from the rest of the ward, he lay with his head on his mother's lap. His eyes were wide, staring, and to my mind implored us to do something. Every moment or two he was seized with a tortuous convulsion. We could do nothing save encourage the attending physician to give liberal amounts of Valium. Anguish, frustration and wonderment about why such tragedies occur occupied our minds as we left that sad scene. Mercifully, the child died a few hours later.

23 April 1988

Tom Durant showed up yesterday. He is an ob/gyn, about my age, and this is his seventh tour to Thailand. Besides that, he has also worked in Afghanistan. This is the first time our paths have crossed, and many ARC workers have said we should meet. There are some differences. He is an administrator at Massachusetts General Hospital, a prestigious position. He is now on the board of ARC, and is here only for a short time on an official visit.

24 April 1988

Tonight at my instigation we are having the MSF group here. I proposed "potluck," a term I had to explain to them. In my self-appointed role of facilitator on good relations between Volags here, I have been most successful with them. Dr. Danielle, tall and bearded, has a pediatric background. He lived most of his life in Brazil, but speaks impeccable French and excellent English. His lady friend, Dr. Odile, is a derma-tologist. We have exchanged hospital visits a number of times and have helped one another.

For our part of the potluck we are providing Coke and fruit salad, and Jip is preparing some mysterious Thai dish that requires much peel-ing, cutting and chopping. Have you ever seen bamboo shoots? They look like long, green turnips.

25 April 1988

Our potluck went very well. We had six guests from MSF, and food and fellowship were grand, with much credit to Jip. She worked all after-noon in preparation. She made two dishes and a salad. One was a Thai version of spaghetti, using wide noodles and a delicious spicy sauce made with chopped-up pork, tomatoes, onions and various spices. The second was a type of spring roll made with short pieces of bamboo shoots. These were partially split and stuffed with a pork-and-egg fill-ing, dipped in egg batter and deep-fried.

Not only did Jip provide this fine food, she also provided a good part of the entertainment. We were all sitting in a circle and she told of 10 rules taught to girls in her youth on preparation for marriage:

1. Get up with the first rooster crow.

2. Prepare husband's bath.

3. Fix breakfast.

4. Help him to dress.

5. Serve breakfast.

6. See him off to the rice fields with a good lunch.

7. Prepare nice dinner.

8. On his return home, greet him, help him with his bath.

9. Serve him dinner.

10. Help him to get ready for bed, a nice massage and then *wai* his feet.

You can well imagine the happy smiles on the faces of the men and the uproar from the feminist women. I forgot the best part: carefully spread the toothpaste on his toothbrush. I can't wait to get home.

19 May 1988

Twanoh Falls

It was dark, the evening of 25 April 1988, as I made my way to the "phone store" in Ta Phraya. The phone store is a typical installation in Thai villages, where almost none of the residents or stores have telephones. An open storefront on a busy street, it is usually presided over by a Thai woman, and invariably there are several people sitting or squatting, either waiting to place a call or just visiting. In the back, there is a doorway opening into the family's living area, which is often dominated by a TV set. To place an overseas call, one pays a 50 baht service charge and then waits, sometimes for a few minutes and sometimes much longer.

I knew that Gwen had had a physical exam that indicated the need for an ultrasound of the abdomen. I had no foreboding thoughts as the Thai lady pointed at me and directed me to the phone booth. I remember little of Gwen's conversation, except the grim words of mass in the liver, necrotic areas, metastatic nodule. I vaguely remember stumbling out of the phone booth, paying the lady and being unable to answer when she asked, "Phone call OK?"

I had ridden my bike to the phone store, and in a melancholy daze made my way back to our house. There my housemates, all medical people, understood immediately the portent of my report, and I experienced the real and tangible compassionate support that springs from our work together. I was to experience this many times in the following days.

Brother Bob Maat drove me to Aranyaphrathet, where I stayed the night. Through Gwen, I had arranged to have her physician call me. She confirmed the grim report. I returned to Ta Phraya in the morning, where, with the help of Jean, I packed my bags; I then returned to Aran, where a taxi awaited me for the trip to Bangkok. The ARC office in Bangkok, already alerted, had made travel arrangements, and did all they could to comfort and support me.

On Wednesday, I proceeded through the departure routine without problems. The 19-hour flight on Thai Airlines was comfortable, and Gwen met me at the airport. Life in Thailand can often be described as bittersweet, and our reunion had this quality. What joy to be reunited, but along with it was the dark cloud of apprehension.

That was three weeks ago. During that time Gwen has had numerous complex examinations. At first the reports continued grim, and then a little ray of hope, finally confirmed yesterday by a special CT scan that definitely revealed a cavernous hemangioma of the liver, a benign lesion, probably present for years and requiring no treatment.

My primary feeling at this time is gratitude: thanks to ARC for the opportunity to experience Thailand and the border, and thanks to my colleagues in Aranyaprathet and Ta Phraya who by voice and letter have given us support. Thanks to the Khmers who—having suffered so much in their own lives—expressed their compassion, support and understanding by letter and tape. Thanks to our friends here who have shared our concern. And thanks to the physicians, nurses and staff of hospitals and clinics who have seen us through this difficult time.

Tour IX

Live in the Here and Now

4 December 1988

Each time I have flown across the Pacific on volunteer tours, I have tried to express in writing my mental and emotional response to this experience. In the past six months we have been privileged to share time with many friends and family near and far. In a very real way I have felt the loving support offered to us. For this we are grateful. If there is any merit in my work over here, all of you share in it.

We landed at Taipei after 12 hours of uneventful flight. The flight from Taipei to Bangkok is about 3½ hours. As we approached Bangkok, my energy and awareness came back, perhaps the result of my little watch alarm going off, telling me it was 5:30 A.M., Twanoh Falls time. The Thais have remodeled their airport, and immigration and customs went fine. I was met by Bob Medrala, ARC Bangkok chief, and we spent the taxi time and an hour over coffee exchanging news. His report was primarily that personnel are different but border problems are about the same.

I'm not sure what time I went to bed, but I awakened six hours later, ready to take on Bangkok.

Opening my suitcases in Bangkok is always a challenge, for Gwen— international-class packer—manages to get each bag full plus 25 percent. The result is that with the zip of a zipper or the turn of a latch it is like "open sesame." All of those items, so lovingly packed by Gwen, seem to spring out. Now when I leave for Ta Phraya, I will have the challenge of getting them back in such a way that the luggage will close.

It is early morning as I write this, and I now must start some errands. No doubt part of this day will be spent in nap time.

10 December 1988

My first 36 hours since returning to the border have been a mix of great reunions with old friends, meeting people new to me and getting my living situation organized. Largely the result of stimulation by Brother Bob Maat and others in ARC, and backed by the UN, today is being observed as Human Rights Day. Classes have been held discussing the significance of this. As usual, along with their interest in such topics, the Khmers have managed to inject a little humor. One of the classes in school told their teacher they would not study that afternoon for it was their "human right" to so decide.

As per usual when I return here, I find some improvement in the status of the Khmers, but this is interspersed with the continuing lack of tangible hope, punctuated with episodes of tragic violence and over-riding hunger for freedom. Progress continues in the dedicated work of the health education workers of ARC. The Khmer health workers are quite able to handle the vast majority of acute health-care challenges, and show understanding and acceptance of preventive measures.

11 December 1988

Daytime temperatures are about 80° Fahrenheit, but I would think below 70 at night, and most every night the wind blows. I brought a long-sleeved sweater, which I put on at night since the little Thai-sized blankets fail to cover my shoulders. This is Sunday, and I did not work. As usual, I got up early only to face a difficult decision—to shower or not to shower, that was the question. Shivering and shaking, I managed my shower, but, man, did I feel good after it was over!

14 December 1988

Yesterday, the Khmer medic chief asked me to see one of his patients. I took this opportunity to do a teaching round. This man, 33, had been wounded by a land mine explosion one month ago, and had been in a military hospital until coming here. He was rendered unconscious by the blast. His current complaints were dizziness, nausea and vomiting whenever he tried to get up. Examination revealed both eardrums were destroyed, healing wounds of skin of the arms and legs, and traumatic amputation of the fingers of the right hand. It is possible that with modern sophisticated treatment his hearing might be restored, but such is impossible here. I shall see if arrangements can be made to send him to Bangkok, but it is unlikely. As I went over this man, I wished that our political leaders could see this example of what happens when they refuse to talk peace and turn to war.

15 December 1988

Edie put on a super dinner last night—quiche, green salad, and topped off with apple pie à la mode (actually it was guava, which in pie tastes just like apple). I think it was the best meal I have had in Thailand.

Ken is an attorney who for eight years was one of the bright young men on Wall Street in New York. He is the nephew of Father John. We met at dinner at the home of our mutual friend, Edie. This young man had the urge to do overseas work for a number of years. He states he has left the Wall Street life forever and plans to stay here for two years. His present work is teaching basic principles of English law to Khmers.

In Cambodia before the chaos, French law was the basis of the legal system in the major cities. In the countryside, law came from the village headman, the elders and the tribal customs. During the Pol Pot chaos, all vestiges of law and order succumbed to the requirements of survival. I feel that as the requirements for survival decline in the camps, it is important that we help the Khmers to reestablish what I call quality of life.

This fine young man, Ken, is doing his part, and it was fascinating and inspiring to spend some time with him.

18 December 1988

The project for Friday was to obtain driver's licenses for me and two colleagues. This was somewhat complicated, starting out with a "physical exam" at Aran Hospital. The Thai woman doctor I saw listened to my heart through my shirt and pronounced me fit to drive—15 baht. Next we went to the district police station, where we sat for an hour while the policeman shuffled through our papers. After a 50 km ride to Sakeo, we waited for three hours until finally the licenses appeared. Such is life in the land of *mai pen rai*.

I spent Friday night in Aran. The chief delegate of the International Committee of the Red Cross had invited ARC members to dinner and an exchange of information. This tall, handsome Swiss man lives in a very nice villa in Aran, and must have an excellent cook, for we were served a delicious meal. The delegate spoke quite openly about the role of ICRC and the current status on the border. It appears that the major impediment to returning the Khmers across the border is the role of the Khmer Rouge. Progress is being made, and it appears that sometime during the coming year small numbers of Khmer volunteers may return.

Some of my colleagues were puzzling over questions that confront all of us periodically—questions about the appropriateness of our role here, questions about how much and how best to help those individual Khmers to whom we feel particularly attracted or who we feel are most deserving of our help. These are the unknowns that disturb us all to varying degrees. Perhaps it is my age, perhaps it is my good fortune in having the opportunity to participate here for intermittent short periods, but somehow I am not as deeply bothered by these questions. I remain convinced that simply by our presence here, we say to these people, "There is a better world, somebody cares."

A postscript to Human Rights Day: for the first time we were allowed to stay in camp until 7:00 P.M., after dark. The final production was a speech by Bob Maat, with a candle-lighting service. Unfortunately, there was a wind blowing, so instead of the steady glow of candlelight, the candles intermittently blew out, requiring relighting. Looking back on it, I realize that this was truly symbolic, for such is the state of human rights in our world, and the flickering and dying candles truly represented the plight of our Khmers and many other groups on our planet.

20 December 1988

Yesterday afternoon ended with me making an ambulance run with two babies in respiratory distress. One of the babies had diarrhea, while one of the mothers, carsick, vomited on the floor. In the hot little tin box of the ambulance, the odor was something else. Arriving at KID, the receiving physician, a French woman, greeted us coldly until I used a few words of French; then she added cordiality to her obvious skills. I was picked up for the return trip to Ta Phraya by one of our drivers, who as usual had the air-conditioning on full blast. So I exchanged the excess warmth of the ambulance for cold. En route, while passing a farmer and his oxen-drawn cart, we received a radio message that resulted in meeting one of our other trucks, which I was to drive back alone. Instead of the fast but skillful driving of the Thai ambulance driver, I proceeded slowly, enjoying the lovely Thai countryside.

21 December 1988

Jan, the internist in charge of Adult Medicine, plays the violin quite well, and of course you know of my talent with the recorder. Somehow the Khmer minister of a little evangelical church heard of our talents, and insisted that we play with his choir and string ensemble for a Christmas program scheduled for tomorrow for Khmer administration. The songs are the familiar Christmas carols, so not too difficult. Two exciting things occurred while we were there. During "Silent Night," a ragged little Khmer boy with a flail leg came in. As he made his crutch-aided way to his seat, I felt sure he must be the namesake of Tiny Tim of Dickens fame. During a break, I sat on the unsupported end of a bamboo bench, fell backward, struck the back of my head against a pew, and spilled coffee all over. Somewhat dazed, I got up, muddy and dirty, surrounded by Khmers, at first concerned, and then giggling. I don't have to worry about whether we have eggs for my breakfast, for I have a goose egg on the back of my head.

Again, my day ended yesterday with an ambulance transfer of a baby in respiratory distress. I frequently point out to my colleagues that perhaps the major good here is to support these people by showing them compassion—and care. It occurred to me on that ride: how could I do that any better than by holding the plastic bag into which the poor young Khmer mother was vomiting?

And so life goes on here at the border.

22 December 1988

The big news from here is that I have achieved my major goal of this tour for Ta Phraya House. We now have a new stove, a beauty. It has four burners, an oven with light and rotisserie and timer. What more could we ask? As it turns out, this stove was sitting unused in one of the other ARC houses. Now all we have to do is learn how to use it, since all of the indicators for On and Off are in Thai sign language. Arlys promises to bake cookies. In celebration, I made scalloped potatoes last night with ham and cheese.

It has definitely been warmer in recent days, and the nights are quite comfortable. I am wondering how the winter weather is there.

My super head cold came to full bloom yesterday, which was unfortunate for it was a busy and demanding day. On arrival at camp, I found two surgery cases requiring transfer—serious enough that I went along with an accompanying medic. Regrettably, I returned just too late to play my recorder with the musical ensemble for the administration Christmas party. I did manage to eat. An important meeting was scheduled for Aran, and I arranged to leave early. The plan was fouled up by another late surgical transfer. I did not go on the transfer, but nevertheless it resulted in my late return home. By that time, I felt badly enough that on arriving in my little room I just dropped everything and plopped on my bed. I awakened in about an hour, drenched with perspiration. No meeting for me. This morning I definitely feel better, but my nose runs and I cough, so I am staying home.

25 December 1988

May joy and peace be with you on this Christmas Day. Yesterday was busy for me. I was the only doctor on the platform and also was Alpha III all day. In the afternoon, we received a transfer from the ICRC surgical hospital: a lady whose fractured jaw had been wired. Since vomiting for such a patient could be fatal, it is important that a pair of wire cutters be readily available. The driver who brought her in had the cutters in his pants pocket, and in a very human way—which I can understand—left with them still in his pocket. When this was discovered, he was a long way off, and there followed a flock of radio calls you wouldn't believe. It being Christmas Eve, fewer people than usual were working, and those who were all seemed to be proficient in speaking Thai, French or Khmer. With my poor language ability, it was most frustrating for me to try to explain our need of wire cutters for a lady with a fractured jaw. We finally dispatched our driver to get a replacement pair. As a result, we were very late leaving camp.

This day had a happy ending, for by the time I returned home the ladies and our new stove had combined to make a delicious Christmas Eve dinner of spaghetti. In the evening, I went to Christmas Eve services at the nearby Catholic compound. The service was beautiful.

26 December 1988

Most of us here at Ta Phraya had Christmas Day off. I spent my time reading, writing, playing chess on my electronic game Elmer, and doing errands. At my suggestion, rather than having a party for our Khmer workers, those of us who work in the hospital decided to buy fruit for them to take home to share with their families. It amounted to about 75 kilos of fruit and plastic bags to put it in. I had made the arrangements for this, and in the morning completed the transaction. I'm sure that for the little old "fruit lady," it was probably her biggest deal for the year. When it came to tallying up the bill it was a great scene. She and her son worked on it, and pretty soon our Thai driver got into it. After much discussion, they came up with the same figure I had arrived at, so we were all happy.

27 December 1988

This will be a busy week for me. Jan will be on vacation. We have an ambitious education schedule, and I fill in for Alpha III when necessary—plus being the only physician in Site 2 South. It certainly makes the time go by quickly.

Last night we had several guests for dinner and then played Trivial Pursuit. Our invited expert on Trivial Pursuit was Father Andrew, a Jesuit priest from Australia. He does amazingly well on questions about America, but failed to recognize the oceans which surround Australia. It was a great game that, thanks to the good Father's erudition and Arlys's good reasoning, we managed to win.

28 December 1988

We hosted grand rounds yesterday. This is a biweekly meeting I set up last tour for the farang doctors and top Khmer medics. Our medics presented two cases, and there was good discussion by physicians from France, Holland, Burma and the U.S., and also from the medics. It was a good time for all of us, and I think of some service to our patients, since we got some good ideas about further investigation and treatment of our patients.

30 December 1988

Yesterday, Jeff and I were invited to lunch at BunSieth's house. He lives in a little bamboo-and-thatch house that is closely surrounded by rows of similar houses. BunSieth is one of the brightest stars in the constellation of young Khmers who have responded so well to the excellent training offered by the ARC Medical Education department. He has no apparent chance for expatriation. His lovely wife greeted us at the door, surrounded by their two children and a group of neighbors' children. BunSieth's father-in-law and his brother were also present. The father-in-law speaks no English, but his face has the marks of nobility. He is a group leader, a minor political post. BunSieth's brother speaks only a little English, but that will improve, for he is on the health worker staff and expects to start nurse's training soon. We ate in Khmer style, with which I am not yet comfortable. BunSieth's wife served the meal but did not partake. The meal was special, with serving dishes of stew, chicken, bits of beef and of course rice. The procedure is a serving of rice on the plate and a sharing bite by bite taken by each from the serving dishes.

10 January 1989

Security on the border for the farangs: In our group we have five radios tuned to the UNBRO security officer's radio. When all is quiet, we are at Situation 0. When there is artillery fire, a mine explosion or a grenade blast in the nearby perimeter, we are advised "Situation 1" and required to stay near a radio and keep the Alpha III person aware of our location. When there is indication of closer military activity, a calm but serious voice announces Situation 2, and we hurry to our assigned places, load the trucks and depart for the Situation 2 rendezvous. There we are to wait until the situation is evaluated and declared safe, or we go back to Ta Phraya. A Situation 3 is called when artillery fire lands in camp. When that occurs, our direction is to run to our assigned vehicle and leave immediately for Situation 3 rendezvous out of camp. The directions for Situation 4 are simple—"Hit the dirt." To the best of my knowledge, there has in recent months been only one Situation 3 and I don't believe any Situation 4. The camp is many acres in size, and most times when a situation is called we have no idea of the precipitating cause.

Yesterday, we had a sudden Situation 2. Our group got out efficiently and we proceeded to the Situation 2 rendezvous. I cannot describe the feeling of shame and compassion that I feel when I see our Khmer co-workers helping us to depart, leaving them to who knows what. The Situation 2 rendezvous is a bare stretch of road. We are required to stay in the trucks, which shortly become stifling hot. After about an hour, an UNBRO security officer came by and described the precipitating scene—an angry Khmer firing two pistol shots at his opponent, no injuries.

Most trucks returned to camp, a few went to Ta Phraya. At camp we were greeted by the smiling faces of those we had left to their fate.

A Walk across Thailand

Most people who come to Thailand as tourists do not have time or opportunity to really experience this country—such a mix of beauty and ugliness, of wealth and poverty, of peace and violence. Come with me then on a half-hour walk that offers a microcosmic experience of all of these facets.

My walk started at Siam Center, a modern shopping center featuring the luxury goods and services of Thailand, mixed with the American influence manifested by Pizza Hut, Dunkin' Donuts and A&W. My goal was to visit the new ARC office. My map seemed to indicate it was only a block away, but experience has taught me that what looks like a Western block often is closer to a mile. Now, I have had lots of experience finding my way in the mountains, hills and valleys of the Pacific Northwest. There are those with whom I have traveled, my daughter Peggy in particular, who would claim I am not too good at finding my way.

My walk started on a busy street, with the roar of traffic and its attendant overwhelming carbon monoxide fumes. Who could blame me for being enticed by what appeared to be a nice shortcut trail, seeming to lead off exactly in the direction I wanted to go? In the beginning, it was about six feet wide, concrete and lined on each side by little storefront-style Thai businesses. It wasn't all peaceful, for, even at the start, motorcyclists were frequent, squeezing by at considerable speed, their handle bars missing my elbows by inches. Soon I came upon an area with an ambience of peace and quiet. It was a Buddhist temple, and I could see monks gliding along in a parklike atmosphere. I am told that in one form of Buddhism the monks are trained to meditate as they walk, and that must have been what they were doing.

A little ways farther, I heard the sound of many children's voices saying a series of words in rhythm with great enthusiasm. It was a grade school. The pupils who were not in class had an appearance of discipline not seen in American schools. The boys all had flattop haircuts, and wore blue shorts and white shirts. The girls all had bobbed hair, and wore blue skirts and white blouses.

My concrete path became narrower, the little Thai businesses more primitive. Most frequent were little eating establishments, open in the front, a charcoal fire going, a woman busily stirring some concoction in a wok, a few chairs and a rickety table. In most, there was a small glass display case offering cigarettes and Mekong, the ubiquitous Thai whiskey.

Onward I walked, becoming aware that my pathway was becoming narrower, dirt instead of cement, and now passing through the area where poor people lived. Their huts were constructed of corrugated steel, plastic, boards and thatch. Many of the people looked at me in wonder, but few failed to return my smile, and I heard many "Benais," the Thai equivalent of "Where are you going?" or "Can we help you?"

My path led me through a swamp, fertile with plants, bugs and treacherous little board bridges over open water. At this point, I belatedly pondered the possibility that I had made a mistake in taking this route. Around a bend, I sighted a broken-down car and knew that I must be coming out. To my delight and surprise, the path grew more substantial and led me to a street nearby the ARC offices. Once again, I was grateful for a wonderful little adventure.

13 January 1989

Rabies is a rare disease in most temperate countries, but it is not all that uncommon here. Recently we had a patient who was reacting to his series of rabies vaccine injections, given after a dog bite. This led me to reading several articles about rabies. It is estimated that about 3 percent of dogs in Thailand carry the virus, but only a small number are symptomatic. As a result, all persons bitten are advised to go through antirabies treatment. I can well remember my early apprehensions about Thai dogs. There are many of them, a few are handsome, attractive animals, but many are thin, scruffy and mangy scavengers. Strangely enough, they are rarely belligerent, and picking up a rock or a stick is usually effective.

Yesterday morning, I mounted a bike to ride over to check on Jan's health. A few hundred meters from our house, I was assailed by two dogs, one on each side of my pedaling feet, their jaws snapping. I tried pedaling faster but could not outdistance them, and it made them even more angry. I considered stopping and facing them, but with two dogs it seemed not to be the thing to do. Finally, after about a block of shouting at them, they peeled off. I shall avoid that area, for that experience left me shaken, and I can't believe that the calves of my legs are intact. Another facet of the mixed life of peace and violence that characterizes Thailand.

14 January 1989

The big bike ride starts at 6:00 A.M. I have my coffee made and my camera loaded. There are eight of us going, led by the indomitable Sister Margo. We will carry a radio. This is the kind of maneuver about which there is no regulation, no permission sought or granted, and the authorities will only know it as a "fait accompli"!

Yesterday was busy. Alpha III for part of the day, many visitors, and a class to teach—all combined to keep me running. Of course such a day could not end without a terminal ambulance run. Besides myself, there were five patients in that little aluminum cubicle. I stood the whole way—no mean trick since we had a fast Thai driver, many curves, and several abrupt slow-ups. En route, I felt one of my shoes becoming moist. I looked down, and saw a green liquid sloshing on the floor. My immediate reaction was that it was some foul liquid draining from one of the patients, but I was relieved to see it came from a swinging plastic bag that a grandmother patient had taken along and hung from a rail. When she saw what had happened, she very apologetically took the bag and drank its contents.

15 January 1989

Yesterday started with the great bike ride from Ta Phraya to Site 2 South. From ARC, there were Betsy (education coordinator), Jip and myself. The remaining five were from COERR, including my good friend John Henderson, and also the leader, Sister Margo. I found out to my surprise that Margo is not a nun. She teaches ocean swimming in Australia for six months of the year. This is her fifth tour.

We met at the market as day was breaking and the merchants were putting out their wares. We bought rice soup to carry out and fruit, and then went to Margo's house, where John had brought by truck from camp a bicycle for each of us. The aura of the departure scene put me in "déjà vu" because it was so similar to scenes I have experienced so often at home, when we were in the departure mode for a mountain climb. People were cinching up their packs. "Did you bring . . . ?" questions flew about. The leader rolled out, and we formed a line of eight bicycles. Even at this early hour, there were many Thais on the street. They watched us, and their expressions clearly asked, "What are these strange foreigners doing now? When they have all those cars and trucks, why are they riding bikes? Crazy!"

We pedaled our way to the first military checkpoint, and passed through to the smiles and waves of the Thai soldiers. How nice the contrast was to our daily rattle and bang of riding in a truck. The sun was just rising, the air was freshened by a light breeze, the birds were singing, and even the occasional water buffalo seemed to give us a quizzical but friendly look.

About one third of the way along, we came to a little village where we turned off on a short road that led us to a delightful pastoral scene. This is rice harvest time. The strawlike rice plants are cut and tied into small bundles by field workers, hauled to this threshing area, and built up into large stacks. The ground here is hard-packed. A worker and his three oxen were threshing. A circle of the dry rice plants, about eight meters in diameter, had been laid down to a depth of about one meter. Directed by the man, the oxen circled over the pile of straw, tramping it, and shaking the rice kernels loose. I do not know how the man could tell when all of the rice was loosened. He must have some way to tell, for eventually he began to pitch the trodden remains to another stack, and there was the rice on the hard-packed earth. We watched all of this comfortably ensconced on the top of a rice plant stack, mesmerized by the circling beasts, the warm welcome of the sun, and the friendly gaze of village children who had come to stare.

We moved on to the shore of a reservoir and ate our breakfast. The last part of our journey was a little more difficult, for our road led us directly into a stiff wind. We arrived in camp a little late, physically tired but filled with gratitude for having had this opportunity.

18 January 1989

Early morning and a demanding day ahead. Jan is off for two days. We have a class today that may be more than usually demanding since, after several coaching sessions, it will be taught for the first time by our Khmer clinic chief, with me as backup.

Last Saturday was Thai Children's Day. More unique was Monday, Thai Teachers' Day. By custom, teachers are given three gifts: flowers, a common grass, and a needle. The flowers symbolize the beauty of learning, the grass the quality of spreading and covering the earth, and the needle the sharpness of intellect. Not being well enough organized to get these things together as a gift of respect to the teachers with whom I live, I drew them on our bulletin board with an appropriate greeting.

19 January 1989

Martha is a lovely young American, trained as a physician's assistant and reputed to be an expert in orthopedics and emergency medicine. When a six-year-old boy with obvious signs of major fracture of the lower leg appeared in our Surgery ward, I sought her out, for she also has the reputation of being a good teacher. There followed a demonstration of the best of traditional tribal medicine combined with the science of American practice. She spent time gaining the confidence of this boy, and with beautiful gentleness commenced her examination far from the site of his pain and deformity. With patience and skill, she did all of the scientific examination required by American medical science, never causing the boy to whimper. It was indeed a privilege for me, and the Khmer medics, to watch and learn. Knowledge, skill and compassion are prime qualities for a health worker here.

20 January 1989

More about rabies. On Wednesday in Surgery we received an infant who, in playing with a dog, had received an abrasion to the conjunctiva of one eye. The rule is that anyone who has sustained a break in the skin or mucous membrane must receive rabies postbite treatment. This includes local injection of antiserum. None of us knew how this is done when the wound is in the eye. We therefore sent Jeff, a nurse, to Ta Phraya to call Dr. Wilde, world-renowned expert on rabies, who works in Bangkok. Eventually, I received a radio message from Jeff telling us that we should make up a solution of the antiserum and irrigate the eye.

I proceeded to Surgery, where they told me they had used all of their antiserum. That seemed only a small problem, so I sent Sok Saly to the pharmacy. He returned promptly to tell me that there was no serum in the pharmacy. I then went to the pharmacy, only to find that the pharmacist was safely locked in the latrine. I waited patiently. When he came out, he told me that I would find additional serum in the antivenom kit in the TB clinic. I walked across the long hot field to the TB clinic, where I was told that the antivenom box was locked and could only be opened with the keys in possession of Alpha III. I carried the box back to the health office, where Pytt, Alpha III, opened it—no serum. About this time, a Khmer from Surgery appeared and reported that further search had produced some antiserum. Our task was completed. The remarkable part of this little story is that, had a similar episode occurred in the U.S., I would have produced lots of adrenaline, anger and frustration. Perhaps I am becoming Thai?

22 January 1989

On a recent evening, I went "downtown" in Ta Phraya for a haircut. John had recommended a shop. When I arrived there, I was taken aback by the appearance, for it looked like a women's beauty parlor. Nevertheless, I entered and by sign language indicated to the young proprietor that I wished a haircut. She looked at my bald pate, giggled, and indicated she only had scissors, no *Bzzz Bzzz,* indicating the action of clippers. I walked down the street to the next shop, a large barnlike room with a barber chair and few tonsorial accoutrements. She too giggled when I pantomimed "haircut," but enthusiastically nodded her head and indicated I should sit in the chair. She promptly ducked out the door and was gone for several moments. It was apparent she had gone down the street to borrow some clippers. She came back, apologetic, saying, "Mai mill" (have none), and indicating I should proceed down the street. Here I found a men's barbershop. A boy indicated I should sit in the middle chair, from which I could see the barber leisurely eating his dinner. I was not without entertainment, for the boy turned on the television, which as usual featured a Thai show of a flashing sword duel with the opponents jumping from rooftop to rooftop, their blades flashing in great arcs—not a good preparation for a haircut. The boy sensed my ennui and changed to an English-speaking station. I was treated to views of the Reagan, Bush and Quayle families.

The barber, having finished his dinner, came in and commenced his ministrations, quite routine in my experience the world over. The unique part was his patient and persistent use of the straight razor to trim the hairs in my nose and ears. Sensitized by the flashing swords, I found that hard to sit still for.

I drove to Aran early this morning, and on return had a nice nap. I encountered Father Pierre, who looked worn and shaky; for the first time in my experience, he looked his age of 75. He had been in an automobile accident, having chosen to hit a tree rather than a motorcyclist. This occurred several days ago, and he still favors his injured shoulder.

23 January 1989

The other night I was driving to Aran with three lady passengers. At the Royal Thai army checkpoint, the driver is to give his RTA number, first name and destination. The soldier who checked us was as usual very formal and polite. I rattled off the required data, he shook his head in wonderment, broke into a great smiling laugh and waved us through. It seems that depending on how you pronounce it, in Thai, "Louie" comes out the equivalent of "go for it."

24 January 1989

We remain on limited access, and yesterday were held out of camp for two hours by a Situation 2. After a two-week hiatus, the Khmer Rouge or the Vietnamese in the surrounding mountains decided to send a few rounds, which landed outside of camp.

A useful Thai expression is "chili and salt." Each of these is good and useful in itself, but together are incompatible in Thai belief. The expression is used when two people cannot get along.

26 January 1989

Recently I was teaching a class on physical diagnosis, and we were studying a procedure called tactile fremitus. To do this, you place your hand on the patient's chest and ask the patient to say "ninety-nine." This ancient procedure allows you to roughly gauge the relative vibrations emanating from the patient's voice box and reaching the chest wall. Depending on your experience and training, you may do this using one hand or two. I asked the class how many used two hands. Three students raised their hands. I then asked, "Is there anyone here who does this exam with only one hand?" With a great smile, one of the students raised his hand, and there was great laughter, for this student had only one arm. At first I thought I had made a great faux pas, but instead it was a time of shared pride and of empathy at this evidence of courage, acceptance and accomplishment by our brother.

28 January 1989

A number of my friends are collectors. They collect stamps, antiques, precious stones, etc. I am not that well organized, but I do have a collection; it is the consciousness of the brave people I have known. Two years ago, I visited a clinic in northwestern Thailand on the Burmese border. Miles of rough mountain road separate it from the nearest hospital. It serves primitive hill tribe people, and is also the scene of considerable violence originating from the opium trade.

Susan Bassett has worked there for many years. Nancy Thompson and Jip have also worked there, and they are in my collection.

29 January 1989

Yesterday was the day for Jeff's good-bye party in Aran, and most ARC people went. I decided to put on dinner for John and Rob. I made spaghetti and Jip made salad. In early evening, Jip, John, Rob and I walked to the mountain. We got back just in time to go to Catholic Mass, and ate afterward. There was also a good-bye party for Philippe (MSF coordinator), and I made a short appearance. It was late by the time I got to bed. I am the only one from Ta Phraya ARC who works today; it is hard to resist a feeling of martyrdom as I go through the morning chores knowing my friends are sleeping.

2 February 1989

I have eaten much Thai food this tour, but my addiction to McDonald's hamburgers remains. Most times when I come to Bangkok, my schedule allows one stop at the Golden Arches. Besides the "good" food, this often gives me another view of Thai life. The National Football League should send one of their scouts here. There was one customer in the line I chose at the McDonald's counter. She paid her bill, picked up her tray and moved to the right. I had just shifted my weight to the right foot, when like magic there appeared before me the back of a Thai lady about my age. How she slipped through that crowd and past my left elbow I'll never know, but it was a move that a pro quarterback would do well to learn. I was so impressed with her skill I couldn't summon any righteous indignation at this violation of American ethics of fair play and taking your turn.

3 February 1989

I moved from the hotel on Sukhumvit (they only had a vacancy for one night) to the Opera Hotel, near the ARC office and now the hotel with which ARC has a connection. It is a step up in quality from the Trocadero.

The Khmers keep track of when we go on vacation, and often ask for some special purchase available only in Bangkok. Accordingly, I had a request for a special ointment (cortisone and gentamycin) and for a French–English dictionary. Both of these required considerable shopping.

Returning to the Opera Hotel as prearranged, I met Tony Jackson, an official in OXFAM. He is working on preparations for the return of Khmers to Cambodia. Tony is a 43-year-old Englishman whose hometown is Oxford. He is a bundle of energy, and unlike myself gives evidence of being well organized. He spent a number of years in various countries, directing distribution of food to the poor and displaced. Currently, his position could be described as a public relations representative and facilitator for the Khmers on the border. Like me, he believes that the continued incarceration of 300,000 Khmers on the border must not continue, and that world opinion must be focused on solving this complex problem.

4 February 1989

Sok Thim is another outstanding Khmer we have the privilege of working with. Five or six years ago, he started working with Bob Maat when Bob was setting up the first TB clinic on the border. With the intense dedication and discipline of his Jesuit training, Bob started this effort with the long-range goal of training the Khmers to eventually take over the total management of this important part of health care for their people. Steadily, Sok Thim proceeded through the steps of becoming clinic chief and Fellow. About one year ago, Bob declared himself super-fluous and Thim became TB coordinator for the ARC team. It now seems probable that Sok Thim will become TB coordinator for all the camps on the border. These two have not only treated a long line of the Khmers for this dread disease, they have provided a challenging example of the development of Khmer self-reliance for the rest of us, which has spread to other Volags on the border.

Unheard of several years ago, Khmers now periodically are allowed to leave the camp to visit and learn from other services and meetings. As usual, Sok Thim is leading the way, for he is en route to Bangkok to present one of his cases to a prestigious medical meeting. He stayed at our house last night. He went to the market with me, and I sensed a feeling of shared joy that this young man must experience in this small taste of freedom after years in the penal camp.

5 February 1989

I'm at House 1, in the midst of a very busy weekend. I worked yes-terday, Saturday. In a hurry, I drove home, showered and shaved, and came to Aran. It was Father Pierre's 75th birthday, and his many friends and parishioners had planned a special observance. The usual Saturday night Mass was crowded with people from both Ta Phraya and Aran, and Father Pierre was at his best. After the service, we all went to ICRC, where a very nice buffet was laid on. There were many people there that I don't get to see often.

From there, I went to ARC House 6, where a group had gathered to hear and speak with Tony Jackson. It was a most interesting and inspir-ing meeting.

This morning I am scheduled to meet Tony and a journalist at Kim Kim's, and then go to Site 2, where there is a big graduation.

Later: After writing the above, I went to Kim Kim's to meet Tony Jackson and Rob Waters, a journalist. We had a nice breakfast. Rob went to camp with me. At camp, I did a little work, attended the graduation ceremonies and escorted Rob around.

Graduation

Today was graduation day for medics, nurses and health workers, and recognition day for Fellows and those medics who have completed three years of faithful work under the guidance of ARC personnel.

I would guess that there were about 200 of us gathered in a large bamboo building. Seated at long tables, we listened to speeches by ARC and Khmer leaders. English was translated into Khmer and Khmer into English. A monk gave the benediction.

It was my privilege to present certificates to those who had completed 18 months' service as Fellows on the clinical wards. First was Sok Thim, Fellow in the TB clinic and now coordinator of the TB service. Under the guidance of Brother Bob Maat, he has become an expert in treating that once dread disease, and now without farang provision is solely responsible for the administration and professional service. He represents Khmer self-reliance in action. BunSieth followed. I have had the privilege of working closely with this fine young man, who in such a wonderful way was able to blend professional skill and leadership talent. Next was Sok Saly. In my early days on the border, we saw many children with malnutrition. It was hard to persuade our medics to work with this condition, for many of the medics, having survived the Pol Pot chaos, had seen hundreds of their people suffering and dying from this condition. A wonderful ARC physician, Dr. Fern Houck, detected in Sok Saly the talent and compassion to treat this condition, and those two established the pediatric feeding center.

As these fine young men approached me to receive their certificates, they bowed their heads and made the *wai* gesture of respect. In truth, it was I who was honored, and I bowed deeply in respect for their courage, compassion and dedication—shown in their bright eyes and smiling faces.

It was a moving scene, and made me sense acutely my gratitude and admiration for the accomplishments of that long line of ARC teachers and health professionals who had made this possible.

7 February 1989

Ban Thad is the camp they installed adjacent to Site 2. It is in two sections, one for Vietnamese who are occupying it now, peacefully, and the other section for the illegals and "non-eligible for expatriation Khmers" from KID. It is reported they will move to Ban Thad the end of April. They are under the protection of UNHCR, a legal situation I don't understand. These Khmers believe there is the possibility this may give them some hope of expatriation.

8 and 9 February 1989

Besides getting up late yesterday, the start of the day gave promise of a busy one. I found that one of the tires on our truck was low in pressure. This required a short stop at a tire repair shop. Then at the market I found my favorite restaurant—the source of my usual lunch—closed. I found another restaurant, but it took time. With many of our team away, I drove alone to camp. It was a beautiful drive, early-morning scenes of Thai schoolchildren, water buffalo and birds attracting my attention.

Arriving at camp, I made my early-morning rounds. All was quiet in Adult Medicine and Surgery, but in Pediatrics they presented me with a 14-day-old infant, pale, blue lips and grunting respirations. The attending medic presented the case history and his diagnosis of sepsis and pneumonia—a dread combination. The rule sounds grim, but logically and logistically defendable: that patients who are moribund, and whose life could not be saved by the slightly more sophisticated procedures available at KID, are not to be transferred and are to be kept in our ward. Despite this rule, I called the ambulance, and on its arrival, out in the bright sunshine and surrounded by a host of curious and concerned Khmers, we gave oxygen from the ambulance's emergency tank. Very quickly the infant's lips lost their blue color.

With this sign of hope, we decided to transfer the baby to KID. In view of the delicate status of this patient, I decided to accompany the ambulance. Again I found myself in that hot little aluminum box rattling down the road. I sat on a little chair in the aisle. On my left sat the mother with the child in her lap. On my right sat a woman going to KID to help some patient there. I held the oxygen mask over the baby's face. Soon I saw the pallor and perspiration of the faces of these women, and I made sure the plastic vomit bag was handy. It was soon needed. Holding the oxygen mask in one hand and holding the plastic bag for the retching mother, I could not brace myself. The inevitable lurch of the ambulance occurred, and I cracked the side of my head on one of the steel rods of the framework. It wasn't all that bad. Soon the ladies felt better, and then I again learned something from these people. One of them reached into her bundle and came up with a container of Tiger Balm, a menthol-wintergreen ointment, very strong. They each applied some to the mustache area and the forehead. They offered me some, and I did the same and also to the side of my head. Voodoo, Krou Khmer, or psychological? I don't know, but we all seemed to feel better; we certainly smelled better. I shall add this ointment to our traveling emergency kit.

Arriving at KID, our little passenger seemed to have survived the trip. The French nurse in Admitting made the trip worthwhile, for she received the baby with a wonderful mix of skill and compassion. She even had kind French, English and Khmer words for the women and me. Thirty-six hours after this transfer, I talked with KID and learned the baby was improving.

10 February 1989

Khmer expression, used when too many things have been scheduled: Hold your arms out, like carrying a large basket, and say, "I have put so many things in my basket. I cannot carry it."

Last evening, driving home, the clutch of our old Toyota van gave up the ghost. An UNBRO jeep carrying a high UNBRO official was right behind us, and so we had immediate help. We were towed home. Our van carries the TB records back and forth to camp, and so we had to transfer them—three huge boxes, heavier than we could lift without unloading. Bob Maat, bless his heart, helped us.

11 February 1989

A number of years ago in France, on a sunshine-bright but cold winter day, I stood on a rise and looked down on the green sward overlooking the cemetery where lie the bodies of thousands of men killed on the invasion beaches of Normandy. I still remember the picture that came to my mind of these young men running over these hills and being cut down by gunfire.

I had a similar experience a few days ago. It was in the morning at camp. Pytt and I heard the steady roll of approaching drums. We went to the nearby road and watched the parade. Before us marched some 500 Khmers, mostly boys and young men and one contingent of young women. Their faces were so serious as they marched in military cadence. I found myself looking at their strong legs and picturing many of them as amputees, for this surely will be their fate. Pytt must have felt something similar, for we returned to our workplace silent and with tears in our eyes.

Later I heard that these marchers, in semimilitary dress, were members of a paramilitary group, and the parade was for a visiting Khmer general.

Last night I had hardly returned to my room when Corinne called me. "There is a car here with a man who has had his leg blown off." The car was from one of the other Volags. This couple had picked up this man on the side of the road. They were so distressed I could not get an understandable story from them.

I examined the man in the car, such a familiar sight, for I had seen many such in the old days at Nong Samet camp. He was a young Khmer, his leg wrapped in a bloody *pakima* and with the lower third dangling. There was no serious bleeding, so I advised the young couple to take him immediately to the nearby Thai Ta Phraya Hospital. Corinne and I went there and arrived right behind an IRC ambulance and officials. The Thai medical attendants had very efficiently bandaged his leg and started an IV. Arrangements were made for the man's transfer to KID, and I rode in the ambulance with him.

En route to KID, while I did my best to comfort and monitor this poor victim, I thought about that parade of healthy young Khmers. I wondered if peace would be served better by another parade, this one with drums muffled and the marchers all the amputees I see walking with crutches in the camp.

Tomorrow I am off but will go to Site 8 to help with pregnancy screening. I have always wanted to see Site 8 camp; otherwise I would not go, for it is a two-hour drive each way, and I have been so busy lately I could use a lazy day.

12 February 1989

Site 8 is a rather unique camp in many ways. It is a Khmer Rouge camp, and as such is often threatened by shellfire. Situation 1, which was called today during our visit, is considered *tomada*—that is, routine.

CARE has feeding responsibility at Site 8, and a responsibility to be sure that only pregnant women receive the augmented ration due them. They are entitled to this extra ration from the fourth month of pregnancy on. Pregnancy screening is carried out in a very regimented fashion. "New" pregnant women at four months are lined up in one section and are checked only by women. "Old" pregnant women are in another section, the one in which I worked. The women are lined up in rows and pass through gates to the checker and the distributor. As checker, it was my job to peruse each lady's prenatal card, and if the size of her belly seemed consistent with the dates on her card, the distributor gave her a ticket for extra rations. If the size of her belly did not coincide, I felt her belly, which caused great giggling of applicant and surrounding ladies.

The grounds of Site 8 are quite neat in contrast to Site 2, and the roads and pathways are well maintained, no doubt evidence of the stern code of the Khmer Rouge. One can admire discipline in a social group, but it is bought at a price. Watching the people a little distance from me, they seemed somber and less openly friendly than those at Site 2. The population seemed to me to be made up mostly of women and children, with very few young men evident. They must have been someplace else. Out on a military mission?

15 February 1989

Last day in camp. I think I have made all the proper arrangements for our little party. This will be a frugal party, but this tour I have worked so much with all the services on the platform, I can't just put on a party for Peds. Pop, ice, cookies and a bar of Lux toilet soap for 170 workers paid for at the grocery, pass in my pocket—what else? Emotions in control?

16 February 1989

Debbie has made all of the bureaucratic arrangements to take nine Khmers for a several-day trip to Surin, a distant border camp where our Khmer teachers will observe and exchange knowledge and experience with other Khmers. En route they stayed overnight at our house.

Debbie bought a wonderful menu of takeout Khmer and Thai food at local restaurants. After dinner, our house rang with laughter and murmured with contented talk incident to a wild card game called UNO and Scrabble and dominoes. When I got up early this morning, I saw the quiet forms of Khmers sleeping on pads in our front room, and I realized that for some of these people it was their first taste of freedom in years. What a wonderful gift Debbie has given them. Arlys and Edie, also teachers on the ARC staff, have also invested themselves in the work, energy and expense incident to such trips—truly gifts of love. I work with some wonderful people.

21 February 1989

I am running the OPD while the rest of the staff is attending a workshop on evaluation techniques. The medical care delivery system here is very different from Site 2. Since the population is a transient one, education of a Khmer health worker staff is not a reasonable goal. As a result, I have no well-trained medic to see the patient, with me in a supporting role only. Instead, here I interview the patient through an interpreter, examine the patient, arrange for lab work and write the prescription. This is also a more sophisticated level of care, with more lab and X-ray available. Today I learned that gastroscopy (a procedure using an optical instrument to see inside the stomach) is available. I wonder what it is like to look at a hookworm eyeball to eyeball?

23 February 1989

I work in the OPD and at a reasonably easy pace. We are assisted by interpreters. While we see mostly Vietnamese patients, there is the occasional Khmer, Lao and Hmong. Here the diseases of sophistication and chronic stress are much more common than at Site 2. Hypertension, depression and functional GI distress are frequent. Much as I appreciate the skill and help of trained medics, it is kind of nice to be back into hands-on medicine.

24 February 1989

I am really enjoying my short tour at Phanat Nikhom. It is different here from Site 2 South in a number of ways. The refugees in camp fall into three general groups. There are those who "have the name." That is, they have been assigned a definite date for their flight and know their city of destination. The people in this group, common to life over here, hold mixed emotions: happiness that their long-held hopes are coming to fruition, anxiety over what life will be like in their new country, grief at parting with friends and family members. Another group has arrived here, having successfully passed many of the hurdles, but still they "don't have the name." For them, incarceration in Phanat Nikhom camp is for an indefinite time, some for years, and for some only disappointment lies ahead. The last group—for one or another bureaucratic or diplomatic reason—has been labeled as "ineligible" for expatriation. They have no further hope along that line, and accept this with attitudes that vary from severe depression to relief. From these groups come the patients we see, and their symptoms are often clouded by how they see their situation.

| *Return*

Like most refugee workers, my emotional status during the last few days of my tour at Site 2 was marked by the conflicting feelings of enthusiastic anticipation of reunion with my wife, family and friends, and the grief of parting with other friends. Reality forced me to recognize that many of these latter I would not see again. I asked Jip what Buddha would tell me about this mortal and emotional conflict. With a beautiful smile, she promptly replied, "Live in the here and now"—simple words, but bearing magic. Saying good-bye to a friend is an opportunity to express and to hear wonderful words of love, admiration and gratitude, thoughts that we often harbor but fail to express in the course of our daily lives. And so, thanks to those simple words, "live in the here and now," my good-bye times in Site 2, Ta Phraya and Aran were really times of joy for me.

I spent three days in Aran, days of shopping, of good-byes, of shared meals, of walks and bike rides. The most remarkable event was Father Pierre's Saturday evening Mass. He started his homily with the unusual statement that he was tired, having had a demanding and discouraging day. He ended it with the statement, "This time of imprisonment for our Khmer and Vietnamese friends on the border cannot go on; it must end, and it will end soon." There are many indications that what Father Pierre says is true. In his prayer, Father Pierre prayed for my family and me. What a privilege it has been to know this great man.

The Trip Home

In Phanat Nikhom, I heard that ICM was looking for a physician willing to fly as medical escort for a sick baby who was to go to Boise, Idaho. This sounded like my type of deal, and I talked further with Dr. Philippe, the French doctor in Phanat Nikhom. He was pleased to have me as a volunteer, checked with the ICM office in Bangkok, and I arranged to meet with them on Friday.

ICM stands for Intergovernmental Committee for Migration. They have the responsibility of making arrangements for the transport of refugees to accepting countries. It is a large organization, employing persons from many countries, including Thailand. At this stage, I was informed of two not so minor complications. I was to serve as medical escort for *three* sick patients and shepherd 50 other refugees on this transpacific flight to the U.S. I could have refused, but learning that this had been done many times, I felt it was well within reason for me to undertake this responsibility. The other problem presented was a change in sponsorship, with the result the little baby and family were to go to Hartford, Connecticut.

The child I was to accompany to the U.S. was nearly five months old. She was born with a cystic hygroma in the neck—a benign tumor that is very difficult to remove completely, often requiring repeated surgeries.

At 4:00 A.M. on 6 March, I made my way to Bangkok General Hospital, where, in the semidarkness, our crowd of immigrants gathered. The sick child, my major responsibility, and an older man with the residual defects of a stroke rode to the airport in an ambulance, and the rest of us in a bus.

At the airport, the ICM shepherd, for that is my name for this work, managed to get us all through the airport and customs procedures.

Our trip across the Pacific was by Northwest Airlines. The flight crew was extremely attentive. The parents of the baby were expert in observations and ministrations. All went well, except that our battery-driven suction machine, theoretically good for 24 hours use, failed us about three hours from San Francisco.

Little Phal Sophany was admitted to San Francisco General Hospital, where she stayed for four days. After two serious episodes of respiratory distress, Phal stabilized, and on Friday we left the hospital.

Our flight across this great country went very well. We arrived at the airport in Hartford late in the evening, to be greeted by the pastor of the sponsoring church and various supporting people. By this time I was fairly mentally fogged. I was taken to a nearby Holiday Inn, and slept well. In the morning, I awakened to a cold but bright day. Imperceptibly, my reentry started—an American breakfast and reading the morning paper, with its potpourri of news, good and bad, depending on how you look at it. Later I took the airport limousine. At the airport, I thought about our country. On this one planeload, I had accompanied 37 immigrants to this land. Three of them had significant medical problems, while the rest presumably were in satisfactory health. Some of these immigrants, like Phal Sophany and family, would find a warm welcome, and some will have to largely find their own way. Amongst the Southeast Asian refugees who made their way here in previous years, there are those who have become scholars, scientists, teachers and social workers. There are many who have set outstanding examples of family life and industry. To this new group of immigrants, I say welcome and wish them happiness in our land.

Tour X

The Sound of Distant Fire

1–2 September 1989
Crossing International Dateline

It was tough saying good-bye to Gwen. We had been through a stress-ful period remodeling a little room in our house. Somehow we man-aged to get things done so that we could have a wonderful 24 hours in town, including a nice dinner, a good movie and a good-bye to Gwen's aging mother. Time passes more rapidly as one ages, but right now six months seems a long time—a significant portion of the time many of us have left.

As I write this, we are high above the Pacific, halfway to Hong Kong. In these hours, thoughts about plastering and painting, social engage-ments and obligations have left. They are replaced by considerations about the situations I will find in Bangkok and on the border, and by thoughts about how I can best serve these people, thus justifying the sacrifices of my dear wife, family and friends.

The flight to Hong Kong and then on to Bangkok went well, as did immigration at the airport. There I was greeted by Bob Medrala, ARC Thailand director. He is a dear friend of a number of years. En route from the airport, he brought me up-to-date. In general, the morale and physical condition of the ARC team are good. This is a tense time on the border. The Minneapolis director of ARC was here recently and experienced a Situation 2. The sound of artillery fire has been heard frequently in recent weeks, but no shells landed in camp.

Bob and I sat and talked in the hotel restaurant for some time. In my little hotel room, I doffed my clothes and crashed, only to awaken bright eyed at 3:30 A.M. The windows here are screened, but at least one mosquito made it through. I have a number of bites on my arms.

3 September 1989

In the U.S. we call them alleys, but in Thailand they are called *sois* and identified either by a name or a number, which forms an important segment of the address. A *soi* is generally a paved road just wide enough for single-car traffic, with a very narrow space for pedestrians. Following the usual Thai traffic custom, cars race down these narrow roadways with little regard for pedestrians, and pass opposing traffic with only inches to spare. It is not unusual to come upon two vehicles headed in opposite directions, hood to hood and drivers arguing about who should back up.

Despite the narrowness of these roadways, they are often the site of an entrepreneurial business getting its start. If, for instance, you wish to start a restaurant and have limited funds, a *soi* is a good place to begin. All you need are some folding tables, a few camp chairs, a push cart bearing a charcoal burner, a few pots and pans, and some plates and utensils. Gather some rice or noodles, green vegetables, spices, a little bit of meat, and you are in business. Actually these stands, and there are hundreds of them, offer some of the best of Thai cooking. This morning, early, as I left for some shopping, I came upon one of these businesses and could not go on without having my first Thai meal of fried rice for breakfast—good! (There I go, writing about food again.)

4 September 1989

Last evening I went to the home of Jim and Elizabeth Anderson and Susan Walker. Susan was with ARC during my early days here. She is now Thailand director for Operation Handicap International, a French organization. Jim is Thailand director for the International Rescue Committee, and Elizabeth, pregnant and almost ready to deliver, is program manager for Joint Voluntary Agency.

These people, besides working hard in their assigned positions, are also very active in international circles here, working hard for the human rights of the Khmers. After a very good Thai-style dinner, we sat and talked for some time, them telling me of changing times here. Talking with them convinced me that, besides working with the Khmers, I want to do what I can to influence the political powers here to take actions that will have a real effect on improving the day-to-day lives of the Khmers and to offer them some hope.

5 September 1989

I left the Opera Hotel by Aran taxi about 1:30 P.M. yesterday. In Aran at House 1, I was greeted by several of the Thai drivers and Bobbie Caraher, field coordinator. She and I drove out to Ta Phraya, where Edie had prepared a very nice welcoming dinner.

As I sit here in this little room and write, it is moderately warm and muggy. Through the open windows, I hear the typical sounds of Thailand—birds chirping, motors, some purring, some growling and some snarling. A few minutes ago, the street loudspeakers gave forth with the pleasant tune of the national anthem.

There are two houses in this ARC compound, the office house and the gingerbread house—the latter name relating to some architect's effort to fancy up the exterior decor. Currently, I am in the gingerbread house, but expect to move to the office house in a few days.

6 September 1989

Before I forget, let me assure you that your many hours of work on making those cookies and individually wrapping them have been very much appreciated. Indeed, it is my understanding that the following conversation took place many times. "Have you heard? Papa Louis has come back." "Oh good, did he bring cookies?"

7 September 1989

To the Babel of tongues here, a new term is added: "log frame," short for logical framework. This is a system coming into use by large companies and now reaching into ARC. It is a system applied to planning for desired changes, an outline of goals, methods, assumptions and expected difficulties, and provides a way to evaluate the pace of success or failure of attaining goals. Rolf Sartorious, from the Minneapolis office, is the teacher and proponent. Like the computer world, it has its own vocabulary, adding new definitions to words commonly used in our language.

Thus, for this old brain, it is like a new language. Like all new learning, one grasps bits and pieces, which in gradual steps develop into understanding. Part of my problem is that the emphasis on this comes at a time when demands are great on the Peds ward.

This is a difficult time on Peds. There has been a change in Khmer personnel, and new leaders are learning to deal with their new responsibilities. There is a change in farang staff too, as several complete their tours and new people assume position. While all this goes on, there has been a marked increase in admissions, mostly infants with gastroenteritis. As a result, there are many IV bottles hanging, a sure sign that there are great demands placed on the Khmer medical staff. If all of the above sounds negative, let me assure you there are still those wonderful people to work with.

8 September 1989

Suddenly I realized that I have failed to talk about the military situation here. It is very quiet, with only the rare and distant sound of artillery. We have had only two Situation 1s, and those I think only because of hair-trigger response by Security sensitized by the events of March and April.

Arlys Herem is in Bangkok and arrives here tomorrow.

9 September 1989

Yesterday was a good day on Peds. Our influx of gastroenteritis cases has moderated and Saeroen, our clinic chief, and Sakun, Fellow, are doing well.

Although the countryside is green, I am told that the rainy season has not produced much rain and reservoirs are down. It did rain heavily on Thursday and a little yesterday. Today, there is bright sunshine, and it is already hot.

10 September 1989

The dinner I put on last night went very well. The coleslaw in particular was good. Yesterday was a full day. I went for two bike rides. At one place I came upon the body of a dog lying in the highway. Seeing the cars dodge around this, I stopped and dragged it off the road. I have done my good deed for this trip. Chris Elias came in the early afternoon, and I spent several hours hearing about life inside Cambodia. Like so much of life over here, his report is a mix of the good and the bad. They are making progress there in establishing medical services, food distribution, etc.; on the other hand, many are living in poverty. The general feeling is that with the withdrawal of Vietnamese troops, war between the Khmer Rouge and the Heng Samrin government is viewed as inevitable. Chris's feeling is that the people from the border will be received without retribution.

11 September 1989

ANTS! Soon I shall try to find a book and read about them, for they cause me anger and frustration, emotions not good to have over here. This must be the season when they hatch, for there are countless numbers of them, tiny ones that are just barely perceptible on the skin, that crawl on your plate or invade your lunch. Surely in the grand scheme of things, they must play a significant role, and perhaps if I learn about them they won't bother me so much.

I worked yesterday, again a busy day. I would guess that the average census for the Peds ward is around 40, but we are at 67. It is no wonder that the little child I will call Tic Tic was sort of lost in the melee. She is two months old, born at home and reported to have weighed 2.5 kg at birth. On admission, her weight was 2.4 kg. The medics have had difficulty in getting a detailed history. Apparently it was a normal birth, but in the following days the mother became ill and gave the child for adoption to a 42-year-old lady. The adoptive mother brought the child in because she had diarrhea. Such adoptions are not uncommon in Khmer life, and often the results are not good. Lacking breast milk, the adoptive mother buys powdered formula in the market. The ambient warm temperature, the lack of potable water, and ignorance on the part of those who care for the baby often result in the baby bottle rolling around on the dirt floor and becoming a culture tube. This little fading flame of life has the aged appearance of malnutrition and dehydration. I fear that despite our best efforts this tiny flame will go out. We shall do our best.

12 September 1989

I have been living in temporary status in the gingerbread house. As a result, I have unpacked only to the degree necessary to function. With Jan and David having vacated the little house on the reservoir, there is much moving around contemplated, and I will likely be moving into the office house, where my old friends Arlys, Debbie and Corinne live. I look forward to getting unpacked and fully organized.

Little Tic Tic is doing better. The maternal-child health ladies found a wet nurse, and this tiny spark of life is eating well.

13 September 1989

Yesterday was a routine day until 4:00 P.M., when Alpha III came running to announce Situation 2. With speed and calmness and a sense of the inevitable, we got into the trucks and drove to the Situation 2 meeting point on the periphery of camp. Once again I experienced that mix of feeling engendered by our leaving these people, our friends, to their fate.

Eventually we were told that a shell had landed in Site 2 North, a dud that did not explode, and no one was injured. With that news we were released and headed for Ta Phraya. Now we await news as to whether or not we can go to camp today.

Every day we hear rumors of events portending military action on the border. I have great admiration for the young people with whom I work, for they continue in their labors unaffected.

14 September 1989

This letter will be written very hurriedly, since I got up late. Yesterday the sounds of artillery broke out, and Situation 2 was called quickly. We evacuated in good shape. Later we were told it was a battle between KPNLF [Khmer People's National Liberation Front] and Hun Sen forces. The old-timers predict that this will go on for months now. Today we are on limited access. I will be in charge of the team in camp, so it will be a busy day for me.

Last night Bob Maat gave me the pleasure of coming by to talk. He looks very good. He lives with his Thai farmer family and has worked through the rice-planting season. It is now the quiet time for farmers, and Bob is writing and awaiting "the Light" to direct his path. He would like to work on repatriation or to work in Cambodia, but for now just waits. What a privilege to know him. He, like many others, asks about you.

18 September 1989

One day last week the medic presented the case of a little four-year-old boy, whom I shall call Supohl. Supohl had fever and vomiting for three days. On the day of admission, his mother noted that he was not walking well. His mother, sadly enough, is typical of many. Her husband, a soldier, died in the fighting three years ago. She lives the best she can on the subsistence-level rations provided by UNBRO. She presented the boy's "Road to Health" card, which was so torn and dirty we could not read it. She assures us he had all his immunizations. Supohl shows paralysis of his right leg and partial paralysis of his left leg. Polio? Guillain-Barré? Beriberi? We probably will not know.

Later—evening

I had a bucketful of potatoes to peel, along with a conviction that I had seen one of those super Thai vegetable peelers in this house—one that I had purchased on a previous trip and now could not find. Very near our house is a Thai grocery/hardware/gas station operated by a Thai man and wife, who are also our landlords. They are very accommodating, and no doubt are building up a nice retirement income from our business. Having searched all possible places in our house, I finally went to the grocery. It took a bit of gesturing plus my repetition of *mah fah rong,* Thai for "potato," until the lady understood what I wanted. She indicated she had one. The lady looked patiently and soon I joined her, lifting and shifting various packages, searching for the elusive object. She kept saying in her broken English, "I know, I know." Eventually, she called her husband from his hammock and he joined the search. Suddenly she squealed a Thai word that could only mean that she had found it. Thirty-five baht poorer, I returned to our kitchen. I spied a dish towel that had escaped my previous search, and sure enough, underneath it was my peeler. I did not have the nerve to return the new one.

The last few days have been militarily quiet. Today I sat on a bench in Peds and talked with one of our new medics. He said that every night there is much artillery firing, and observed, "It is strange that if such firing were occurring in the daytime it would be Situation 3 for the farangs, but for the Khmers at night it is Situation 0."

Another Khmer joined us and said, "I know why that is—the farangs are much more valuable than us." Sad. Sad.

23 September 1989

It is Saturday and here I sit at the computer. During my lesson with Edie the other day, I made a long list of notes about how to get this machine going, and I now can only hope that I have it right. On the ground floor of this office house there is a large room dedicated to this computer. The whole thing is somewhat complicated from the start. First, you must know and remember the numbers for the combination lock to get in here. Next, you need to open the grate door to ventilate the air conditioner. Then, you turn on a series of switches in proper order to activate the air conditioner, the monitor, the computer and the printer. Consulting my list, I find the proper help keys, which in computer language direct me how to get started. At this stage in my learning, I can only hope that when it comes to printing I will punch the right button.

It is a temptation to ramble on about the irony of sitting in this air-conditioned tomb, operating 20th-century equipment, while only a few feet from me a group of construction workers do their thing with centuries-old tools and methods, and on the street carts pass drawn by oxen or men much like they have done for years. I should hasten to add that this is not a peculiarity solely of ARC's but common to most of the Volags here. It really is a manifestation of the current emphasis on evaluation, programs and goals. I should also point out that the air-conditioning is for the benefit of the computer, not for the operator.

Lana has moved to the house previously occupied by Jan and David, leaving a room open in this office house where Debbie and Arlys live. I had planned to move into Lana's old room, but I think for the time being I will stay in the gingerbread house. After I finish this letter I am going to really unpack at last. In contrast to previous tours, all of these houses operate on an "each individual for himself" basis. In view of this, I think I will just stay in my own little room away from the commotion of the office house, which has an aura at times like a bus station, somewhat like the old House 1.

My screen tells me that I have now started on page 2, so I might as well keep going for a while. I do think I am typing a little faster. The spell checker on this instrument operates a little differently than the Brother. It is activated at the end of a document, and starting from the beginning sorts out each misspelled word and gives you the choice to correct or ignore. I fear that will take me some time.

It is time for me to try the printing operation. If you hear a loud noise, you will know I have goofed up 1½ hours of work. It took me a half-hour searching how to get out of spell checker into printing mode, and more time to figure out how to exit.

23 September—later

I hope my long word processor letter reaches you. I spent several hours on it this morning. I work in camp tomorrow along with Annette Frost, who is platform nurse. She comes from farm country north of Minneapolis. She is a very nice person and easy to work with. She lives in Aran. I invited her to come to Ta Phraya early for breakfast. That's a long explanation for why I am writing a second time today—so I will have time to fix breakfast.

25 September 1989

Yesterday, Sunday, was my day to work. It was a quiet day. Only two people work on Sundays, an MD and a nurse. Annette was sick on Saturday and got worse by noontime yesterday, so she went home.

In recent letters, you expressed concern about the military situation here. Thus far, all the action has been distant from us, and furthermore you can be sure that UNBRO and ICRC are very protective.

On the steps of the office house, where we leave our shoes or flip-flops, there are often ants. Yesterday, when I came down the stairs and slipped on my shoes, I realized they had been invaded and these were stinging ants. I fully expected my feet to be swollen this morning, but they were not.

28 September 1989

I am now in the ARC office in Aran. The first floor of this building is comprised of a large gathering room, and the remainder is warehouse-storage. The second floor has the office—a large L-shaped room, with Brian occupying one part and several desks in the other part. The other room upstairs is the guestroom. Unlike the office, it is not air-conditioned and gets very hot in the afternoon, since it faces west. Hence, I am sitting in the AC comfort of the office.

My vacation was scheduled Tuesday to Saturday. Actually, I came to Aran on Monday night and stayed here in the office. I was still undecided about where to go. I decided to go to the Rayong Resort. It turns out that this is a new and very fancy resort located on the beach looking out toward Ko Samet. It was beautiful, with lawns, coconut trees extending down to the sand, and surf. It was also expensive and just a little too nice for my taste, so I only stayed overnight. On Wednesday, I traveled about 20 km to Ban Pay, and there took a bus to Bangkok. I checked into a cheapie hotel, where I showered and slept. This morning, I took a bus to Aran and here I am. As I look back on the past 72 hours, it seems like most of the waking hours I spent on a bus.

This does not sound like much of a vacation, but I did see the central part of Thailand, the "mountains," and a lot of verdant agriculture. It must have been enough vacation, for I found myself eager to get back to Ta Phraya and will return tomorrow, a day early. I didn't have any particular adventures during these days.

29 September 1989

On arriving in Ta Phraya, I found several letters waiting for me. I guess I didn't tell you that Pytt has moved to the reservoir house to live with Lana. Michael moved to House 4 in Aran for the social life. That leaves Suwit (Thai driver) and me here. However, Lori, Edie's replacement, arrives tomorrow and is expected to move in here.

Edie was just here. Apparently, spotter planes report that there is a big military buildup around Site 2, and evacuation is imminent. I'm not sure at this point whether I will work tomorrow or Sunday. Once again, I would remind you that I am decided to tell it like it is and also that ICRC and UNBRO are determined to do everything to keep us safe. I do not consider myself a brave person. For reasons I don't understand, I am not made fearful by this situation. I take comfort that by the time this reaches you the events of the next few days will be history, and you will know that I am all right.

30 September 1989

It is not too bad to awaken to the sound of birds chirping and roosters crowing. This morning I was awakened at 5:00 to the sound of distant artillery fire. Gradually, the sound gets louder and nearer. A few minutes ago, I heard a rapid-fire gun for the first time. Our house trembles with the reverberations. I hesitate to write this, since here I sit in comfort and relative safety, while some kilometers away Khmers cringe in ditches, bunkers and flooded rice fields. If this is the expected offensive, the artillery fire will cease and the infantry will advance. In their hands and hanging from their belts are weapons made by Russia, the European countries and, to our shame, the United States.

The radio announces that we are on limited access, and I will remain in Ta Phraya. Right now the sound of guns has silenced. The people of this little village have been through this many times, and I hear the sounds of normal life here: carpenters pound, local cars growl by, and the conversation I hear is calm and routine.

Lori arrives tonight; she will have quite an introduction to life on the border.

1 October 1989

The official news, reliable or not, is that the KPNLF forces won the battle yesterday against the Heng Samrin forces, and have taken over the old Nong Chan and Nong Samet area. A force of 300 Heng Samrin forces remains about 2 km from Site 2, but it is believed they will not fight further.

I am skeptical about such reports, but for now things are quiet.

Site 2 is closed today and scheduled for limited medical access for to-morrow. Yesterday, I was on standby and made two ambulance trips from Ta Phraya to KID, with patient transfers from our medics in Site 2. No shells landed in Site 2. Michael is on schedule for tomorrow, so it appears I will have both today and tomorrow off, except for standby duty today. I should get some correspondence taken care of.

Yesterday, I typed a medical report on Tep Chan Thou, Sok Saly's wife, who has asthma, to send to Glenda Potter, lawyer and Khmer advocate in Minneapolis. In trying to get into spell check, I managed to press a magic button and all my typing disappeared—irk, irk. Will try again tomorrow.

3 October 1989

Today I am scheduled to work, but whether or not it will be camp closed, limited medical access (one MD, Alpha III, and one nurse) or full hospital crew is in question. In the distance I hear artillery fire. It was quiet last night, but this morning they are at it again.

4 October 1989

We awakened again to the sound of distant artillery fire, lots of it. What will that mean to our schedule today?

5 October 1989

The sound of distant artillery fire has been so frequent here that it becomes a part of life.

Yesterday morning we awakened to those dull thuds. After making our usual morning preparations, we gathered around the office porch and listened to the UNBRO radio, which would tell us whether or not we could go to camp. Eventually, we were told to proceed as far as Kok Prick, a crossroads, and wait there. A little restaurant provided us with coffee, and we waited. Word came we were to return to Ta Phraya.

Midmorning, back at home, I wrote a little and played a game of chess with Michael, who is a beginner but whose razor-sharp mind gives promise that he probably will be winning soon.

Once again the radio summoned us with the announcement that a limited team could go to camp. Arriving there, it is always satisfying and a little surprising that the Khmers have things so well in hand. Nevertheless, I see additional lines of worry and stress etched into their faces.

Work went well through the noon hour. Once again the distant thunder started. We were at Situation 1. I know not how the Khmers made the diagnosis, but as the frequency of distant rumbling increased, the Khmers began to load our trucks with the materials to go. Slowly the noise increased, and to no one's surprise the radio announcement of Situation 2 came—the signal to evacuate. Being sure that all were accounted for, I drove our van out onto the road. Words are poor tools in my hands to describe the feelings I experience as I drive by the crowds of Khmers walking toward their huts and families. There is a feeling of concern for them, for my colleagues, a frustration that all of this represents an unnecessary tragedy, a feeling that by our flight we are deserting the people we came to serve. These feelings are augmented by the laconic radio voice that announces Situation 3, shelling in camp or very close. At the Situation 3 meeting place, we are checked out and proceed to our homes. Our bodies are sweated and dirty as usual, but the pour-on shower fails to remove that layer of doubt and questioning—why is it that we are chosen to escape while those poor people remain?

Later we learn that land mines within 2 km of the camp exploded, causing the Situation 3. No casualties. It is morning as I write. Birds sing, insects buzz, roosters crow and motorcycles snarl. In the distance, there are dull booms.

9 October 1989

Sok Thim stayed with us over Saturday night. After dinner we played Scrabble, Sok Thim, Arlys, Lana and I. It was one of those games where I tried to play all my letters to no avail. Arlys did the same, and Sok Thim beat us solidly as a result. I came out a miserable third.

Today, we should be back to our regular schedule, since there has been little artillery fire the past few days. Today marks the 12th anniversary of the founding of the KPNLF, and I understand there will be parades. Once again I wish I could get a group of amputees to march.

11 October 1989

In all my time here in Thailand, I have never experienced as many crawling and flying insects as the past 24 hours. A few days ago, on the steps of the office house, I found a huge colony of ants. With water, broom and finally ant spray, I got rid of them. Two days later, there was a recurrence. I passed them by to complete my errand. When I came back a few minutes later, the ants were replaced by some larger, black insects that fly. These black predators apparently are nature's answer to ants, for they appeared to have eaten them all. As a result, there are now far fewer ants, but the air is full of these black bugs. Our kitchen is not screened, and the air is full of them. They bounce off one's head like raindrops. They invade whatever you are eating or drinking.

Last night was unusual for me: I did not sleep well. My single sheet caused me to perspire, and whenever I shifted it off my skin, I was immediately attacked by insects. Finally, I awakened enough to turn on my fan, which both cooled me and seemed to discourage the attacking insects. The last part of the night I slept well.

There is a definite improvement in the performance of the Peds ward. On his day off this week, the chief medic worked hard until 2:00 P.M. He had been on call the night before. He told me that during the night the Thai ambulance driver had indicated a child should be taken to KID. Khmers are easily intimidated by farangs and Thais, but this medic, confident in his training and experience, examined the child and with courage told the ambulance driver that the child should stay with us.

14 October 1989

Each day brings its problems, more so recently it seems. A few days ago, a young man was admitted to the adult ward with malaria. Despite his strong and healthy-appearing body, he failed to respond to treatment and went into coma. Despite excellent care by medics, nurses and health workers, he remained in coma, and after several days he died.

It was obvious that this young man was high in the social and political structure, for his bed was constantly surrounded by a group of family and friends. Soon after the death, a man, apparently a family friend, made a formal threat of death to the attending medic and the Khmer hospital administrator. It was taken very seriously by the farang and Khmer staff. As a result, there were meetings yesterday and a steady parade of security people. The saddest scene was the Khmer medic, shaken by fear, bewildered by the question of how this could happen to him and overwhelmed by the danger to himself and his family. His tearful wife sat by him, holding their youngest child.

This situation was made all the more poignant for us who consider Savan one of the most knowledgeable, skillful, reliable and self-giving of medics. For now, all we can do is offer what comfort and protection we can, and see that his family is hidden in a "safe" house.

The grace, beauty and generally kind behavior of this people tend to make us forget that there is a thread of violence manifested by the Pol Pot era and the still present, unyielding hatred of the Vietnamese.

I'm sorry to send such a grim account for today's letter. Aside from this, my work in Peds goes well, and yesterday for the first time in weeks the situation was "o" all day.

18 October 1989
Bangkok

Sok Thim—"We Had Only Our Hands"

The "border." That word describes a meandering strip of land, where artillery shells land, where land mines lie in wait for those who would pass, and armed men watch for trespassers. A rather indefinite line that marks the territorial limits of Thailand and Cambodia, it also marks two segments in the life of Sok Thim.

Born in 1955, Sok Thim grew up in a middle-class family in the suburbs of Phnom Penh. His father was an engineer by training, but in the early '70s was a member of the body guard of then president, Lon Nol.

The fall of the Lon Nol government and the beginning cataclysm of Pol Pot made escape imperative, and Sok Thim and family fled to Battambang, a large city in western Cambodia. Here this family hid its former identity and melded into society.

By 1976, the Khmer Rouge were to be found most everywhere. Sok Thim, then 21, was sent to the rice fields. Working from dawn to dusk, it was hard and frustrating, for they had no tools or equipment. Lacking plows and beasts of burden, they were required to tramp through the rice paddies in the vain hope that their feet would prepare the paddy for planting. Rice culture is dependent upon careful management of water levels. Dikes and dams are needed, and these Sok Thim and his group were required to dig, transport and construct of mud. They had no tools, and of this time Sok Thim says, "We had only our hands."

In 1977, Sok Thim decided it was time to marry—a difficult thing to arrange, since their every moment was observed and governed by Khmer Rouge overseers. Those of us who have had no direct association with the Pol Pot minions tend to picture them all as monsters, but strangely enough Sok Thim's overseer had retained some spark of human compassion, and he aided Sok Thim in gaining permission to marry. Late that year their first child was born.

Through 1977 and 1978, Sok Thim continued his daily toil in the fields. By 1979, the Vietnamese and Heng Samrin forces had expelled the Khmer Rouge. Sok Thim was approached and offered a minor position of leadership, but he declined, preferring to work in the fields while his mind pondered what would be best for the future of his family.

In 1983, at great risk, Sok Thim and his family crossed the border and entered the Nong Samet camp. The Khmer camp administration, recognizing his abilities, referred him to the American Refugee Committee, and there he met his first volunteer worker, Marike Keuning Landstrom from Holland.

Months of training followed, and Sok Thim became a medic. A new chapter in his life began when he met Bob Maat, a Jesuit Brother and physician's assistant. Brother Bob, a wonderful combination of skill, personality and disciplined Jesuit training, had persuaded the authorities to allow him to try setting up a TB treatment program on the border. Already Brother Bob had the dream of guiding this program to the point that it could become totally Khmer operated. In Sok Thim, he found his compatriot. With Sok Thim as coordinator, the ARC TB program became the first truly Khmer-operated therapeutic center in 1987. Later, Sok Thim became UNBRO TB coordinator for all the border camps.

One of the techniques of interviewing is to ask the patient to describe a typical day in their lives. For Sok Thim, the day begins early. On arising, he writes. He writes stories of imaginary people and places. Later he gets these reproduced, and then his wife assembles them in a little booklet. They then are distributed to eager customers for sale or rent. From this activity, Sok Thim derives additional income for his family. Having finished his writing, Sok Thim proceeds to his daily work as UNBRO coordinator of TB treatment on the border. At the end of the day, this good father returns to his home, where he spends an hour after dinner with each of his two children, reviewing their schoolwork. When one realizes that much of this activity is carried out in a bamboo hut, with only the dim light of a little lantern, one senses the measure of this fine father. He not only has contributed greatly to his people but also is preparing his children to serve their generation.

To Sok Thim and his family, to that unknown minor Khmer Rouge leader, to Khmer administration, to Marike, to Brother Bob, and to untold others who have aided Sok Thim, we offer our thanks and admiration. Not only have hundreds of Khmer been successfully treated for tuberculosis, but you also have shown us a path worthy of following.

19 October 1989

Last evening and this morning, I worked on the AIDS course. It reminds me of when I was in medical school and studied the dread diseases—to the extent that I became convinced I had Hodgkin's disease.

I often have some minor skin eruption on my hands, and this course really emphasizes the acquiring of AIDS through exposure to broken skin. I'm glad AIDS has not yet been detected in our Khmer population. This course would indicate that a number of medical workers have turned HIV+ from this type of exposure in the past several years.

20 October 1989

The Narai Hotel, site of the 12th Annual Conference of the Committee for the Coordination of Services to Displaced Persons in Thailand. This is a relatively new and modern hotel. The theme for this anniversary meeting was repatriation. It was an all-day affair, well worth attending.

25 October 1989

Yesterday, we awakened to the sound of intense but distant artillery fire. It continued as we prepared to go to camp. We were approaching camp when our radios summoned us to return to Kok Prick, a village on the outskirts of Ta Phraya. There we waited along with our colleagues. After about one hour, we were allowed limited access to camp.

Strangely enough, the sound of artillery fire was even more distant from camp than it was in Ta Phraya. The Khmers seemed unusually comforted by our arrival. It was a quiet day. The census on the Peds ward has declined markedly.

26 October 1989

He was tired, wet with perspiration and dirtied with mud and with the mental and emotional residue that clung to him. Only a few hundred meters separated him from the barbed wire enclosure of Site 2 and the relative peace and comfort of the bamboo hut, his home. Too fatigued to watch where he walked, his eyes wandered, or perhaps the skill of the man who planted the land mine was unusually great. So near to home, his life was changed in an instant of unimaginable noise, flame and flying fragments of steel.

There were others nearby, and they picked up his shattered body and made it to the barbed wire, and then to the nearby ARC OPD 2. Martha was there, and with her crew of Khmer medics bundled this man into the back of a truck for the bumpy ride to the hospital.

We farangs who work in Site 2 have heard artillery fire and land mine explosions many times in the past weeks. Insulated by distances, and out of the usual line of military triage, we have not seen much of the scene at the site of those distant explosions. This changed with a radio call from Martha alerting us that she was bringing in a wounded man, hereafter known as a double amputee.

A crowd of Khmers, sprinkled with a few farangs, quickly gathered as the truck backed in. Eager hands grasped the stretcher bearing the man, his head spattered with blood, his lower legs a mass of gore with one foot dangling.

In the old Nong Samet days, other farangs and I were often present in similar situations, our hands engaged. But time has passed, and we have developed confidence in those we have taught. We stood back, and in awe and pride watched our Khmers in action. There was no doubt that Sok Saly was in charge. The mangled legs were bandaged, IVs started as if by magic, and in the few minutes it took the ambulance to arrive, the man, still in shock, was ready for the trip to KID hospital.

As the stretcher exited, I looked about me. Farangs with moist eyes looked stricken. A Khmer stood by the door, his rugged face had an expression that seemed to say, "This is what happens when Khmers fight one another." My own thoughts were of that mechanical device, the land mine, no doubt manufactured in some distant, so-called "civilized" nation.

America, America . . .

And crown thy good
With brotherhood
From sea to shining sea.

The writing of this has caused me inner turmoil, and I don't have it to go on to other things.

[A later letter completes the story: The double amputee died; he was a KPNLF soldier returning to Site 2 for R & R.]

29 October 1989

Today is Sunday, my day off and Debbie Webber's departure day. I slept in until 6:00 A.M. and did my usual car chores. Then I went to the market to buy pineapple, papaya and eggs. Debbie did not want a good-bye party. We settled on a family-style Sunday morning brunch. Arlys made delicious pancakes from scratch, I fried eggs, and we had the fruit and delicious percolator coffee provided by Lana. It was a very nice time.

30 October 1989

Louise Ross followed Denise as coordinator of midwifery. In the '60s, she and her husband, Chuck, were in Vietnam with International Volunteer

Service, and so we have a common bond. They were not in the highlands where I was, but we had some of the same experiences.

While Louise is here as midwife, her husband is here, writing a book on teaching industrial arts to learning disabled. They live in Aran. Louise is a very strong member of our team, with great understanding and compassion for the Khmers. Once again I am grateful for this opportunity.

31 October 1989

I am in the throes of one of my super head colds, with nasal congestion and a sore throat. I am considering staying home today. As if that were not enough, yesterday a chunk of tooth chipped off—not my old friend, which seems to be doing well. It is a right upper molar. I saved the piece and perhaps Dr. Arakasaka can glue it back in. I suppose I could spend this time going to Bangkok, but it is not a kindness to expose one's dentist to a cold like this.

1 November 1989

I have often written boastfully of what we have taught the Khmers. Today, Sakuen, our pediatric Fellow, taught me something. A bulging fontanel [soft spot on a baby's head] in this setting is all too often a sign of serious disease, such as meningitis, hydrocephalus or brain tumor. Today, Sakuen presented the case of an eight-month-old child with that fearsome sign. In listing the differential diagnosis in his soft voice, he mentioned overdose of vitamin A. I wasn't sure I had heard him right, but made a mental note to read up on this.

A genuine pediatrician would probably have had this information readily in his mind, but for me it was necessary that I look it up in *Nelson's Pediatrics*. The native diet of these people contains minimal vitamin A, and as a result, a potentially serious eye condition called xerophthalmia is common. Treatment for it is 100,000 units of vitamin A. I looked it up in the pediatrics book, and sure enough an overdose of vitamin A can cause bulging fontanel.

My Khmer friend had indeed taught me something. But be assured the Khmers have taught me many things. They have shown me courage, determination and self-discipline. They have taught me much about real values in life. They have taught me patience and acceptance. They have taught me more than I have taught them.

4 November 1989

I did make an appointment with the dentist. The trip to Bangkok was OK—I managed to sleep about half the time.

Dr. Arakasaka was her usual kind and skillful self. Instead of just gluing the fractured piece of tooth in, she chose to rebuild it. This required a great deal of drilling, all of which was without local anesthetic. Would you believe it, I don't think my pulse or blood pressure went up a point. I am indeed getting better about dentists.

The bus trip from Bangkok to Aran seemed endless. On arrival in Aran, I found the guest room in the office house available. I was to have my regrets later, for one of those outdoor movies with its chaotic sound effects was located nearby.

5 November 1989

Sovan, the medic in Adult Medicine, asked me to help with a patient. She is 54 years old, and the marks of a hard life are on her face. Her story was that her neighbor found her unconscious. After her arrival at the hospital, it was determined that she probably had some sort of heart failure and that life hung on a slender thread. I advised that we transfer her to KID, and because of her fragile condition I would ride in the ambulance with her.

A patient transferred to KID is allowed one accompanying family member. The only one available in this case was a 10-year-old granddaughter.

When I got in the ambulance, this girl was seated across from her grandmother and was using the grandmother's chart to fan her, for it was very hot. This is a common Khmer response to illness, and this little girl, obviously frightened by the whole experience, was determined to do the best possible job for her grandmother.

With the bumps and swaying of the ambulance the IV bottle was swinging back and forth, threatening to disconnect. Gently, I tried to indicate to this serious little girl that she should move to another seat so I could secure the IV bottle. Her black eyes sparkled as she shook her head and remained in her seat. After several attempts, I firmly indicated she must move.

I fixed the swinging plastic bottle securely and then indicated the girl could move back to her seat. Feeling very much the ugly American, I reached in my pocket and found 15 baht, which I tied in my red bandana and pressed into her hand. Now her beautiful eyes were wide and soft, and she brought her hands to her forehead in that beautiful expression of thanks. Later, I nearly dozed off only to be awakened by a sob. There were tears running down the cheeks of my little companion and perspiration on her brow. It was obvious she was carsick. I supported her thin little back against the lurching of the ambulance. We arrived safely at the hospital and I have hopes our patient will survive.

Once again I have learned something here: for those who are fortunate, a special love exists between grandchild and grandparent. I recalled with gratitude the special love that has existed between our children and their grandparents.

8 November 1989

Last night, I came to Aran to share dinner with three people who work with the Mennonite Central Committee. Stan and Myrna work in Phnom Penh, and Alan works in Phanat Nikhom. Stan is a sanitary engineer, Myrna is a veterinarian and Alan teaches English. There were 10 of us around the table, a variety of home countries were represented, and as usual there was a parade of Thai food. As we ate, I could hear bits of conversation common to life over here. Descriptions of home, experiences with the Khmer, pondering of the great questions of philosophy and the future—it was a great smorgasbord, both gastronomical and emotional.

9 November 1989

I did not complete my letter yesterday. The phone rang; it was UNBRO announcing that the periodic census of the population of Site 8 would occur on this date. The phone rang again, and it was Cheryl (she is the new field administrator who follows in Brian's position). Anne had stayed at her house, and Cheryl was calling to report that Anne had been sick all night with the GIs. I was faced with handling the big polio day, hosting the visit of the Mennonite group to Site 2 and greeting the U.S. ambassador to Thailand and the State Department undersecretary. It was a busy day. I made a few mistakes, but all in all it went off reasonably well. Somewhat aided by the unexpected census in Site 8, the pediatrician there had to postpone the polio immunization. One of the UNBRO officers was a big help in entertaining the Mennonite visitors, and so, as often happens, things were not as bad as I thought. The day ended with a meeting of Ta Phraya Volags to discuss plans for observation of UN Human Rights Day on 10 December. I am finding it hard to deal with this irony, since for the Khmers it is hard to consider human rights.

10 November 1989

We have had a total of 16 possible polio cases. Clinically, about four or five of these have classic signs and significant residuals. They appeared at a rate of about one per day for two weeks, and there have been none for six days. Little as I know about epidemiology, I am tempted to conclude it is over and that what we have seen is better termed an outbreak in a population fairly well protected by oral polio vaccine. We have had no deaths. A neurologist and pediatrician will come today to review our status. A more serious epidemic was experienced at Site 8.

11 November 1989

Dr. Paul, a neurologist from Eugene, Oregon, was still reviewing our polio cases when one of our medics came to get me. A two-year-old had presented at the Peds ward in critical condition. He had been passing blood in the stool for the past week. In exemplary fashion, our medics had assessed the problem, obtained a hemoglobin test at the lab in rapid time and started an IV. The hemoglobin was 3.3 grams, the lowest I have seen here. We started plasma, and I rode in the ambulance.

There are signs of wear and tear as we approach the halfway mark in this tour. My jumpsuits have holes in the pockets. I am running out of toothpaste, Basis soap, etc. But as for me, I am doing fine.

14 November 1989

Sometime during the night of Sunday–Monday, I became aware of cramping abdominal pain, soon followed by the first of several episodes of diarrhea. Following this, I developed general body aches and a feeling of fatigue and weakness, which except for trips to the bathroom kept me in my bed in a semisleep without even the energy to read. By late afternoon, I was able to get up to shower and shave and then back to bed. Until evening, even pineapple did not tempt me, and I took cold water only as therapy for developing fluid imbalance. To my surprise, I slept very well until 3:00 A.M., when I awakened to thoughts about not having written on 13 November—but even then I dozed for another hour. I have just had a butter-sugar sandwich and my first cup of coffee since the onset; so you see, I am well again.

The few times I have been ill have taught me something about what my patients have experienced. During these hours of illness I have thought often of the Khmers during Pol Pot times, of how they must have gone through many similar days without any comforts and knowing that failure to work meant the end of life.

18 November 1989

As I wrote recently, we hear rumors of impending battles but nothing threatening. There was a Situation 2 going to 3, back to 2 and then to 0 on Thursday when I was in Bangkok. It seems that two Khmers got into some argument, and when they couldn't settle it with axes, one of them went home and picked up two hand grenades. He threw the first one too far, and apparently it caused no damage. He threw the second grenade more accurately—enough that his opponent caught it and threw it back. Its explosion was close to both of these angry men. One died and the other was seriously wounded. Along with these tragedies, six onlookers were slightly wounded.

Some of the current tension is self-induced. It has to do with the approach of Human Rights Day, 10 December. Several of our colleagues have spent many hours pondering the imponderable, seeking to answer the unanswerable and turning out position papers. I often approach such things in an oversimplistic way. In this case, I believe that the Human Rights Proclamation of the UN says it all, and the statement that there are no human rights in Site 2 is adequate and accurate.

The other approaching source of pressure is social. Edie departs on Monday, and today we hold a good-bye open house.

Thursday is Thanksgiving, which the whole team will observe in Aran.

20 November 1989

Edie leaves this morning. The party went off very well.

The guns thunder in the distance, and the house again shakes. They sound a little closer, and I wouldn't be surprised if we will be disrupted in our work again.

Snakes are a big subject again. Suwit, the Thai driver who lives with us, killed a small cobra in his bedroom yesterday. Layne, operator of Fargo's, told us of killing a large cobra a few days ago that was found in the storeroom of the restaurant. They chased it out to the shouts and screams of patrons standing on chairs. I have developed several defensive measures: being careful where I step, watching for suitable weapons, and checking the menu at Fargo's for any new items.

Such is life in Thailand.

24 November 1989

The Thanksgiving party went very well. Arlys and Lori baked the chickens, and they were very good. Faced with 10 kilos of potatoes to peel, I schemed to entice Langi, our maid, to help me. First I made an omelet for breakfast, and she agreed to eat breakfast with us for the first time. While she did the dishes, I put out the bag of potatoes, brought out pans, two peelers and two stools. At this time, who should show up but Brother Bob Maat, who promptly sat down and picked up a potato and began to peel. There on the back porch in the pleasant sunshine we peeled away.

Pytt, a fundamentalist Christian, started our Thanksgiving by a short explanation of the origin of this holiday. This she ended with a prayer to the God that we believe in, whether we are Buddhist or Christian.

26 November 1989

There is heavy artillery fire in the distance. Occasionally a really loud one occurs and our house shakes a bit. None of it is close, and except for noise our local situation is calm. As a result, we have been able to work consistently with our Khmer health workers. There are moments of real satisfaction when a child has been helped by the right decision made. One of our recent encouragements was a little boy whose polio had left him unable to swallow—the only residual he showed of this devastating disease. We fed him with a nutritious liquid delivered through a nasogastric tube. Every morning I would see him, his face marred by the ever-present nasal tube, his large shining eyes looking at me, seeming to ask "Why," his grubby hands holding some morsel of food. His mother sat nearby; she too was awaiting a miracle that we could not deliver. But suddenly the miracle occurred. Every three or four days, we had removed his tube for clearing and tried him with a little water. Two days ago he drank. Yesterday, I saw him taking a thin porridge. What joy shone in his mother's eyes. The boy's eyes too seemed to express thanks. The thanks goes to the Khmer health workers, whose care had kept him in good nutritional state and avoided pneumonia.

3 December 1989

I am in Aran, sitting on the bus to Bangkok awaiting departure. I find it most convenient to go to Aran on the night before departure, but that isn't all that simple since I must be ready for whatever transportation I can arrange to Aran. This time it was an UNBRO car driven by Joe Hagenour, a clinical psychologist who once lived in Seattle. We had much to talk about.

In Aran, I went to dinner with Cheryl, field administrator, and Chuck Ross.

Arriving in Bangkok, I checked in at Uncle Rey's Guest House, a current favorite with ARC. A guest house generally has small, simply furnished rooms, no bellboys and no restaurant. This one is clean, has hot water for showers and costs 350 baht, whereas hotels of modest character cost about 700 baht and fancy ones are 1,000 to 2,000 baht.

4 December 1989

Last evening, I went to dinner with Nancy Greene to the Whole Earth Restaurant. While they feature vegetarian food, they also have a Thai menu; I had beef.

Nancy Greene is one of the interesting people who make life here fascinating. She graduated in international relations and then spent a number of years in business and public relations. During the Carter years, she was in charge of the advance party for Mrs. Carter and subsequently for President Carter. It was interesting to hear her talk about the Carters. It seems that they remained genuine, nice and kind people through it all.

5 December 1989

Here I am again in the guest room of the office house in Aran. My trip to Bangkok went well. Dr. Arakasuka was indeed on vacation. Her alternate was a young Thai lady to whom I was not introduced, so I don't know her name. She drilled out what must have been all of the old amalgam filling and put in a temporary. Within a week or two I am to return for a crown.

8 December 1989

One of the things I am noted for in Ta Phraya is my battered-up old pair of tennis shoes, which I wear with only the bottom holes laced so that I can slip into and out of them easily. I have a pair of dress oxfords here, which I wear only in Bangkok. On arriving in Bangkok recently, I noted that these shoes were disreputably scuffed. I knew by experience that finding a shoeshine in Bangkok is difficult and came up with a stroke of brilliance. I went into a nearby fancy hotel and asked the bell captain if it was possible to get my shoes shined. First he asked what room I was staying in. When I told him I was staying in the guest house across the street, he looked at my shoes again and with some reluctance directed me to room service on the fourth floor. There I found several young men standing around, no doubt awaiting summons from their high-class guests. When by pantomime and pointing I indicated I wanted a shoeshine, the young man who spoke some English approached and carefully looked at my poor shoes and asked, "Do you want both of them shined?" I could scarcely hide my incredulity, but managed to say "Yes." A half hour of waiting and 50 baht later, I left this group of young men; as I walked down the hall I could hear their mumbling and laughter.

11 December 1989

The rice field is where the weekly ration of rice and fish is distributed to the residents of Site 2, the largest refugee camp on the border. It is perhaps both appropriate and ironic that the rice field was chosen as the place to celebrate Human Rights Day. UNBRO arranged the celebration. There was music and there were speeches, including one by Haing Ngor (former ARC medic turned actor who plays the part of Dith Pran in *The Killing Fields*). They were both part of a recent fact-finding tour in Phnom Penh. There was also Khmer dancing and singing.

A small group of representatives from various Volags met nearby throughout the day. It was our position that where there is war, human rights suffer. We fasted for 24 hours and spent the day in prayer, meditation and contemplation of what we can do to foster peace in this difficult situation.

13 December 1989

Thoughts on going home:

My commitment for this tour was from 1 September to 1 March. It was a commitment which both Gwen and I were determined—if in our power—to fulfill. For a number of years, Gwen has had occasional extrasystoles, a minor heart irregularity. Several weeks ago these extrasystoles became much more frequent. Gwen consulted her physician and medication was prescribed. Shortly after this, she came down with flu and/or severe reaction to the medication. The medication was discontinued, and after a few days a second one was tried, which seems to be effective. Gwen and I talked frequently through this time. After pondering this situation, it became clear to me that I should come home.

While I regret the problems this brings to the American Refugee Committee, I feel it was the right decision.

Saying good-bye to the Khmer health workers was both hard and easy. It was hard because, as usual, there is no way to know their immediate or long-term future. On the other hand, it was easy because I have been so impressed with their continued development of skill and the dedication to helping their people.

The Ta Phraya, Aranyaprathet and Bangkok staffs of ARC were accepting and supportive of my decision. I left Aran on Tuesday.

The flight home was the most comfortable I have experienced. As we approached final landing, as if it were specially ordered for me, we passed over the Olympic Mountains, down Hood Canal and within sight of our house where Gwen awaited me.

So ends Tour X. An airport van took me to Port Orchard, where Gwen met me. I found her looking better than I expected. A short drive and rapid reentry into the delights of home—a comfortable bed, a great shower, automatic heat, a refrigerator full of goodies—this was reality in this world. But my mind goes back to that other world, and I remember with gratitude the support and best wishes with which Khmer and farang greeted the news of my early departure. I remember the feeling of satisfaction when one little effort brought forth such thanks and appreciation. I remember the excitement of not knowing what challenge this day will bring. I also remember the support of friends and family to Gwen and me during this tour. My thanks to all of you.

Tour XI

"Oh, May I Go A-Wandering until the Day I Die"

Editor's note: Louis's daughter, Peggy, was also working on-site during this tour.

1 October 1992

Yesterday was Jacques's last day, and as of 3:00 P.M. I was in charge of Adult Medicine and Surgery. That sounds formidable, but those services are so well organized that it's mainly a matter of making teaching rounds and seeing the occasional, unusual patient. After rounds yesterday, I went to KID to deliver my last package. I saw a number of my friends from previous tours, including Sharoem, Mali and—sadly enough—Sa Rithy, a Khmer man who was unfortunate enough to be shot in the back by an errant bullet. He has made a little improvement, but it is a sad case.

The last two kilometers of the road to the entrance to Site 2 comprises the perimeter of the camp. Enough rain has fallen so that this lightly forested area is green, and creeks and small ponds abound. In this arboreal setting, one can see what I believe Khmer life was like before the chaos. There are young mothers doing their washing in the ancient way. There are toddlers playing in the red mud, and there are older children swimming or carrying water. It is a beautiful scene.

2 October 1992

I think I am adjusting. I did not require an afternoon nap yesterday. I saw several interesting and challenging cases. On the Surgery ward, we have a two-year-old with a strange swelling in the neck. Puzzled, I was very grateful to have a wonderful pediatrician available for consultation.

Rice, the staff of life here, is also the medium of exchange. En route to KID yesterday, we saw a number of carts laden with 50 kilos of rice, headed out of camp. I asked Chun Roeun where they were headed and where they came from. He explained that every Khmer in camp receives an adequate amount of rice. Those who have jobs receive 1½ rations instead of monetary payment. This leaves an excess, which they sell to traders. The traders bag it and haul it to a rice market where the UN buys rice. Thus, it is conceivable that a single grain of rice may make repeated trips to camp. It does seem that there might be a better way.

4 October 1992

Today is Sunday and I had the day off while Peggy worked. I spent the day alternating between sleeping, reading, working on CPR [the Coalition for Peace and Reconciliation] stuff and a bit of bike riding. Last night Cindy put on a vegetarian taco dinner. Ya Ching made a great green salad. We played Scrabble after dinner, and when it wasn't a person's turn to play, we stuffed envelopes for CPR. Today, I stamped a return address on 1,000 envelopes.

I have heard some of the workers say it's not as much fun as formerly. I think part of the reason is because at the hospital we have the added burden of paperwork for repatriation of sick people, and here at home we have CPR work. I guess I am working up an excuse for not writing as frequently as on previous tours.

5 October 1992

This morning we had one of those torrential rains native to this place. Peggy and I were fortunate in our walk to and from our market breakfast, for there was a brief hiatus each way. Sister Josephine lives in a small house next door. She is a Franciscan, and yesterday, being the Sunday dedicated to St. Francis of Assisi, she invited us to attend the special Mass in honor of this friar, renowned for his special prayer of peace. Sister Josephine had written out the sentences of his prayer, and we were each to draw one. Mine was, "It is in pardoning that we are pardoned." How appropriate that was, for much of the pain and suffering of this place has its roots in the unwillingness of people and nations to pardon.

Today was a busy day with a number of medical challenges, a few small victories, and a few small successes. I spent an hour or so being taught by Peggy the intricate paper pathway that Khmers must follow to leave this penal colony and to reach their homeland. I have found it easy to criticize the UN effort here, but I now better understand the difficulty of moving thousands safely and equitably. We remain hopeful that they will find peace and happiness.

It is hot and muggy this evening; my ankles itch from many mosquito bites, but my heart is filled with gratitude for the opportunity to be here.

6 October 1992

Peggy is putting on dinner tonight—spaghetti. She baked muffins this morning for the staff meeting. You have probably noted the tattered look of the glue edges of these aerograms. I don't know if it is poor quality or the high humidity and heat. I'm just about through with the ones I bummed from Peggy and will have to buy some new ones.

This morning I went to Aran. I needed to go to the bank. My first stop was at "Fat Man's Market"—you remember the propensity of the people here to pin unique names on people and things. Next, I stopped by the "Book Store" to buy a paper, which I read in great contentment at Kim Kim's while I enjoyed an excellent American breakfast. Cashing traveler's checks at the bank was per usual—a time to watch my documents pass from one clerk's hands to another's. It certainly seemed to give a number of people the opportunity to discuss the weather, what they had for dinner and the latest family news. James, field coordinator for ARC, picked me up, and we drove to camp. There was a long noontime team meeting and then a busy afternoon of work. And now, it's over to the spaghetti dinner.

7 October 1992

I have finally developed a fairly regular routine. We get home from camp about 5:00 P.M. By that time I am usually sweaty, tired and hungry. I try to have some sliced pineapple in the refrigerator and have a little snack of some of that delicious fruit, some cheese, and a slice of bread, while I read a bit. Then it is shave-and-shower time. Slowly but surely the water for the pour-on shower is getting colder, and I search for some system to temper the shock of the first pour. Inevitably, I feel very refreshed when it is over and it is time for a little nap. Dinner is usually about 7:00, whether we eat at home or at a nearby restaurant. I have fallen into the habit of spending a half hour working for the CPR. Thus far I have stamped a return address on 3,000 envelopes. My next little project is one or two personal letters and then to bed, about 9:00.

Today was a particularly busy day, since Peggy took the day off. We have a virtual epidemic of pneumonia in Infants. At the end of the day, I found myself looking for one infant not struggling for its next breath. If this continues, there will be some deaths, I'm sure.

8 October 1992

I bought a little notebook yesterday to fit in my back pocket. My idea was that in the course of a day I could record various thoughts and observations.

My little notepad for today says "Dramamine." The Khmers leave Site 2 in buses. For some of them it is only a few hours' ride; for others it is many hours. Fifty Khmers are loaded on a bus with luggage, plus their dogs, cats and a few chickens. What little durable goods they have go in accompanying trucks. Past experience has resulted in a policy of giving every Khmer a dose of Dramamine for motion sickness. The dogs also receive their dose of Dramamine, for lacking it they make a mess. The cats and chickens apparently are better travelers.

9 October 1992

Peggy and I just got back from dinner. Peggy had vegetable curry and I had beef in oyster sauce. When I order that I usually eat the vegetables and half of the beef and take the other half home to use as a sandwich for lunch the next day—works well.

Yesterday, the Fellow in Adult Medicine presented me with a voucher to sign—to order a new stove for the Surgery department. The stove is a hibachi-like structure that is used to sterilize implements in boiling water. Trying to be a good supervisor, I went to the back room and checked. Indeed, the grate in the old stove was all crumbled. When I showered last night, it seemed to me that the water was appreciably colder. When I arrived at camp this morning, I went to talk to the Fellow. His colleagues pointed me to the back room. There I found the Fellow taking a nice hot shower using water heated on the new stove. Ah, such is life here. Rank indeed has its privileges.

11 October 1992

On Sundays only one MD works, one Alpha III, one pharmacist and a driver. We only stay until noon. This afternoon I had a nice nap and then peeled potatoes, and with Peggy's help made a big pan of scalloped potatoes. Peggy made salad and guava pie. Chuck Schroll just returned from Cambodia.

12 October 1992

In the past days, I have had a good excuse for bicycling in camp. Unfortunately, the excuse was grim: two cases of death at home requiring a death certificate, and two cases of cancer being treated at home by our Fellow.

Like all cultures, the Khmers have their own customs when it comes to death. Somehow, they very promptly get some mournful music playing from a loudspeaker. The result is friends and neighbors gather, and we foreigners find the house by homing in on the music. We are greeted with solemnity. We ask our questions and do a brief exam of the deceased. As we leave, we are thanked profusely, for what I am not sure, but the surviving spouse and family seem very grateful for our appearance. Off we go, riding our bikes down narrow alleyways, dodging chickens, dogs and little children. Indeed, it is a privilege to be here.

13 October 1992

This has been a little different day. Peggy and Lori went to Aran for some meeting. I arrived home just before the customary drenching shower. I lay down and read for about an hour. Actually, I was just delaying my shower, since it seemed quite cool and I was sure the shower water would be cold. Cindy called to me that she and Ya Ching were going out to dinner and would I like to come along. En route to what we call the ARC restaurant we met Phillip and Marjorie, schoolteachers with COERR. We found the ARC restaurant was closed. Phil suggested we go to a restaurant he had recently found. It was in an unlikely quarter of town and there were no other customers. Upon being seated at a table, we were surrounded by a circle of young Thai ladies, all giggling, and it soon became apparent that none of them spoke English. It must have taken 15 minutes to establish our order. As we waited, we wondered what our orders would turn out to be. To our surprise we all got what we ordered.

On returning home, I took my shower and now am just a few words from jumping into bed. All goes well.

15 October 1992

The other evening I went to the CPR office to do a little labeling of envelopes. Peggy was there ahead of me and had a tape player going—old hymns. One of the things I miss most over here is hearing those old hymns. It once again made me wonder how such hymns as "Abide with Me," "Let the Lower Lights Be Burning," "Rock of Ages," and "Blessed Assurance" can be allowed to pass from our scene.

My work continues to go well. In the Surgery ward, we are seeing an unusual incidence of abscesses and infected lymph glands. In Adult Medicine, we have had several severe cases of malaria. Most of these originate in the area of Pallim, a village in Cambodia. Sick people in the Cambodian provinces adjacent to the border often head for our hospital—a sort of affirmation that these people recognize the quality of medical treatment here.

Along with a number of other medics, our longtime friends Saeroeun and BunSieth are scheduled for repatriation next week. We will miss them.

16 October 1992

I decided not to go through the rigmarole of getting a Thai driver's license. It would require two days out of camp, and I am here for such a short time I don't think it is worth it. The powers that be allow me to drive in camp, so I can be independent there. Today, I took Supohl with me in the search for a lady whose EVI [extremely vulnerable individual] form was not quite complete. We slithered over many meters of those narrow little alleys between the bamboo huts that comprise Site 2.

18 October 1992

Bob Maat returned from Cambodia. We have received varying reports about the situation for the repatriates in Cambodia—some discouraging, some encouraging. Bob says it all depends on where you look. Bob did see Sok Thim. Apparently his first job did not work out well. He is now working with CARE and is located adjacent to the ARC unit in Pursat.

A letter from a Khmer to Papa Louis:

Dear Papa Louis,

Hello Papa! How are you doing? I miss you so much. I have learned from Liz that you are in Ta Phraya now. Are you visiting or working? You still enjoy living in Ta Phraya and working with ARC people very much, don't you? I guess so, that is why you come back.

My family and I got to the destination safely at Kandal Province. But up to now we have not received allotment of land yet. My family and I still live with my friend in Phnom Penh.

I have been working for UNTAC's [United Nations Transitional Authority in Cambodia] Human Rights Component as a training assistant in Phnom Penh. I like my job because my work is neutral. We work to promote the peace and the respect and the understanding of human rights for everybody. In contract, because our job is to investigate the case of human rights abuses, review or observe the prison condition to make sure there is no detention of prisoners without trial, etc., then the authority people such as police dislike us. They criticize UNTAC Human Rights Component very badly. I feel uncomfortable to accompany the officer to meet them (powerful people) for interpretation. Anyway, I hope you are well and healthy. Best wishes for good luck and LONG LIFE.

19 October 1992

We have several cases of tropical ulcer in our Surgery ward. This condition tends to occur in persons with poor nutrition. It apparently starts with minor trauma, often from an insect bite. The ulcer itself is very deep, becomes wider and deeper, penetrating through the skin, underlying tissue and muscles. Bacteriology studies reveal a variety of organisms, and treatment with various antibiotics is not very successful. I invited the German physician who works in the leprosy clinic to see these patients. He confirmed the diagnosis and recommended we apply a mix of honey and sugar. We will give it a try.

It is definitely getting cooler as the days go by. The Thai word for cold weather is *now,* and in the morning we can hear our Thai friends using that word often. For us it is quite comfortable.

20 October 1992

BunSieth is one of the most highly regarded and loyal Khmer medics who works for ARC. A week ago, his name came up on the list for repatriation. Like so many things here, there is a bittersweet taste to repatriation. All of us who know BunSieth wished for his freedom. At the same time, we know we will miss him. The process of repatriation required that BunSieth, his wife and children, along with all their possessions, go to the staging area this morning.

I was aware that ARC had adopted a rule against our providing the moving of the returnee's family and goods from their home to the staging area. I was taken aback when BunSieth asked me if I would drive them in one of our trucks. Knowing of the courage and dedication with which BunSieth had served ARC and through ARC served his people, I decided, rule or no rule, I would drive him.

When I pulled up to BunSieth's now empty bamboo hut, I found a gathering of neighbors, his excited children and his beautiful wife—whose face showed a mix of happiness and sadness. UNBRO had provided every returnee with strong plastic bags, and BunSieth had six of them filled. There must have been books in them, for they were heavy. These, plus a few conventional-type carry-on bags, a bicycle and a blackboard, comprised this family's accumulated possessions.

Good-bye kissing and hugging, common to our culture, are not a part of Khmer custom. Instead, there were just melancholy expressions on the faces of friends and neighbors as we pulled away.

21 October 1992

I wanted to finish the BunSieth account.

Our Toyota light truck was heavily laden with baggage, on top of which rode BunSieth and his oldest boy. It was a slow and bumpy ride to the staging area, punctuated by greetings and waves of many passersby who recognized BunSieth and the significance of the blue bags.

At the staging area, there were several hundred Khmers, from babies to aged; some were waiting patiently, some were busy arranging their packages in neat piles. All had the blank look of acceptance—learned, no doubt, from past experience.

I helped BunSieth unload the truck. It was the end of a chapter in the life of BunSieth and his family. As I mumbled good-bye, I recognized that it was the end of a smaller chapter in my life as well, for this gifted young man has done much to help me in my days on the border.

As I drove back to the hospital I felt very good about having helped my friend. I had helped him in a very practical way, and he had helped me when he told me that Lori, our director, had suggested he ask me to drive him to the staging area. I was really pleased that she had recognized the debt that ARC owed BunSieth, but also the friendship which existed between him and me.

24 October 1992

Last evening was the first annual meeting of CPR in honor of the anniversary of the signing of the Paris Accords, aimed at bringing peace to Cambodia. It was, primarily, attended by ARC's members. The leaders of this group are Bob Maat and Liz Bernstein. Bob is a Jesuit brother who has spent more than ten years on the border. Liz came to the border with one of the NGOs. They have become known as foremost leaders in the quest for peace, not only for the Khmers, but also for the world. At a CPR meeting, one can hear quotes from all of the great religions and philosophies of this world.

The return of 100,000 Khmers to their homeland is a marker for peace, for they have left the border camps, which are anything but peaceful. Some of the individual Khmers will not find peace where they settle, for factional and political strife remain, and many leaders can only look to violence to achieve their ends.

On the brighter side, there are many Khmers who in their years of incarceration have learned there are alternatives, and many of these Khmers seek to lead their people in paths of peace.

What can we as individuals do? We can support organizations such as CPR. We can write—to our editors, our politicians, our church leaders. We can talk with friends and families and neighbors. We can seek peace in our own lives.

27 October 1992

I worked Sunday at camp, covering the Surgery, Adult Medicine and Pediatrics wards. It was a fairly routine morning. In the afternoon it was my turn to be available at the staging area. For a thousand Khmers this was the crucial day six of the repatriation process.

Coming in groups of 50, they pass through a gate that symbolizes a line between Thailand and UN territory. At the gateway, the Khmers' documents are inspected, and medical personnel observe the Khmers for any obvious signs of illness and advanced pregnancy.

The heavy baggage has already been loaded, but each family carries hand baggage. Many carry pet dogs, cats and chickens. Of course, the procedure requires much standing in line, and there are frequent halts of the line. The Khmers are expert at standing in lines.

Their quietness and acceptance are quite in contrast to what the scene would be if they were Americans or Europeans.

Words fail to adequately describe the ambience. On their faces there are expressions of happiness in some and anxiety in others. In the hearts and minds of the volunteer workers are feelings of compassion and hope that these people's time of terror and oppression is over. Best wishes to you Khmers, may peace and comfort be yours.

28 October 1992

One of our minor struggles here is with computers. As I have previously pointed out, the moving of 250,000+ people back to their homeland in a fair and safe manner is a very difficult task. The UN decided to use computers as the shepherds. In my opinion, they failed to employ real computer experts in designing the system. As a result, we have forms where the concerned person's name is hidden in the fine print in the middle of the page. We have spent hours searching for those names.

Ah, the foregoing sounds pretty grim. Do not be concerned. I remain grateful and happy to be here at this time. Every day I have opportunities to admire the character and talent of our dear daughter.

It's bedtime—getting close to three-blanket weather.

29 October 1992

I have a cute little story to tell you. Early this morning, while I was just getting ready for the day, Ya Ching came dashing into our house announcing that a Thai "walking fish" was outside. Now I had never heard of a walking fish, and I thought Ya Ching was putting on some sort of a joke. Nevertheless, I followed her out to our courtyard.

We had a stormy and heavy rain type of night, and our yard was speckled with mud puddles, as usual after a rain. On the ground between two puddles was a fish, about five inches long. Using its fins to propel itself, it was making its way to another puddle, leaving a snake-like trail. It was surrounded by several of the cats, which have found favor with the ladies who live in the office house. We harried the cats away, and this strange creature continued its pilgrimage. It was obviously hard work, for the fish paused periodically, obviously gasping for breath. When it reached its watery goal, it plunged right in, swam across and crawled out and headed for the next puddle. We watched it for several minutes and pondered how to ensure its safety. We couldn't come up with anything and left it, hoping that neither car wheels nor cats would end its peculiar life.

30 October 1992

I have experienced some heavy lightning and thunder and rainstorms here, but this was the fiercest. It started early this evening shortly before we headed for a nearby restaurant. By the time we got there we were just moderately soaked. The unique feature of this drenching storm was its persistence. All through dinner it poured, and through the south-facing windows the lightning lit up the skies. We dawdled over the last of our dinner, trying to wait out the storm, but it only got worse.

Thinking about the probability that our rooms were getting wet, we finally left the restaurant. It was like stepping into a shower. In a moment, we were soaked. The streets were flooded. We had planned a Scrabble game but cancelled that. I went around our house pushing shutters closed. My waiting bed is damp, but not too bad. The rain has ceased now, and the frogs are croaking. Ah, Thailand.

More on the Thai walking fish. Watching the fish crawl out of one pond and head for another was an awesome experience. I read an article somewhere by a scientist who maintained that at some stage of evolution some fish developed the physiological changes that equipped it to propel on land and to breathe air. Seeing this fish, I felt like I was seeing the earth millions of years ago. From these fish, reptiles evolved. But how does one explain this little fish, eons behind its progenitors?

Bill and Josie Heegaard arrive tomorrow. Bill is scheduled to work in OPD. Soon a Burmese doctor will take over TB, which will relieve Peggy a little.

1 November 1992

I really dozed off. Woke up at 2:00 A.M., and decided that was a sign to give up and try again today to write. Josie and Bill Heegaard arrived last night—surely is great to have them here. I picked them up in Aran; they agreed it's a far bigger, busier town than their last tour here. Every time I go there for meetings or to run errands I'm grateful to live in peaceful little Ta Phraya.

We had a pleasant ride back. This is a pretty time here even in eastern Thailand, not the most scenic of areas. The rice fields are in various shades of green, and the countryside looks fresh and scrubbed, very different from the brown barren scenes of the cool and hot dry seasons.

On arriving at Ta Phraya, we found the house transformed for Halloween. About two weeks ago Corinne's parents sent two boxes, one with beautiful dried waxed leaves and cones, the other with lots of Halloween decorations—hanging paper skeletons, streamers, some great masks, a set of fanglike teeth, big ears, a tape of horror sounds. Besides hanging up the skeleton and streamers, Corinne, Ya Ching and Cindy had carved a watermelon (they're round here), a squat papaya and a guava, all like pumpkins, and put candles in them to make jack-o-lanterns. They put several balloons in the hammock strung across the porch, with the ugly gorilla mask at the head, and folded the hammock around the balloons, so it looks like a gorilla lying on its side. The tape of horror sounds was playing as we came in the house.

Bill and Josie thought it was great. I think our neighbors are convinced more than ever we're crazy. Our landlord's son comes every Sunday to pick up empty bottles, which we keep on the porch. He's maybe seven or eight years old. Corinne was watching from inside the house behind the shutters as he bounded up the steps, halted abruptly as he saw the skeletons, and took a wide detour around the hammock. But Corinne said he was laughing as he went back downstairs.

There are also some capsules with some red foamy dye—you suck on them for 30 seconds, then chew, then open your mouth and red foam oozes out. We've joked about taking all this stuff to Site 2 and trying it out, but with the number of mad dogs we have, plus the number of guns around, maybe we won't try that.

Today was a pleasant day on the wards. I think our pneumonia epidemic is over—much less than last year. Also, I think the camp is significantly smaller. We're doing a total camp census these two weeks, so we'll know more in three or four weeks. Anyway, I know our census in Peds is way down.

We're still having occasional patients with dengue, and as seems to be our pattern this year, we have many fewer with dengue, but the few we have are much more likely to bleed than the kids we saw last year. We're also seeing one or two cases of malaria each day—it's unfair to have those seasons overlap!

Our little TB patient, Em Sy Nae, continues to eat well, gains some weight, can be off oxygen for a few hours, then needs it again, but I still think she's slowly improving. She hasn't been immunized against measles, which I expect will be our next outbreak. And I don't know when to try immunizing her. I would anticipate her nutrition status along with her TB would make her immune system so poorly functioning that I'm afraid the measles vaccine wouldn't be effective. But she'll get measles if we wait too long and may well die from that. By now we're all attached to this child. I want to prevent measles—I just am not sure how.

Screening in the staging area today was fun. Twenty-six orphans entered on their way to Siem Reap. Seeing all these kids without parents was a sad reminder of how much people have lost in the past 15–20 years. A couple other interesting scenes: One little boy brought his pet monkey; the Thai officer working in immigration playfully asked his name while checking the family book. Then there was one threesome in a family group—a 75-year-old woman, a 78-year-old woman, and a nine-year-old boy. The 75-year-old looked quite frail and wobbly. I was just about to stop her to check more closely when she picked up the huge cloth bag I'd seen immigration struggle with. She put it on her head and trotted off to catch up with the other two. I think she'll be OK.

1 November—later

This letter should have been written last night, but it was a busy day and evening. My work at the camp was fairly routine, but not without a little spice. Coming out of Surgery ward who did I see trudging by but Father Pierre. Since I last saw him he has survived a major auto accident and has just recently returned from France.

He was accompanied by a young Khmer man, whose eyes were filled with tears. Father Pierre explained that this young man's wife was in the Maternity ward, and he was very concerned about her. "Now that I have found 'Papa Louis' I'm sure everything will be all right," said this good Jesuit Father.

I walked to the Maternity ward, lacking confidence and trying to figure out what I should do. Khmer custom forbids male presence in the birthing area, and the Maternity service is in the capable hands of Cindy, the ARC midwife. As so often happens, it all turned out fine. The Khmer midwife assured us that the lady was in very early labor with every indication of a normal birth. This young soon-to-be mother came out in the hall, reassured her worried husband, and we males departed feeling much better.

Today is Sunday, a day off for me. Peggy is working. Bill and Josie's arrival was a great reunion. We talked for a long time and then went to dinner at what we call the ARC restaurant. After a very good Thai meal, we moved to the Team restaurant for ice cream and coffee. This morning I took Bill and Josie to the market and introduced them to the pineapple girl.

3 November 1992

Of vitamins, proteins and trace elements. The most frequent condition we are seeing in Surgery ward is abscess—cellulitis of the skin and sub-cutaneous tissues. Often the patient does not remember any injury. In that event, we assume some insect sting occurred. Very frequently the dorsum (top) of the foot is the location.

A few days ago I noted a peculiar redness at the base of my left great toe. I didn't think much of it until yesterday, when I saw there was some swelling in the center and a black spot—indicative of necrosis. During the day I was aware of periodic discomfort walking. I felt fine during the ride home but had moderately severe pain on getting out of the car and was seized with a shaking chill.

I really didn't feel generally bad, but I couldn't face a cold shower, so I heated some water and soaked my foot. After that I crawled into bed, where I was quite comfortable until the phone rang. Getting out of my warm bed and running to the phone I had another chill. I managed to get dressed and go to the team meeting, but with all those medical people I couldn't hide the fever and chills.

Second half follows in next letter—to be written this evening. In short, my two doctors (Bill and Peggy) put me on penicillin and I am much better today.

3 November—later

Infected foot account continued: The meeting was short and I went to bed without dinner. Peggy came to check on me, and with that serious look told me I was not to go to work today. Both Peggy and Bill examined my foot. I'm not sure which one is my primary care doctor and which is the second-opinion doctor, but somehow they come up with the same diagnosis and prescription.

I was a little restless during the night due to drenching perspiration. When I got up this morning I felt well and my foot looked much better. The Khmers we have seen with similar infections usually end up in the hospital with intravenous medication. In an excess of optimism I gave credit to my general good health and my system loaded with vitamins, proteins and trace elements. Now I have to moderate those happy thoughts, for my foot is again swollen, and I have an enlarged lymph node in the groin. My doctors are mumbling about my not going to work tomorrow. We shall see.

4 November 1992

My doctors insisted that I stay home again today. My foot and inguinal node are much better, and I will go to work tomorrow. I spent the day alternating between lying down with leg elevated, writing letters and preparing dinner. (Omelet, cabbage salad, fruit salad for dessert.) Bill loaned me his radio and I heard the election returns all morning long. The Bush administration is now history.

6 November 1992

My letter writing is really getting harder and harder to fit in. Wednesday evening I had lots of typing to do, so as soon as the typewriter was available, stopped my letter. Our computer is once more in Bangkok being repaired; with my poor typing skills, I really miss the word processor function of the computer. I've had a number of pieces of fairly official correspondence to type recently. One plus: they've all been things that needed to be faxed, so use of whiteout is not as obvious. Anyway, I was typing till 1:00 A.M., so didn't get back to letter writing.

Then last night I spent in Aran at a talk given by the chief police psychologist of Australia, here to visit Australian UNTAC troops in Thmar Pouk. This man's specialty is handling incidents of "critical stress"— e.g., in police work, when a policeman shoots an innocent bystander. While he spoke specifically about police work, there are some crossovers with our work, and he had some good points. This was followed by a dinner meeting with one representative from NGOs still on the border.

At dinner we almost got into a shouting match. We discussed the U.S. elections, then somehow got on to capital punishment. We had three Australians, one Canadian, one Frenchman, one Filipino, one Bangladeshi and three Americans. I was the only one adamantly against capital punishment, and the Australians and the Bangladeshi were for virtually instantaneous public execution once a murderer is apprehended. It was a spirited evening anyway. I got back to the office at 11:00 P.M. and decided to put off for one more day finishing this letter.

Now it's 8:30 P.M. I promised it'd be lights out at 9:00, and I'm hoping for an easy day tomorrow and then Sunday off.

5 November 1992

My foot is essentially healed, and the lymphadenitis in my groin is gone. I worked today and all went well. We had a little party on the Adult Medicine ward to honor President Clinton's election.

This evening Peggy has gone to a meeting in Aran. She did not feel like going but thought she was obligated. It was ironic because the meeting is to be a lecture by some Australian on "how to handle stress," and my answer to that problem is to avoid those evening trips to Aran as much as possible.

Josie loaned me a book she had brought, *Run with the Horsemen,* by Ferrol Sams, and it is excellent. It is a moving and comical story of a boy growing up on a small cotton plantation in the South during Depression years.

7 November 1992

I had plenty of time to write last night, but often in evening, due to general demand on the power system, there isn't enough voltage to start the fluorescent tubes. My little bed lamp works then, but for writing it casts enough heat along with the light to make writing a sweaty job. So I read instead.

In the past 12 hours I have had a series of problems with local animal and insect life. Last evening when I went to the bathroom to shower, I found it inhabited with countless mosquitoes flying various aerial patterns in preparation to land on me as I showered. There are always a few mosquitoes present when I shower, and they make life interesting, but this crowd was too much. I went over to the office house and borrowed a can of mosquito spray, which took care of them well.

During the night I awakened to the sorrowful yelping of a dog, which seemed to go on for a number of minutes—gradually dying out as if the dog itself was dying. I kept thinking the dog was in the jaws of some snake. This morning it was Epiphany (strange name for a cat). This favorite member of the group of four cats belonging to the ladies at the office house had found one of several ways to get into our house. Meowing, entangling my legs and jumping on the breakfast table, she did not get my day off to a good start. Of course, any chastisement of this animal could bring retribution down from the otherwise lovely and reasonable ladies at the office house.

8 November 1992

Sunday morning, and I have just completed getting my day pack ready to load into the high-suspension Toyota truck to go to camp. If you are in the market for a truck I would recommend strongly against a high-suspension type. They are a real stress and strain to the neck and low back on rough roads.

The Thais and the Khmers wonder what effect the new Clinton administration will have on their world. I also wonder: can we make a difference in the next four years?

Today I work and do the screening for a small movement of Khmers. Extra farang help is increasing. Actually, most of them are Thais, so I am not sure if it is proper to term them "farangs." We have added drivers and Thai nurses. Areeya is Alpha III and does a great job. She often asks about you and remembers well her short visit with us.

Being the only doctor in camp on Sunday is certainly more of a privilege than a chore. Although neither the Khmers nor the Thais have the tradition of Sunday as a day of rest, Sunday is usually a quiet day in the camp. While the Sunday doctor has responsibility for all the wards, it is not necessary to make formal rounds. The medic in charge of each ward has almost always identified one or two cases he feels he needs help with. These are often a challenge, and thus it was on Peds today.

A 10-year-old boy with a six-day history of fever, chills and weight loss was presented. He is very anemic, but the remainder of the lab work was negative. I wish I could report some outstanding diagnosis, but that was not to be. It was one of those times when I got more out of the hour I spent with him, for he was so cooperative and accepting. Well, perhaps that outstanding pediatrician of the border, Dr. Peggy, will come up with a brilliant diagnosis tomorrow.

11 November 1992

This "cold" weather continues here, and most of us have three small blankets on our beds. It makes it more difficult to make the bed, since the relative dimensions of bed and blanket do not match. The biggest domestic news here is that Lanci, our maid, has purchased a washing machine. It seems that her hands have become sore from scrubbing our clothes.

When I returned from work on Sunday afternoon, I lay down and enjoyed a great nap—made better when on awakening I realized I didn't have to get up quite yet. As I lay there I became aware of a young gecko, about two inches long, making its way across the screen over my window. The sun was shining through the window, and much of the body of this little lizard was translucent. I spent 15–20 minutes studying the X-ray-like vision of its body and pondering the reason for its various movements. Another project for when I get home: read up on geckos.

13 November 1992

I have just returned from a very nice dinner with a wonderful group of friends. Dinner was at Team, a nearby restaurant. Attending were Peggy, Lori, Corinne, whom you know, Kirsten, a nurse with YWAM, and John and Naomi, who are working in Bangkok with a peace group. John is a young graduate in peace studies and political science, and Naomi is a young lady from northern Japan.

Currently things are going quite well, and the mood is quite upbeat. Bill Heegaard is very popular in OPD. We have a Thai nurse by the name of Kitya in Adult Medicine and another Thai nurse by the name of Saru in Surgery. They have been very effective in improving nursing care on the wards.

15 November 1992

Today is Sunday off for me, and I have loafed most of the day. I did go into town and got a haircut. I brought a book to read, and before I knew it, the barber gave me a monk job. The Khmers will really have a big laugh tomorrow.

Peggy went to Aran in the afternoon. In late afternoon the Peds medic came to me for help. He led me to two beds containing four children, all of them having been in the hospital for several days and still running high fevers. Peggy had done all the appropriate things, and I couldn't think of anything different. I don't think I have ever seen four siblings sick at one time like this.

Tonight Peggy is making spaghetti for dinner, and I am making cabbage salad and fruit salad with ice cream. Papayas are plentiful in Aran but for some reason have not reached Ta Phraya. We have a mango tree in our back yard that is heavily laden, but the mangoes will not be ripe before I leave.

17 November 1992

A mixed day of triumph and defeat. In the past two or three days we have admitted several elderly ladies in congestive failure. They really bring to mind the contrast between the modern-day practice of medicine in medical centers and the rather primitive level at which we practice here. In a sophisticated center these ladies would have the benefit of all kinds of electronics and computerized and radiographic studies, which would identify the nature, the cause and the indicated treatment.

Here, like the doctors of a half-century or more ago, we are limited to history and physical exam. What we can learn by touch, sight and hearing leads us to some sort of diagnosis. Our choice of treatment confirms its rightness if the patient improves, or leaves us wondering if the patient's condition worsens. Generally, patients in congestive failure respond to diuretics and judicious use of digoxin. Sometimes their recovery is dramatic, in which case we applaud ourselves. Our three ladies are spread out between these extremes. Challenges like these certainly are part of the attraction of work over here.

19 November 1992

A few days ago in the Surgery department we received an aged lady with first- and second-degree burns on her back. These were incurred when she sat too close to a fire. Sorn, a little Thai nurse, has become quite interested in traditional medicine. The day following the old lady's admission, Sorn showed up with a bag of leaves—swordlike, with raised little bumps. Sorn asked permission to make up a poultice from the leaves to apply to the first-degree burns.

Slightly skeptical, I nevertheless agreed. She peeled the skin off the leaves. The inside was a clear, jelly-like mass. Mixed with water, this was applied. My skepticism was somewhat ameliorated when one of the Western nurses identified the leaves as aloe. Happily, the areas Sorn is treating are healing well.

20 November 1992

I have purposely not dwelt upon eating in my letters this tour. As I look back on the menus of the past seven weeks, I realize that each item has its advantage and disadvantage, and there is a rather dull sameness to it with only the occasional bright spot.

Our local grocery is primarily aimed at its Thai clientele. The proprietors do maintain a small stock of food bought mainly by farangs. Understandably, these items are fairly expensive. For instance, a large box of cornflakes costs about $4.00 US. Strangely, that is my chosen breakfast most every morning. By keeping the box in the refrigerator the flakes remain quite crisp and ant free. Many mornings I round out breakfast by a quick walk to the market with Peggy, where we have a bowl of *quittio*—noodle soup. There we also buy fruit.

Lunch is either made here or bought in camp. Here I make a sandwich of tuna fish or sliced cheese, both of which are expensive. If I buy lunch it is at a Khmer restaurant, Apsara. I also order #7, Chinese noodles frying. This amounts to noodles covered with vegetables and a sauce. Most dinners are taken at Team, a Thai restaurant where my usual dish is fried rice with chicken. That is usually topped off with coffee and one scoop of chocolate ice cream. Now I have to add that all of these meals are generally garnished by pineapple, bought from that beautiful-smile girl who trims it out so beautifully.

I'm ready for some lean, fried hamburger, mashed potatoes and gravy and a tossed lettuce salad.

21 November 1992

Bill and Josie are off on vacation, and Peggy is in Bangkok through Tuesday. As a result, I work this weekend. On Sunday there is a big screening of expatriating Khmers, so I will be in camp until late. I am glad Peggy will be away for a few days as she has been working very hard.

Thursday of next week is Thanksgiving, and we work only until noon. From 11:00 A.M. to 1:00 P.M., I will host a lunch at the Apsara Restaurant for 50–60 Khmers. In the afternoon, we will have a typical feast including turkey. On Friday, Peggy and I will go to Aran to spend the night, and Saturday I will go to Bangkok by taxi.

I remain in good health and happy to be here.

[Louis's reflections, written after his return home 1 December 1992.]

Oh, May I Go A-Wandering

My last days of my time in Site 2 and in Ta Phraya were a summary of my experiences of the past 12 years.

The awesome development of medical and surgical skills by the Khmers was demonstrated. Their survival skills, born in the Pol Pot days and of necessity maintained during their years in the camps, were still evident as they faced the present uncertainties. The dedication of the expatriate workers to lifting at least a part of the load from the shoulders of the Khmers remains remarkable; the willingness of these workers from foreign lands and varied cultures and traditions is inspiring.

It so happened that my last day in Ta Phraya coincided with the American holiday of Thanksgiving. Inspired by the meaning of this fete and drawing upon their seemingly endless supply of energy, the inhabitants of ARC office house put on a Thanksgiving feast. The traditional food, only slightly moderated by our special separation from America, was delicious. It was even more remarkable to stand and watch 40 people from eight different nations, and hear them in various tongues and accents.

For some inexplicable reason, one of the ARC Thai workers demanded that I sing them a song. Now those who know me well know that I love the songs of my youth, but I have near zero ability to sing them. And there was also the problem of choosing a song. Inspiration came to me. Enlisting three beautiful female voices, we sang "Oh may I go a-wandering . . . until the day I die." Not only did those three female voices sing it beautifully, but the words also expressed a part of my philosophical feeling at the time. A line from that song goes, "I wave my hand to those I see, and they wave back to me."

Tour XII

Echoes of Hope

26 August 1993

There is an aura of unreality to this trip. Perhaps it is because part of my mind pictures familiar places such as Aranyaprathet, Ta Phraya and Site 2 and friends of previous trips. The other part of my mind tries to deal with the fact that, while there will no doubt be some old friends, Volags and Khmers, I will have to learn this new situation and how to work with new acquaintances.

My situation this instant is unreal, for as I write this, I am sitting in a fancy hotel room in Tokyo. I thought by now I would be in a little room in the Bangkok Christian Guest House.

Yesterday was departure day. On previous trips, I had struggled to find some profound thoughts regarding the start of another trip. Northwest Airlines seemed to have redesigned their planes along the lines of those I flew in on my early trips, for we were packed in like sardines.

Those who have noted my propensity to deal at length with gustatory experiences will be surprised and relieved when I will only say I ate the dinner they served and then slept most of the way. Due to our late arrival, our connecting flights were long gone, and we were told that NWA would keep us overnight in a Tokyo hotel.

While I only spent about 12 hours in Tokyo, Japan gave me a number of interesting experiences in that short time. They put us up in a very fancy hotel. I noted while showering that there was a soap dish at appropriate height for one who is showering and another one lower for one sitting in the bath. On the counter there were a number of toiletries, including soap, shampoo, a toothbrush and a minute tube of toothpaste. I used some of everything the bathroom had to offer—except the hair dryer.

Arrangements had been made for those of us who were scheduled to go to Bangkok to take a Japan Airlines plane. On arrival at the airport

I found the notice that our flight was delayed from 11:00 A.M. to 11:30 A.M. And the man who checked me in said that departure was dependent on the typhoon.

I am not one to worry along the line of "what might happen," but I must confess that as we boarded I could not banish thoughts of articles I had read about wind sheer. The takeoff was indeed rough, and moderate swooping and tipping of the plane brought some anguished "oohing and aahing" from some of my fellow passengers. The balance of the trip was smooth and comfortable—enough so that I slept through most of it.

The modern Bangkok airport bears little resemblance to my early experiences. The procedures are carried out very efficiently, and my baggage arrived without problems. I was met by a taxi driver sent by Bob Medrala, ARC's Thailand director. The driver was armed with a large sign on which my name was printed in one hand, and a picture of me in the other.

My next venture was the ride from the airport to the Christian Guest House. I was received with a warm welcome.

28 August 1993

At 6:30 A.M. I had breakfast and then went to the airport to catch a plane—on to Phnom Penh, an experience for which I had yearned for a number of years.

It is now 2:30 P.M. as I sit down to write in the common room of the Tokyo Hotel in Phnom Penh, a one-star hotel at best. My little room has all the necessities such as a bed and bathroom and a few niceties such as a TV.

Yesterday in the evening Bob Medrala took my old friend Jeff Nelson and me out to dinner in Bangkok. We went to "Bobby's English Pub," where I had roast lamb, Bob had filet mignon and Jeff had shepherd's pie.

We sat and talked for some time, sharing tales of mutual friends here and in the U.S. Jeff is ARC field coordinator for an effort to bring basic medical care to Burmese refugees on the Thai-Burmese border. He told of visiting different camps in the jungles, which involved travel that requires two four-wheel-drive trucks, each fitted with an electric winch. A recent trip required three hours to get to the camp and two days to get back, the result of getting stuck. They spent two nights in the jungle. It was obvious that Jeff loves the job he is doing.

29 August 1993

Despite a long nap in the afternoon, I slept well through the night. This morning I got up at 6:00, showered and dressed, and went to the balcony, which serves as a restaurant. Finishing his breakfast there was a friendly man of about my age, whom I engaged in conversation. He is a supervisor with the American Friends Service Committee, a Quaker organization. He has been here numerous times since 1979 and before that to Vietnam. As you can imagine, there followed an hour-long conversation exchanging tales of adventure and philosophy. His name is David Elder, another acquaintance to add to my collection of personal benefits arising from my visit here.

29 August—later

If I sounded somewhat critical of the Tokyo Hotel, I should point out some of the good things. Last night I sat at one of the desks in the common room to write. One of the staff must have noted that, for this morning when I came back from my first little walk, I found my little room neatly made up and this nice little desk and a chair had been moved in here. Also, I do have air-conditioning. While I am not overly fond of air-conditioning, I must admit that when I come in from the out-of-doors all perspired it is indeed most pleasant to feel the coolness.

Brian, Cambodian field director for ARC, took me sightseeing after lunch. We went first to Toul Sleng, the Death Museum. This building was once a high school. The Khmer Rouge converted it to a prison where thousands of their fellow Khmers were tortured and killed. Perhaps psychiatrists can explain what transformed a segment of this generally kind and happy population into killers. It is more difficult to understand why they preserved and mounted the pictures of their victims on these walls and decorated one of the walls with their skulls. It is impossible for me to explain what attracts people such as I to go to view this tragic scene or to define how it affects one's thinking after seeing it.

Later we went to the banks of the Pussac River where we viewed boat people—mostly ethnic Vietnamese. Enough for now—it's off to Battambang.

31 August 1993

The act of writing on this aerogram says I have arrived. Yesterday I once again packed up and moved bag and baggage to the ARC office. Brian delivered a one-hour orientation, the best I have had in my experience here. Graham Abutt, Brian's first assistant, and very efficient, took me through some additional paperwork and then we left for the airport. En route we stopped at a clinic called "World Access." The proprietor is an Englishman and his business is immunizations. I had my encephalitis injection, but they were out of rabies vaccine. Perhaps I will get that on some later trip.

The Phnom Penh airport bears very little resemblance to the behemoths of SeaTac and Bangkok—except, like them, it tends to be crowded and there appears to be a line formed at every beckoning window, door or desk. Thary, office manager from the Phnom Penh office, carefully directed me. En route to the airport, we talked about Pol Pot days. Her father disappeared and is assumed dead. Upon return to Phnom Penh, she went to Toul Sleng and found the pictures of her two uncles.

The plane to Battambang was a WW II vintage, prop-driven carriage for about 50 passengers. I marveled at the fact that in my early flying experiences I had flown about the U.S. in similar planes.

1 September 1993

I am still not really settled. ARC has two settled houses in Mongkol Borei and one rented but not set up. I am temporarily staying in John Hollister's room. He is an engineer for ARC and currently away for a week. This is the office house. Arlys and Supohl, my translator, are my current housemates. Nou and Picune currently take their meals here but live in House 2. A Khmer cook and maid work here.

Diet: Every meal here thus far has had rice as the foundation and usually three side dishes of various vegetables with bits of meat. I have found this very good. My only complaint is lack of pineapple. I am told that pineapples grow here but haven't seen any. I am also told there are no restaurants here, so my accounts will probably not dwell as much on menus.

Our schedule seems to be to arrive at the hospital at 7:30 for morning report, which is attended by all the medical staff. Making rounds on one of the wards takes about two hours. Then Supohl and I go across the street to one of the kiosks for coffee. We leave the hospital at noon for lunch and siesta at home, then return to the hospital at 2:00 P.M. Afternoon is spent seeing acutely ill patients. We return home at 5:00. I shower and shave and then usually read either medical material or a novel. Dinner is about 7:00, and then there may be a Scrabble game or it is writing time. To bed about 9:00.

We work five full days and a half-day on Saturdays. The Khmer staff attend the hospital at night and weekends, so this is not a bad schedule at all.

The hospital is located about 3 km from here by car or about 1k if we walk. As soon as I learn the route I will walk. Gradually my role there is becoming clearer to me. The medical staff is comprised of Khmer men of ages I would guess from 30 to 40. There is also an ICRC staff of doctors and nurses whom I do not really know yet—except I gather they all come from Switzerland. I talked with one of the Khmer doctors about his training. He spent seven years at the Faculty of Medicine, Phnom Penh. Following that he had one year of internship, and spent three years in provincial and district hospitals. I gather that in the stratum of medicine he is at the bottom. He wishes he could become a specialist but apparently lacks the money or perhaps the necessary scholarship.

Here I am to play the role of consultant. It is important that I do so in a collegial and diplomatic way. I must remind myself that Phnom Penh medicine is largely French in origin, which means different in significant ways. I must remind myself that, though much of their formal training was didactic, these very young-appearing physicians have practiced for several years in a milieu where tuberculosis, tropical diseases and deprivation are common. I must remind myself that they are practicing in a situation where finances are scarce, and physical equipment (and pharmacopoeia, to a degree) is limited. I'll do the best I can.

2 September 1993

Today I made rounds in Pediatrics. This is the dengue fever year. There are about 60 patients on Peds, and at least one-third of them has hemorrhagic dengue. Last month there were seven deaths. There are also a number of malaria cases, almost all of the falciparum variety—the bad kind. There is a sprinkling of meningitis, pneumonia and gastrointestinal disease. At least half of these have IVs going, and in my opinion about half of these are not necessary. We had the same problem on the border. The origin of this problem, as on the border, is that it makes the family, and to a degree the attending physician, feel better. I haven't figured out what I can do about it yet.

3 September 1993

I just realized that I have missed writing of some recent events. Brian, his assistant, Graham, and Thary, the office manager, came for consultations with Arlys. They arrived on Wednesday afternoon and left this morning. On Wednesday and Thursday evenings we had board games—chess, Scrabble and backgammon.

Today, Supohl and I made rounds in the maternity and TB wards. The Khmer doctor in OB stands out among his colleagues, for he demonstrates great care for his patients and works very hard. There were about 40 patients in his ward. Many presented great challenges to anyone in the OB or gynecology field. I was humbled and very impressed with his skill and dedication.

Rounds in TB were different, partly because the young Khmer doctor had just taken over that ward, and it was a learning experience for both of us. During my tours on the border I had some contact with the TB ward, so I knew something about the basic principles. Also, I had prepared for these rounds by reading several articles. It was nevertheless awesome to see some of these wasted people and to look at the X-rays showing the destruction of their bodies by this terrible disease. Modern treatment of TB is somewhat technical but continues to require consistency and discipline—qualities difficult to bring to bear in the type of lives these people have had in the past 20 years. It will be a long time before this disease will be conquered in this country.

6 September 1993

I am staying this weekend at the Inter Hotel in Aranyaprathet. The last time I stayed here it was a single-story collection of structures, like a motel in the U.S. of 30 to 40 years ago. I was, therefore, very surprised when the *tuk tuk* which brought me here pulled up in front of an imposing multistory, fancy hotel.

The trip from Mongkol Borei, with Arlys expertly driving, took about 11 hours. The highway is smooth but speckled with bicyclists, motorcyclists, horse carts and slow-moving farmers' carts. We proceeded to Kim Kim's, where I had a chocolate shake, a hamburger and fries and a cup of coffee.

Arriving at the hotel I immediately took a hot shower and then a nice nap.

7 September 1993

Here I am back in my little room in Mongkol Borei. Actually, it is not my room, for today I will move next door to House 3 and can finally get my bags unpacked and my things organized.

8 September 1993

I have often heard that moving next door is as difficult as moving far away, and now I believe it. Monday after work, Supohl and I moved from the office house to the newly rented house next door. In the past I have found Thai stairways sometimes difficult, but Khmer stairways are much more so. They are steep, with narrow and widely spaced treads and no risers, almost like a ladder. The Khmer guards and maids were a big help, but nevertheless the move required many trips up and down for me. It is a relief to be permanently settled.

Patients—there are hundreds of them. Right now the Pediatrics ward, which could comfortably accommodate about 40, has 63. The excess is in an adjacent tent. Many of them have hemorrhagic dengue, a viral disease spread by a daytime stinging mosquito named *Aedes egypti*. These children are often admitted in shock and dehydration, requiring IV fluids and later transfusion. They often hemorrhage into the skin or

GI tract. It is frequently fatal. In Khmers, dengue occurs only in children, for to be an adult Khmer means one who has survived dengue and developed immunity.

We are in an area where the most difficult kind of malaria, falciparum, is common and more difficult because it is resistant to chloroquin, and therefore in most cases requires quinine. Cerebral malaria is the worst complication and not rare here. It occurs in both adults and children. Then there is "black water" malaria. This means the patients pass urine laden with broken-down blood cells, so many that the urine is almost black.

We have about 80 cases of TB in all stages. We can be grateful that modern treatment is available and quite effective. Respiratory infections are also common, and while pneumonia usually responds to antibiotics, the occasional infant or child fails to respond.

Last night we had the loudest thunder and most prolonged lightning I have ever experienced. It was followed by a drenching downpour, which stimulated a chorus of bullfrogs to follow the thunderstorm.

9 September 1993

Our house is located about 3 km from the hospital. Part of the way resembles a miniature Grand Canyon. There is a shorter route if we walk, and Supohl and I choose to walk if there has been no recent rain.

The dirt street (in our country it would be called an alley) leads to the market. It was Monday morning, and vendors and customers absolutely jammed the narrow pathway, on either side of which hopeful merchants had laid out fruits, vegetables and all manner of precooked somethings. It took us a number of minutes to make our way. From the crowd a young woman cried out, "Papa Louis." We could do no more than wave and smile at each other. This lady had worked with us on the border. Like many, she appeared much happier than during her days there.

Several days ago a mother bearing her tragic tale appeared at the hospital. She had come seeking help for her four-year-old child. This child had been normal in development until eight months ago, when she fell from a roof, sustaining a head injury. She recovered the ability to walk about but lost her ability to talk, became hyperactive and developed the condition called pica, a tendency to pick up dirt or any other material and try to eat it. She has regained two or three words of vocabulary. Since that time her mother has had to keep her right with her, for the child wanders away and cannot find her way back. The father and mother have done the best they could, but it was too much for the father, and he became an alcoholic and left the family. The mother spent all of her savings—some $400—seeking help from native healers (Krou Khmers). Now she came to us for help.

I had heard that Dr. Dan Savin, a young psychiatrist I had known on the border, was at Sisophon, and when I was there recently I asked if he would see this child. He was very willing and came yesterday. It is my opinion that a physician who wishes to treat the whole person of his patient must in some intangible way "get that person in the palm of his hand." It amounts to conveying the message: "I care about you. I will do my best to understand what you are going through. I will help you to the best of my ability, and I will be honest."

In a few minutes Dr. Dan had this mother and her child in the palm of his hand, for the little girl sat quietly near him, playing with his fingers and the mother listened attentively to his every word. Of course, it was a great help that Dr. Dan speaks fluent Khmer. The conclusion was sad. Dr. Dan felt that this is a permanent defect and that no medication would help.

13 September 1993

Supohl, the translator employed by ARC to work with me, is somewhere in his 50s. He worked with ARC on the border for a number of years. His first work was with maternal and child health. After a year or two with MCH, Supohl took medic training. I believe he is the oldest of the medics. A full head of slightly curled hair, now flecked with gray, is part of his dignified appearance. His posture and stride are that of a confident man who knows where he is going.

In the last few months of the border experience, medics had opportunity for early repatriation and found well-paying jobs with UN organizations. Typical of Supohl, he chose to stay to the end, serving his people. He has paid for it too, for he has only been able to find a few short jobs here.

There are two groups of Khmers here: those who stayed and survived the Khmer Rouge and the Vietnamese depredations, and those who fled to the border and lived there for years. Those who stayed tend to look down on those who went to the border. One of the political effects of this is the refusal of the government to recognize the excellent training and experience of the border medics. As a result of this, medics such as Supohl are prohibited from practicing their skills.

Supohl is employed as a translator and cannot apply his medical skills and knowledge except through me. It is a somewhat atrocious waste of talent. There is some movement toward establishing provincial training centers to bring the skills of the border-trained and the Cambodian-trained medics to a level, and grant them all certificates of equal merit.

15 September 1993

Two days ago we admitted a young man with malaria, his dark red urine indicating he had the dreaded "black water fever." He was started on the routine IV quinine treatment but failed to respond, becoming more lethargic and his urine progressively darker—finally the blackest black water I have seen. This morning it was found that he was not producing any urine (anuria, an almost inevitably fatal situation).

Later in the morning, in some mysterious way, word of his status reached a family member. In a further mysterious way, this family member encountered Father Bernard Diynaz, parish priest and family friend and spiritual guide. Late this afternoon a car drove up to the Adult Medicine ward, and I encountered the good Father, who had come to check on his parishioner. Our meeting was a continuation of these mysterious circumstances, for Father Bernard confirmed what I had heard as a mere rumor: that the MSF team in Battambang was doing peritoneal dialysis for those with anuria. After 12 hours of anuria, it was our opinion that the prognosis for this young man was 100 percent negative. Father Bernard reported that the group doing dialysis reported 50 percent success.

It was 4:30 P.M.—an almost impossible time to arrange ambulance transportation. With that 50 percent figure in mind, I rushed to ICRC and encountered Fernanda, chief nurse for ICRC, just the one I needed. She contacted their ambulance base by radio, and within minutes the ambulance was on the way to pick up our patient. A Khmer nurse to accompany was necessary and our chief nurse agreed immediately.

As I write this, our patient has arrived in Battambang. Only in the future will we know the result, but I am most grateful for those mysterious coincidences that gave this young man some chance.

17 September 1993

Coffee, as you know, is part of my life. Here, instant coffee is routine. Gwen sent a pound of French gourmet coffee grounds for me to use for special occasions. Yesterday I noted that we were out of instant coffee and suggested to Supohl that we should buy some more. Supohl replied that we had more coffee. A little later he came to me with a puzzled expression. In his hand he held a cup with hot water and floating coffee grounds. He had mistaken the ground coffee for instant coffee.

19 September 1993

A week ago we expected the arrival of our new housemate, Luc, who did arrive on Friday afternoon. He is a nurse from Quebec and speaks English and fluent French. He served a tour on the border, and we both think we have met before.

Every morning at 7:30 there is an assembly of the Khmer staff. They line up in formation before the Cambodian flagpole, and a clanging cymbal is struck. Dr. Serim says a few words and then we gather in a classroom.

This meeting starts with a Khmer administrator reading the 24-hour statistics. After the reading, a few announcements are made, and then we disband. On Saturday morning I dared to introduce Luc in French—quite an accomplishment for me.

Communication is difficult. Most of the persons I need to talk to have Khmer as their native tongue, French as a second language and a small vocabulary of English. Sometimes it is frustrating.

The Dutch UN army group will pull out next month. In preparation, they have brought a considerable quantity of medical supplies to the hospital (much appreciated). Fernanda is the chief nurse and in charge of such things. She approached me the other day and said that the Dutch had given her several hundred eyeglasses, and "Would you like to pick out a pair for yourself?" Now that was nice and considerate. Then she said they had also been given a number of hearing aids. "Would you like one?" Completing her assessment of my social security status, she then said, "There are also a number of sets of dentures, would you . . ." Ah, life over here is unique and wonderful.

22 September 1993

My trip to Battambang started yesterday morning with a 1½-hour lurching ride in the back of an ICRC Land Cruiser. That rough ride brought on a little headache, but it soon went away. My colleague and host, Olivier, suffered far more than I, for—as he said—he had a "hangover" from his departure party the night before.

On arrival in Battambang we went directly to the ICRC Rehabilitation Center. Here they deal primarily with amputees, fitting them with much more sophisticated prostheses than we had available on the border. I was particularly impressed by the fact that, with the exception of two French supervisors, all of the technicians were Khmer. I was also impressed with the variety of challenges they have incorporated into their "walk again course"—stairs, concrete stepping stones, rounded obstructions to maneuver over, and, of course, the parallel bars. It seemed to me that on this planet, while some men are using their talents for destruction, here there are other men using those same talents to help the victims. That is peace.

On the border, the basic approach was to use appropriate technology that required the use of locally available materials and involved the victim in fashioning his own prosthesis. Here we are not dealing with refugees, rather we are dealing with citizens of Cambodia, and it does seem appropriate to be teaching and applying the level of technology that hopefully will be available in the Cambodia of tomorrow.

Our next visit was to the Handicap International Center, where we were graciously received by Tess, Filipino veteran of six years' work on the border and good friend of Peggy's. We toured the present HI Center and then the new center, which is just under construction. HI deals with the physical and occupational therapy of all sorts of disabilities.

After the tour we had a meeting dealing with how we could improve communication and transfer of patients.

We were invited to lunch at the ICRC Delegation House. ICRC brings a considerable amount of European lifestyle and culture along with them to these foreign posts. The Delegation is housed in a stately mansion, and lunch was a leisurely affair with most of the conversation in rapid-fire French. As a result I had little to say except for a short conversation with a Canadian. He insisted that Seattle is the origin of a new style of rock-and-roll music. I'm not sure what he was referring to, but I doubt it would appeal to me.

After lunch we visited the MSF headquarters, where I had the privilege of talking with Dr. Eve for a half hour. He is the French physician who has promoted peritoneal dialysis for renal failure patients in the Battambang Hospital. He was very happy to report that the patient I had sent there is responding very well to treatment.

Olivier next delivered me to the Catholic Relief Services office, where the staff informed me that Lori would return in about two hours. While this office is located in a run-down part of town, they had managed to install a lovely rooftop terrace with comfortable furniture, a roof for shade, potted plants and even a patch of lawn. There I stretched out on a sofa, and after reading a short time, of course, fell asleep.

I awakened about 5:00 P.M., and soon a parade of wonderful friends from border days commenced. There was Kosal, Somall, Sorn, Som Nang, BunSieth, and finally Lori. What a grand reunion it was.

We arranged to go to dinner together. We went to a Khmer restaurant where we had a wonderful and long dinner. I could not possibly describe all the dishes; I can only say that, as I spooned some sort of stew onto my rice, I wondered what all it contained—but I have been here long enough not to ask.

On returning to the nice house where Lori lives, we sat in a circle and talked.

We all got up this morning at 5:30. I went for a walk after the others left. Just beyond the market the road parallels the river, and I found a stairway leading down to the water's edge. There I sat for an hour watching the river traffic and taking pictures. Across the river, there was an old man sitting quietly in his slim little skiff. It was apparent he operates a ferry service. Eventually his service brought him to the foot of the stairway where I sat. Using sign language and waving a 10-baht note, I communicated to him my desire to go across the river and back. His craft was small and narrow. I crawled onto the foredeck and we were off. With single oar pivoting from a post, he skillfully and with little effort took me across the river. He had a somewhat mystified look when I indicated I wished to return. Once again at the stairway he smiled and repeated "Aukune, aukune" (thank you), when I gave him the 10 baht. It was a blissful experience for me.

25 September 1993

I am seated once again in a comfortable room in the Inter Hotel, and I have my *pakima* thrown over my shoulders to ward off the chills. I am in the middle of a severe cold. I had not intended to come to Aran this weekend, but the thought of air-conditioned comfort, hot showers and the opportunity to do my own schedule of eating and sleeping was too enticing to resist.

On the border we often talked of "appropriate technology." For instance, there we had only sporadic electricity; thus it did not make sense to teach diagnostic instruments that required electrical power. Although a somewhat higher level of technology is available in Mongkol Borei, it still behooves us to teach simple procedures to those physicians, who may find themselves practicing in deprived situations.

Currently, we are trying to persuade the Khmer physicians to adopt the SOAP system for their daily progress notes. *S* is for Symptoms— what the patient tells. *O* is for Objective findings, also termed signs— what the physician finds on physical exam, X-ray and lab. *A* is for Assessment—patient's condition (is it improved, unchanged, or worse?) and diagnosis, if one can be made. *P* is for Plan—discharge, discharge medications and directions, change of medication, further diagnostic workup.

The hospital campus covers about four acres, and there are a number of buildings. Some of these were built by the Khmers in pre-World War II. The Japanese occupation forces built one building, and Pol Pot built one. Most of the buildings are masonry. The oldest, now the TB ward, is of wood. The hospital has a capacity of about 300. Recently, in response to an epidemic of dengue fever, they had to erect a large tent over a concrete pad. One cannot avoid thinking of the term "pesthouse" in use in the Middle Ages, for with malaria and dengue fever being mosquito-borne, I'm sure there is a fair amount of cross-infection.

27 September 1993

I dread going to work today. By last evening, as a manifestation of what I call the cluster effect in medicine, we had six children and two adults in critical condition. At the morning meeting they present on the blackboard a statistical report of hospital status with columns showing admissions, discharges, etc. One column shows deaths, and it is not unusual for Peds to be listed as having one death. I will not be surprised if this morning it shows more than that.

It is now afternoon and my grim foreboding is not borne out. There was only one death in Peds listed. After the meeting, I hustled over to the ward and found most of our charges doing surprisingly well. We had done the best we could and were thankful.

28 September 1993

There are two ways for us to get to the hospital or return home. One is to go by car about 4 km—a route that requires crossing a one-lane bridge over the Mongkol Borei River. The bridge is interesting. One or more amputees station themselves on either end of the bridge. Since the bridge is too narrow for two-way traffic, the amputees govern the traffic by waving their caps. As the car passes them they hold out their caps for donations.

There are two walking routes. The one we use most takes us through the market and then across a sturdy wooden bridge over which pedestrians, bicycles, motorcycles and the occasional horse-drawn cart compete for right-of-way. This is a covered bridge, and on a hot day, if we have time, we take advantage of the shade and the breeze from the river to sit on the rail and cool off.

The other walking route requires we use the suspension bridge. While not quite as exotic as the bridges constructed of vines, its sturdy steel cables do swing and wiggle as we walk across.

In general we choose to walk to and from the hospital, about 1.5 km each way. It is sometimes made more challenging by the mud in the road and always gives us more of a close-up view of life in Cambodia.

The patients we care for seem to represent a cross-section of the Cambodian people. Some come to the hospital accompanied by supporting friends and relatives, and still others who seem to be walking a lonely path through life.

The nursing service is based on the assumption that the patient will have one attending family member or friend. This person helps with bathing, fetches water and extra food, summons the nurses or doctors when the patient requires and is often the patient's communicator or advocate. The patient who is not fortunate enough to have such an attendant is at an obvious disadvantage. Single mothers who come to the hospital with a sick child are in a particularly difficult situation.

One of the problems I face every day is that I come in contact with many of these poor people. There is no way that I can give to all of them. Picking out one to help is not altogether good, since their fellow patients soon become aware that the chosen one is receiving help that they would also like to receive.

Despite the inherent problems I chose to help Sanaven, a young widow who had come seeking help for her little girl, one year old. This infant had diarrhea, and her thin little body and wide staring eyes somehow drew me. When this mother told Supohl that she had no money to help feed her baby I could not resist. As a result, every day for the two weeks that they were here either Supohl or I would slip 10 baht under the covers when we examined the baby. Later every day the mother would find us in the hall and give us a thanking *wai*.

2 October 1993

As I have written before, I have been determined to get the Khmer doctors to order stool specimens on all of their patients who have symptoms or signs of parasitic infection. Their reluctance to do this seems to be the understandable reluctance to deal with that part of our physiology and the fact that the laboratory is not cooperative in this. As a result I have heard a myriad of excuses why, in clearly indicated cases, stool specimens have not been ordered. Yesterday I was told the ultimate in excuses. A lady was admitted for severe diarrhea. To my inquiry of the

Khmer doctor about a stool specimen, he looked me in the eye and said, "She did not pass stool at the proper time."

3 October 1993

Travel to and from Aran is made much easier by the presence of Luc Payant, our latest team member. His Thai wife and five-year-old girl live in Aran, and he desires to go to Aran every weekend. Not only that, he is a willing and a very able driver, so I travel relaxed.

4 October 1993

Our trip home yesterday evening went very well. At Kim Kim's, I bought some bologna and Dijon-style mustard and Kraft cheese. While the others ate small barbecued fish and pork fat with rice, Luc and I had American-style sandwiches and pea soup.

The above was written this afternoon. It is now 7:00 P.M. and I do not feel like writing. Today was a very busy day with an overdose of seriously ill and challenging cases. The bed in back of me is beckoning, and so I guess I'll make my way to the latrine and go horizontal.

5 October 1993

A great night's sleep and I'm ready for another day. Yesterday we received a man about 30 years old who has had severe digestive problems for a number of months. His thin frame and sunken eyes indicated that, unless we could find his problem and do something about it, death would come soon. Wonder of wonders, his medical records came with him—the best records I have seen this tour.

It steadily becomes cooler here. It won't be long until it will be one-blanket time and sweater-in-the-morning. We have had very little rain during the past couple of weeks. Luc, Supohl and I like to ride bicycles to work when it is dry. ARC has three nice bikes, so for the time being that will be our transport.

A couple of days ago the surgeon from ICRC sent us a patient to take care of during her terminal days. They had performed a simple mastectomy several days previously. In the postoperative period she developed jaundice. There was little doubt that her deteriorating condition was from metastatic carcinoma of the breast.

Today, she was surrounded by family. One of the young men approached me and in excellent English asked if they might take her home. He explained that he realized there was little we could do for her and that she wished to die in the comfort of her home. I asked this young man where he had learned to speak English so well. He had been in Khao-I-Dang in 1980–81 and remembered Peggy very well. He now lives in Australia, where he is a mental health counselor. I was, of course, most willing to sanction their taking the mother home, for in our conversation this young man brought out the best of Western and Eastern concepts of death.

7 October 1993

For the past week our team has been somewhat split, with half the team working in the *khums* (*khums* are collections of villages within a district, which is within a province). With Supohl working out there, a different translator was assigned to me temporarily. Saveth is a tiny Khmer lady who worked on the border. Early on, I said something to her in French. She replied in English, "I do not understand your French." In English I said, "Ah, I'm sorry, I do not speak French very well." "Oh, I quite agree with you," was her response, a deadly blow to my lingual ego.

19 October 1993

A number of years ago a young physician, Dr. Fern Houck, served a tour on the border. Faced with the onslaught of respiratory disease, she conceived the idea of a steam cabinet for children with croup and bronchitis. Aided by Jeff Nelson, a nurse at that time, she directed the construction of this cabinet. The steam originated from a pot boiling over a charcoal fire and was piped to the cabinet. It was my good fortune to follow her tour, and I was convinced that this simple apparatus, compatible with Khmer life, saved a number of lives.

Here in Mongkol Borei, we are facing another wave of respiratory disease. Soon the dry and relatively cold season will be upon us. Indeed, we already have a number of little ones struggling for breath. Shortly after arriving here I proposed to John Hollister, engineer on the ARC staff, that we design and build a similar structure. John was very willing and commenced drawing plans.

His concept was to build a very modern and lasting structure, with hot water provided by electricity, flow of water governed by float valves, and walls of thick clear plastic. I could agree with his idea—except for the problem of urgency with the impending onset of respiratory disease and the estimated cost of $3,000 at a time when budgets are tight.

20 October 1993

It seems like every evening for the past week we have been treated to a thunderstorm. I don't really mind such things except that the roads and paths get so muddy that bicycling is impossible, walking is difficult, and we are often reduced to riding in the car. While the bridge that was blown up is being replaced, our cars have been forced to use the wooden bridge. This one-lane structure connects the market to the hospital side of the river and in the morning is a mass of humanity, bicycles, horse carts, motorcycles and cars. About half of them want to go in one direction and the other half, the opposing direction. Two or three soldiers are assigned to the job of directing traffic, armed with two-way radios; despite their efforts it is bedlam. Reports are that the repaired bridge will be open tomorrow, so perhaps things will be better.

21 October 1993

The dead in Cambodia are either cremated or buried. Cremation is a religious ceremony held in the *wat* and there is some expense involved. As a result, mainly the poor are buried. Dr. Supul told me that Khmer custom is to bury the body with the head in the direction of north or east, never to the south or west. As a result, it is also Khmer custom to sleep with the head in the direction of north or east. Having learned this, I quickly got out my compass, and sure enough, my bed requires my head to face south. To change it would make it impossible to read in bed, so I think I'll leave it the way it is. It's nice to think that at our house in Twanoh Falls, our bed allows our heads to point toward the east.

22 October 1993

Yesterday morning on arrival at the hospital we found a motorcycle cart in which a young man was stretched out. The driver reported that he had brought his friend in because he was sick, but the driver wished to get him off-loaded and to depart. It was evident that this man's legs were paralyzed and his arms and hands very weak. We off-loaded him and put him in a temporary bed.

In response to Supohl's questioning, we were presented with a problem. This man insisted he was alone in this world, with no friend or relative who could help him. Now this is a real problem in this hospital system, for except for technical functions like tending IVs, injections, and taking blood pressure and temperatures, virtually all bedside nursing care is done by supportive friends or relatives.

This is so much a part of the system that the medical and nursing staff maintained we could not admit this patient. Luc and I insisted he must be admitted, and when I pointed out that we could hardly lay him out in front of the hospital to die, I got that blank Khmer look and turn-away that says, "Do what you want, we won't have anything to do with it." As usual, they were being realistic, for already this man's pants were wet with urine, and it was obvious he would require much personal care.

This man took up most of our day. History and physical exam pointed to dry beriberi, and we started an IV with vitamin B-1. I went to my reliable friend Fernanda, who said ICRC could pay if we could find a willing support person. She also gave us a couple of *kromas* (large pieces of cloth they wrap around their body when not wearing Western clothing) from the charity box. It was late in the day before we found a lady to undertake his care. In the meanwhile, he was rapidly improving, so perhaps our problem will not persist for long.

23 October 1993

Today has been a good day. On arrival at the hospital I found our paraplegic of yesterday no longer paraplegic. Indeed he was quite happy to show us how he could walk. In addition, the lady we had hired had washed his pants, bathed him and had seen that he was fed. Another day or two and he can be discharged. Most of the paraplegics we see here are tragically permanent, so it is indeed a joy to see one who responds to a simple medication like vitamin B-1. Now if we could only persuade him to eat unpolished rice along with some green vegetables and some fruit.

24 October 1993

I have been trying to reach Bob Medrala in Bangkok. We received 60 pairs of eyeglasses from ICRC. There is an optometrist on the ARC staff, and we are trying to arrange for him to set up a clinic to fit them to needy Khmer. The other thing I am working on is the steam cabinet. Already we have two infants with respiratory disease, so time is of the essence. In Aran there is a Mr. Rongsen, a Thai who worked with ARC at Site 2 for several years. I have employed him as my "gofer." He will purchase the pot, butane tank and grill, the pipe and the plastic for the steam cabinet. This is estimated at $300 U.S. A contractor at the hospital is building the fencing and the framework at 3,900 baht for an estimated total of $500 U.S. If it saves one of those little lives, it will be worth it.

26 October 1993

The mud and the condition of the bridge across the river have forced us to use the suspension bridge when traveling by foot or bike. This bridge jumps and swings with each person's steps. Today I followed Supohl on the bridge. Ahead of him was one of the nurses from the hospital. When she was almost to the end of the suspension part, she saw Supohl coming and paused to jump and swing. She did not notice this old man following behind Supohl. We had a jolly jumping time of it. When we arrived at the hospital, I told her about what an exciting trip she had afforded me. At first embarrassed, she dissolved into laughter and then told the assembled group what she had done, and everybody had a good laugh.

30 October 1993

Luc and I came into Aran early today—it being a Khmer holiday (Sihanouk's birthday) and we didn't have to work. Yesterday the ICRC

Surgical service honored me once again by asking me to see one of their patients. I describe it as an honor because I hold Dr. Johan Serat, the surgeon, in such high regard. The patient was a four-year-old girl from Poipet. She came in two days previously, having sustained a devastating gunshot wound. The bullet struck her right thigh, shattered her femur and deflected upward, lacerating her femoral artery, perforating her bowel in two places and lacerating her liver. She was unconscious on admission and taken directly to Surgery, where an above-knee amputation was done, bowel resected and liver repaired. Twenty-four hours post-op, she was awake enough to complain of pain, but subsequently lapsed into coma. When I saw her I could not find a definite reason for her coma but felt that her surgical care had been excellent. There was nothing I could suggest to help her, and she expired two hours after I saw her.

No one seems to have been able to find out about the origin or reason for the gunshot. I suppose that the NRA folks would maintain that the Khmer population, as in the U.S., has the right to have guns. I wish some of them had stood at the bedside of this child.

1 November 1993

We believe that we have seen our first case of cholera. A 15-year-old female was admitted two days ago in shock and dehydration. The shrunken face of a Khmer in advanced dehydration makes those eyes stand out like beacons of fright. Her mother had been seized with diarrhea and vomiting a few hours before her. The mother died at home within about eight hours. Our young patient arrived in time and with IVs and tetracycline improved promptly; by yesterday it was apparent she would recover.

Our tent, set up for overflow, is now set up as the cholera ward. Special procedures for isolation, use of disinfectant, and waste disposal are in place, and public health organizations units advised. We hope that this may not be the start of an epidemic.

Needless to say, there has been an increase in hand washing and discretion about what we eat or drink.

I had one of those humbling experiences yesterday that are part of life here. It was a busy morning on the ward for Dr. Supul, and there were a number of worried mothers awaiting admission procedures for their sick children. I spied a four-month-old child on an examining table and decided to do the admission physical. With Supohl's help on the history, we learned that this child had diarrhea for the preceding 24 hours and had not breast-fed well. The only examination finding was a respiratory rate of 20, each respiration very deep and ending with a *cheep*-like sound. Someone had already started an IV, and I wrote an order for a blood test, a stool specimen and a blood sugar and sent the child to the ward. In the afternoon, the Khmer physician saw the child was not doing well and started oxygen. I was called soon afterward and saw the child was in extremis. Shortly the child died. The blood test was negative, but the blood sugar had not been done.

Today at the morning assembly I felt constrained to present this case. My diagnosis had been electrolyte imbalance. Other diagnoses and treatment suggestions were offered, but it was hindsight and of no help to this child. I felt badly for the child and the mother.

7 November 1993

I'm back in Mongkol Borei. It is very hot today, and I was ready for a nap with the fan wafting air over me. On awakening I headed for the hospital, passing through the market. There I found a nice lady selling pineapples of size and appearance similar to those I remember from Ta Phraya days. I picked out two.

At the hospital I found my good friend Dr. Supul had the duty. He seemed quite happy to see me and presented three patients. One was the little girl we had worried about for the past several days. She has a definite pneumonia and some other disease causing liver enlargement and jaundice and anemia. We have presented her to every doctor who comes by, but none of the suggested causes seem to fit. For several days she seemed to be on a terminal course, but happily today seems considerably better.

8 November 1993

Today is a holiday but I worked anyway. During the middle of the day I was in my room writing letters when there was a tap on the door. It was an ICRC nurse who speaks mainly French. Her message was that at about

11:30 A.M. a UNHCR person would arrive to inspect the ARC work at the hospital. I quickly got on my bike and pedaled off.

There was no sign of any visitors at the hospital, so I sat in the combined lounge and Fernanda's office and read, periodically checking the gate in full view. By 12:30 P.M., I was tired of waiting and hungry. I told Fernanda I was going to the coffee shop for noodle soup,

On return to the hospital I came upon tragedy. A nurse in the World Food Programme had brought in three mine victims. A family had been gathering wood when the mother stepped on a mine. Her left foot and lower leg were hanging by a shred of skin. The father's right foot was bandaged, but it looked like he would lose the foot. Their beautiful teenaged daughter had sustained shrapnel injuries to her chest. I spent most of the time with her. X-rays and surgery indicated she had sustained a lacerated liver. It was quite an afternoon for a day off.

10 November 1993

It seems to me that my letters have been rather full of tragedy. I look for some comical experience. First I must tell another sad tale—the most recent mine injury. A teenaged boy walking in the woods triggered a mine, which took off a leg, and shrapnel spattered his chest and perforated both eyes. He was brought to the hospital and survived surgery but died the day following. The surgeons were at a loss to explain his death. I prefer to think that God in his mercy recognized the agony of being blind and an amputee in Cambodia and called him home. Rumor has it that the Khmer Rouge are replanting mines in "cleared areas." I believe God may have some judgment to make about this and also the countries that are manufacturing and shipping the mines.

11 November 1993

As we rode to the hospital on our bikes yesterday, our way was temporarily blocked by a long funeral procession. Children wore their school clothing, dark-colored shorts or skirts and white blouses or shirts. The coffin was carried in a trailer behind a motorcycle. A loudspeaker gave forth with somber Khmer music and was followed by young men and older folk, apparently arranged in order of age. Supohl told me that the deceased must have been a revered teacher, and the cortege was made up of his students, recent and past. It was an impressive tribute.

Yesterday we admitted a lady with cholera. She was in shock. She had come in "sick-on-a-stick," and in helping to lift her into bed her hand swept across my lips. Visualizing those cholera germs, I pursed my lips and hastened to the sink to wash and gargle with that strong Khmer soap.

14 November 1993

From Aran: The steam cabinet is complete, and its first trial run went well. We have two locked doors on it, and I had to get some extra keys made. Past experience served me well, for I brought the locks along as well as the keys to be reproduced.

The same key man I had patronized years ago was there and using the same hand tools, not the machine-type. I sat and watched him work. He filed, tried the lock and filed again, repeated a number of times until the lock yielded. It took a long time to make the four keys, but I enjoyed it.

Last night two drummers, right outside my window, practiced their booming rhythm. This was alternated with firecracker explosions.

This morning, a full band, dancing dragon, marchers and a pickup truck—from which lighted firecrackers were thrown—passed in front of our hotel. When I went on my errands it seemed that every crossing I needed to make was blocked by this noisy parade. It seems that this is a Chinese holiday. Of course, they would not be aware that visitors from Cambodia would not react favorably to the blasts of firecrackers.

16 November 1993

Recently we heard that UNTAC, upon its withdrawal from Cambodia, returned to the four Khmer factions armaments—including land mines—that they had yielded up in the stand-down, part of the peace agreement. This, to me, is atrocious, irrational and contrary to everything we have tried to do here. I have written a letter to the editor of *Time* magazine.

19 November 1993

Meetings, statistics and goals are a big part of life here. Fortunately I am not much involved, since I am allergic to meetings, skeptical of statistics and rarely meet the goals I set for myself. It's not that I object to the goals; it is mostly that one must prove one has reached the goal, and to do so one must prove it by statistics, which are subject to so many variables here that they become meaningless.

For instance, the literature is replete with articles about how indigenous practitioners tend to use too many IVs and that this can be decreased by persuading patients to drink ORS [oral rehydration solution]. I am quite sure that most of the authors have not tasted ORS. I have, and it is terrible. Besides that, it is virtually impossible to convince a Khmer that IV solutions do not contain some magic potion that will ensure recovery.

As a result, pressure is put on the Khmer doctors to use IVs. Today when I asked a Khmer doctor why his soldier patient, who did not seem to be ill, was getting an IV, the doctor replied, "Because he is a soldier." I told the Khmer physician to ask this patient if he would like to go home. The patient's answer, as he pointed to the half-finished plastic IV flask, was, "When the IV is finished."

Early in my tour here I assumed a goal of reducing the number of IVs. It seemed simple statistics, for all one had to do was make a daily count of patients and of the number of IVs and calculate the percentage. That seemed good, but it failed to take in the variables that are so much a part of life here.

23 November 1993

My time here has dwindled to hours, and despite my determination to accomplish departure chores ahead of time, I have much left to do. Each day has brought forth some complicated challenge, and on my way to the hospital I wondered what it would be today. I soon found out.

A mother appeared bearing her seven-year-old boy in her arms. He had developed a nonspecific illness one week previously, and she had taken him to a local physician, who had given him an injection of some medicine in each thigh. On the fourth day of illness he was unable to move his left leg, and the next day was unable to move his right leg.

On examination he clearly had polio. It is well established that the onset of polio is often nonspecific, but the paralysis is stimulated to occur by any injection. Obviously it is difficult to convince Khmers that the paralysis is not specifically caused by the injection.

Here in Mongkol Borei we had the first case of reported cholera this season and now the first case of polio. I quickly reported this case to Arlys, and she drove to Sisophon to report to the public health people. Mobile teams will visit the village and surrounding environs, and they will educate, advise no injections and vaccinate all children with oral polio vaccine.

Our seven-year-old patient was admitted. By midafternoon his respirations were labored, and he died this evening.

28 November 1993
Tokyo Hotel, Phnom Penh

I awakened at 3:00 A.M. with severe abdominal cramping, followed by the most profuse diarrhea. This continued until 6:00 A.M., by which time I was weak and thinking about hypovolemia and electrolyte depletion. I went out to the hotel office and with some effort managed to buy bottled water, most of which I drank in the next two hours. At 8:00 A.M., Dr. Frank Bleed arrived to drive me to the airport, and what a lovely surprise to find Mary Dunbar there as well.

After checking in at the airport, we went to a coffee shop, where I drank a cup of coffee, a glass of water and a glass of orange juice. By departure time I felt in pretty good shape.

It was a prop plane carrying about 50 passengers. On arrival at the airport in Bangkok I again felt weak but managed to get through the immigration formalities without difficulty. One of the sweetest sounds one hears in this kind of travel is the thump of the official's rubber stamp, which means he has found no problem with your passport and forms.

My baggage and I were soon reunited, and I proceeded to the taxi stand. The ride into the city was swift, and the Bangkok Christian Guest House had my room ready.

Having taken nothing but liquids all day I felt I should eat something. Nutritionists will shudder when they read this, for I went to a nearby McDonald's and had a small hamburger, a chocolate milkshake and a glass of water.

December 1993—Back home

Seated at my word processor in my little attic office, I hear the rain on the roof. Through the window, which often provides me with a beautiful view of mountains and water, I see nothing but gray fog. This is the sixth day since my return from Cambodia, and I am still making great use of jet lag as an excuse for hours of napping.

My return schedule brought me to the Seattle area airport early in the morning on 3 December, where Gwen and I were happily reunited. We stayed at a nearby motel for the day. In the evening, we went to First United Methodist Church in Seattle to meet Peggy and participate in a sing-along *Messiah*—our favorite way to begin the Christmas season.

Reviewing the little notebook I carried with me every day in Mongkol Borei, I find a few notes from my last days there.

An Assessment

In the final days of my tour in Cambodia I was frequently asked what I thought about the status of this troubled country. A facile and essentially meaningless answer would be: there are some bright spots and some dark spots. Three months in Cambodia do not make one an expert. I write this in the belief that there may be some interest in my observations about ARC's role, which is inevitably affected by the problems that exist.

Violence

While the violence of the Pol Pot days is no more, violence is common to the Cambodian scene. Small-arms fire is often heard in the neighborhoods, and distant artillery fire and the sound of detonating land mines are occasionally heard. ARC protects against this by restricting travel and activities at night when violence is most common.

Lack of Reliable Security

Burglary and robbery are common. Recently a medic who works for ARC had a personal reason to travel from Battambang to Pursat, about 50 km. He traveled by small taxi, which was halted at gunpoint 50 times by soldiers along the road, who demanded tribute from the driver, a few baht at a time. The ICRC unit at the hospital was recently burgled, with loss of a large quantity of drugs. ARC has thus far avoided such losses by traveling only in flagged and labeled vehicles, employing night guards, avoiding night travel and ensuring excellent maintenance of vehicles, which are driven mainly by professional Khmer drivers.

Financial and Administrative Problems of Cambodia

Obviously the fiscal state of Cambodia was destroyed as a result of the Pol Pot years, followed by the Vietnamese invasion. Even prior to these events, the Cambodian government accepted graft, corruption and bribery as a normal part of business. As a consequence of the above, administration at all levels is unreliable. Administrators promise delivery of goods or services but are unable to deliver, and the people have little confidence in the government.

Health

ARC's effort in the province of Mongkol Borei is divided into the clinical work in the hospital and the public health work in the villages. In the hospital, our role has been primarily that of adviser and counselor to the medical staff and the nursing staff. The medical staff is young Khmers, recent graduates from the medical school in Phnom Penh. Their training was in the French system, in some ways quite different from the American and English systems. There are cultural, traditional and social pressures that affect the Khmer physicians. I believe that ARC's work in the hospital is very worthwhile and should continue for several years.

A province in Cambodia is about the size of a county in our country, and the provincial hospital is comparable to a county hospital here. The people who live near the provincial hospital are able to come for outpatient care or direct admission. Care at this level is restricted by minimal laboratory support and limited pharmacy. Nevertheless, very seriously ill patients are cared for, with good results in many cases.

People who live a farther distance away may go to the district hospital, which usually has six to ten beds; there is a small nursing staff, and a Khmer doctor may periodically visit. Most serious cases are sent to the provincial hospital if transportation can be arranged. Minimal care and treatment are available to the less seriously ill.

In villages far from the district hospital there may be a "health activist," a volunteer with minimal training. This person may promote public health measures, treat minor illnesses and advise transport of seriously ill patients to the district or provincial hospital.

It is obvious that to improve the general health of the Cambodian people, health education must start at the village level. ARC's move in that direction is, in my opinion, very appropriate and needed.

Education

Education is an important and necessary part of dealing with the problems listed. It is a major part of the infrastructure of a stable society. It seems to me that, even as ARC has sought to aid in the field of health, American educators should be encouraged to consider a similar effort in the field of education.

Challenges Facing ARC

1. To maintain its reputation for excellence of service to the Khmers combined with education leading to Khmer self-management.

2. To continue its role in advocacy for the Khmer returnees and for refugees in other parts of the world.

It is my opinion that the United Nations needs to consult and listen to what the Volags feel about actions before they are committed. The option for land offered to the Khmers when there was not enough mine-free land available; placing highly paid UNTAC personnel in Cambodia without calculating the deleterious effect upon the economy; and the returning of land mines to the factions—these are the kind of actions that I think might have been avoided had the Volags been consulted.

Since I started working with ARC in 1981 I have felt that it was *the* outstanding organization in service to and advocacy for the Khmer people. I am grateful to and have great admiration for that long line of volunteers and staff people who have made ARC the outstanding organization that it is. In this regard, I think of people like Karen Johnson Elshazly, Bob Medrala and Arlys Herem.

I have read articles that seem to indicate there is a sharp dividing line between emergency care and development. I do not believe there is such a line, and in the case of Cambodia, I believe there exists a social emergency that can only be treated by aiding the reestablishment of the infrastructure. Education and encouragement at the village level are where it needs to start, and I am glad to see that ARC is going to be there.

Acknowledgments

The American Refugee Committee would like to acknowledge all the people who contributed, each in his or her own way, to make the publication of the book, We Shared the Peeled Orange, *possible.*

To Gwen Braile, wife of the late Louis Braile, M.D., and to Peggy Braile, his beloved daughter, our heartfelt gratitude for sharing Louis's letters with us, and for allowing us to share them with the world.

To Patricia Benson, project editor and publishing consultant, our sincere appreciation for your professional guidance, creativity and enthusiasm for the project.

To Bob Gaertner, our many thanks for your skilled and caring manuscript review and editorial support, which was invaluable in launching this project successfully.

To members of ARC's Board of Directors and ARC staff who took a special interest in this 25th anniversary project, our deep appreciation for your support and unwavering commitment:

American Refugee Committee Board Members and Supporters

> Mary Tjosvold, President, Board of Directors
> The Neal Ball Charitable Fund
> Sonia and John Cairns
> David Duclos
> Luke Ellis
> Barbara Forster
> Mel Goldfein
> Jean Jachman
> Steve Miles, M.D.
> Holly Myers
> Nancy Roberts
> Carol Winslow

ARC Headquarters Staff

Hugh Q. Parmer, President
Karen Johnson Elshazly, Senior Advisor to the President
Karen Frederickson, Vice President
Therese M. Gales, Public Relations
Martha Naegeli, Marketing Communications

About the American Refugee Committee

The American Refugee Committee (ARC), based in Minneapolis, Minnesota, is an international nonprofit, nonsectarian organization working for the survival, health and well-being of refugees and internally displaced people (IDPs) caught in the cross-fire of war or civil conflict. ARC was founded in 1979 to assist refugees uprooted by the conflicts in Southeast Asia. Since then, it has grown to nearly 2,000 employees providing humanitarian assistance and training to more than one million people in Africa, Asia and Europe.

ARC is committed to involving the people it serves in the planning and implementation of its efforts. This participatory approach is critical to the success and sustainability of ARC's programs, a critical factor in a world where people might now live for decades, even generations, as refugees and IDPs. Current programs in Africa, the Balkans, Central Asia and Thailand provide health care, clean water, shelter repair, legal aid, trauma counseling, micro-credit, community development, and repatriation assistance.

The American Refugee Committee is a nonprofit, nonsectarian 501(c)(3) organization that depends on private donors to do its work. Roughly 91 cents of every dollar donated goes directly toward its international aid programs. As a result, ARC was named one of *Worth* magazine's Top 100 Charities for three years in a row. In 2003, ARC was listed by *Reader's Digest* as one of its Top 12 Charities. And ARC has earned Charity Navigator's highest rating, four stars, for its fiscal responsibility.

Between war and peace, there is hope.

You can help ARC restore hope and rebuild lives shattered by violence. To learn more, visit www.archq.org or call 612-872-7060 to request more information.

The American Refugee Committee (ARC)
430 Oak Grove Street, Suite 204
Minneapolis, Minnesota 55403 USA

Abbreviations Used in Text

AFS	American Field Service
AFSC	American Friends Service Committee
ARC	American Refugee Committee
BCMG	Border Control Medical Group
CAMA	Compassion and Mercy Associates
CARE	Cooperative for Assistance and Relief Everywhere, Inc.
CDC	Centers for Disease Control
CME	Continuing Medical Education
COERR	Catholic Office for Emergency Relief and Refugees
CPR	Coalition for Peace and Reconciliation
CRS	Catholic Relief Services
EVI	Extremely Vulnerable Individual
ICM	Intergovernmental Committee for Migration
ICRC	International Committee of the Red Cross
IRC	International Rescue Committee
JVA	Joint Voluntary Agency
KID	Khao-I-Dang Holding Center
KPNLF	Khmer People's National Liberation Front
MCH	Maternal-child health
MSF	Médicins Sans Frontières (Doctors without Borders)
NGO	Nongovernmental Organization
OHI	Operation Handicap International
OPD	Outpatient Department
OXFAM	Oxford Committee for Famine Relief
UNBRO	United Nations Border Relief Operation
UNHCR	United Nations High Commissioner for Refugees

UNTAC   United Nations Transitional Authority in Cambodia
VN   Vietnamese
WFP   World Food Programme
YWAM   Youth With a Mission

To order additional copies of *We Shared the Peeled Orange*:

Web: www.itascabooks.com

Phone: 1-800-901-3480

Fax: Copy and fill out the form below with credit card information.
          Fax to 763-398-0198.

Mail: Copy and fill out the form below. Mail with check or credit card
          information to:

          Syren Book Company
          5120 Cedar Lake Road
          Minneapolis, Minnesota 55416 USA

Order Form

Copies	Title / Editors	Price	Totals
	We Shared the Peeled Orange / **Braile, Louis E., M.D.**	$18.95	$

Subtotal	$	
7% sales tax (MN only)	$	
Shipping and handling, first copy	$	4.00
Shipping and handling, ___ add'l copies @$1.00 ea.	$	
TOTAL TO REMIT	$	

Payment Information:

__ Check enclosed __ Visa/MasterCard		
Card number:	Expiration date:	
Name on card:		
Billing address:		
City:	State:	Zip:
Signature :	Date:	

Shipping Information:

__ Same as billing address __ Other (enter below)		
Name:		
Address:		
City:	State:	Zip: